DECOLONIZING
AMERICAN
SPANISH

ILLUMINATIONS:
CULTURAL FORMATIONS OF THE AMERICAS SERIES
Jorge Coronado, Editor

DESCOLONIZANDO EL ESPAÑOL AMERICANO

DECOLONIZING AMERICAN SPANISH

EUROCENTRISM AND FOREIGNNESS
IN THE IMPERIAL ECOSYSTEM

JEFFREY HERLIHY-MERA

UNIVERSITY OF PITTSBURGH PRESS

Published by the University of Pittsburgh Press, Pittsburgh, Pa., 15260
Copyright © 2022, University of Pittsburgh Press
All rights reserved

Manufactured in the United States of America
Printed on acid-free paper
10 9 8 7 6 5 4 3 2 1

Cataloging-in-Publication data is
available from the Library of Congress

ISBN 13: 978-0-8229-4726-4
ISBN 10: 0-8229-4726-9

Cover design by Joel W. Coggins

Para Alejandro

CONTENTS

Preface
When Do We Improve upon Silence by Speaking?
ix

Acknowledgments
xv

Introduction
Colonialism in US Spanish Departments
1

1: *After Hispanic Studies*
On the Democratization of Spanish-Language Cultural Study
31

2: *Vetting the Decolonial Turn*
53

3: *Multilingual Cognition and Ethno-Lingual Relativity*
Expanding "Spanish" Maps of Meaning
97

4: *Spain*
The Arabized Province of Latin America,
or, Which Quijote Do We Need?
120

5: *On the Puertoricanization of US Higher Education*
or, The Awkward Constraints of Using One Language
147

Conclusion
Overcoming the Tradition of Silence
169

Notes
193

References
227

Index
253

PREFACE

WHEN DO WE IMPROVE UPON SILENCE BY SPEAKING?

> When do we improve upon silence by speaking?
> **Vamsi K. Koneru (email to the author, December 28, 2018)**

> Allowing the Spanish to exist in my text without the benefit of italics or quotations marks a very important political move. Spanish is not a minority language. Not in this hemisphere, not in the United States, not in the world inside my head. So why treat it like one? Why "other" it? Why de-normalize it? By keeping the Spanish as normative in a predominantly English text, I wanted to remind readers of the fluidity of languages, the mutability of languages. And to mark how steadily English is transforming Spanish and Spanish is transforming English.
> **Junot Díaz, qtd. in *Weird English* (Ch'ien 2004, 204)**

> Spanish has been a part of my life [in Los Angeles] since my infancy. . . . My formal education with Spanish did not start until I started my seventh grade year. . . . I enjoyed linguistics courses, but detested mandatory surveys of Golden Age literature. A class on heritage language education was new and exciting, but a mandatory survey of Don Quijote was not. I wanted to engage with Spanish as a social study—not just a language maintained in letters and prose. In essence, I wanted to understand *how Spanish had saturated my world here and now.*
> **Adam Frederick Schwartz, in "On Imagination and Erasure" (2009, 16–17, my emphasis)**

Spanish is by far the most common language in this hemisphere. There are more Spanish-speakers in the United States than in any other country in the world, save Mexico—more than in Spain, Colombia, and Venezuela, and more "than in all of Central America (Guatemala, El Salvador, Honduras, Nicaragua, Costa Rica, Panama), plus Uruguay and Paraguay thrown in for good measure" (Lipski 2009, 48). Nevertheless, nearly all US institutions of higher learning hold tight to English as the sole language for degree conferral, accreditation, instruction, funding opportunities, admissions applications, scholarly awards, institutional communication, and so forth. The academic foreignization directs literacy itself toward English and away from Spanish in a way that pushes many communities toward political and social obligations that shape not only literacy and graduation rates but also access to public funds, democratic participation, and the nature of belonging and citizenship. In concert with this tradition, Donald Trump eliminated the Spanish version of the White House website.[1]

Any scholar interested in reforming these conventions of Spanish-language cultural pedagogy is confronted with two immense problems: (1) the received institutional mischaracterization of Spanish as a foreign language in the United States, and (2) the subtle power of Eurocentric traditions that have dominated the field for generations. By foregrounding local cultures and language varieties, and a shift in conceptualization from foreign to domestic, the ideas developed in this book gesture toward creating new conceptual maps, revising inherited ones, and institutionalizing marginalized and silenced voices and their stories. My views on foreign vis-à-vis domestic myths are largely influenced by the ways Spanish and English occur at my institution—the University of Puerto Rico.[2] While Puerto Rico is often described as "foreign in a domestic sense"[3] in relation to the United States, our university has developed many institutional relevancies that would be readily applicable on the mainland, especially in Spanish-dominant communities.

Conventional Spanish-language cultural studies often engage spatially clustered themes around geographic regions that are sometimes combined with a historical period. As a result, many tenure-line announcements use terms like "Mexican," "colonial Southern Cone," or "Peninsular golden age" and so on, a tendency that tacitly applies a limited set of categories that establish the boundaries of critique and knowledge creation. A quandary with this circumstance is that these grammars generally rely on a priori presumptions about cultures, epochs, languages, communities, and individuals.[4] The performances under analysis may confirm, nuance, or dialectally resist these centers, but the received unity is understood to exist across both time and space.[5]

Privileging rupture and disunity that characterize the decolonial turn, this study gestures toward new forms of localism (*pueblos*, as per Enrique Dussel[6]) that are external to a degree from these conventional approaches and their centers. In addition to shifting focus from Spain toward the Spanish-language cultures local to each university, my argument bases perspectives on realms of the human condition like cultural displacement and multilanguage use (instead of transnational or political status, periodized views, among other conditions) in ways that unlink pedagogical attention from Eurocentric exigencies and allow critique to develop new questions and uncertainties.[7] Focusing on how new conceptualizations of "local" circumstances influence aesthetics, poetics, community sentiments, and creativity, among other topics, this book gestures toward perceiving, studying, teaching, performing, and creating in ways that allow these depths to become part of our intellectual endowment. Reconstructing value from localized, group perspectives (that engage nontraditional latitudes of "local"), this framework provides methods to develop attuned contextualized knowledges of each particular community, region, and institution, toward emic structures that de-emancipate the already-power of Spain-centric teaching and learning.

This book examines the university not as a neutral institution but as one of the main levers of political and social power that supports the misrecognition of Spanish as foreign in the United States. I argue that the overwhelming Eurocentrism at US universities obfuscates local varieties of the language and culture in ways that are detrimental to students and the communities served. My theoretical approach questions the self-evidence and value of the monolingual/monocultural university as an institution, and queries the relevancies of how geographic, transnational, and regional constraints of conventional approaches have been institutionalized;[8] a specific focus of my critique concerns the area-studies/periodization model that explicitly neglects US/Latin American cultures vis-à-vis Spain. Departing from the tacit presumptions of uniformity across time and space (myths that inform many area-studies epistemes), I dispute the degree to which traditional centers and their grammars are meaningful containers of emotion, community, and cultural performance. My focus on local cultures and lived experiences endeavors to add dimensions to the existent collection of critical categories, to shift focus toward nontraditional subjectivities, and to reconsider what may be understood as legitimate (and thus hirable) faculty specializations, opening the possibilities of intellectual connections and concentrations that do not exist at the present time.[9]

Decolonizing American Spanish imagines post-Eurocentric Spanish-language cultural study not as ahistorical but to a degree postapocalyptic: a present connected and disconnected to various pasts and many narratives and myths. I want to anchor an anxiety in perspectives that are disintegrated to a degree from conventional canons, protagonists, narratives, and conceptual presumptions and prescriptions—and do so *within* the already-institutionalized conditions of pedagogy and scholarship. That is, if conventional structural mechanisms remain intact (the corporate university and its courses, degrees, publications, conferences, hiring processes, and so on), what realms of inquiry have the potential to open new contours of being, forms of localization, and threads of emancipation? What new centers can enunciate local cultures in generative (non-Eurocentric) ways? In a post-Eurocentric academy, how will traditional Peninsular studies evolve? Such questions participate in a long, slow demise of a colonial project: namely the myth that all Spanish-language material has an a priori relation to a master Euro signifier (and thus performs a contaminated iteration thereof) conceptualized within linear continuity. Subtly and violently, such myths enforce the structural notion that contemporary cultures (largely but not exclusively in the Americas) may be understood as dualistic successors to pure essences in Spain—performing relational ties to distant Euro centers (merely reorganized in time and space). In places like the United States where Spanish is externalized as "foreign," such cultures and languages are commonly conceptualized as non-generative, ungrammatical, impure, and/or contaminated—and thus invalid vis-à-vis their equivalents in Spain. While these local cultures have profound histories, traditions, aesthetics, narratives, and myths, the structures of the academy require (if these materials appear in pedagogy, which does not regularly occur) that they be studied, recognized, and institutionalized as minor and unimportant in comparison to Spain.

My contact with the languages and cultures discussed in this book grew partly out of boyhood experiences in Aguadilla—experiences that ultimately developed into the passions and visions that would crystalize into academic inquiry. When considering undergraduate and graduate education, the ingrained Eurocentrism in the Massachusetts of my youth meant that attending the Universidad de Puerto Rico-Aguadilla, walking distance from my grandparents' home at 164 Calle E, would have been (and indeed was) inconceivable. Upon the advice of those surrounding me, including my grandparents, my studies were realized in Boston (Brandeis University and Boston College) and in Barcelona (Universitat Pompeu Fabra). While I do not dispute the merits of those universities, semester after semester in Waltham and Chestnut Hill were dedicated to Díaz de Vivar, *La Celestina*, Siglo de Oro, and the Guerra Civil (*which Guerra Civil never needs clarification*). There was never mention of why MBTA bus 114 was called *guagua* in Chelsea and *autobús* after crossing the river into East Boston. Or that across the same river *fácil* became *mamado* or *chiche* (or that *chiche* and *mamado* had other meanings in other contexts) or that terms for food, drink, family relations (and the ceremonies of each) have similar variations. Walking from East Cambridge across the Prospect Street bridge to Union Square in Somerville, the Spanish changes and so do the traditions, styles, music, and art; in the "Spanish" classrooms at elementary, secondary, high school, and university levels in those communities, though, there was no notion that these cultures existed. They were not studied. They were not recognized. We were to think about Spain—and I did.

And in Barcelona, my studies offered no context as to why employees in L'Hospitalet bakeries greet customers *"no tinc pa"* or *"no tengo pan"* or a mix of the two—or how one's order can determine the language of response from the clerk. Or that cultural maps of many *barris* in a "Spanish" city like Barcelona, aside from *catalanisme*, percolate with Latin American cultures—and the local (*castellano*) language, when spoken by Spaniards, is often variants of Andalucía or Extremadura. While these are existential and distinguishing characteristics of those places, just as they are in Boston, the institutions of higher education did not recognize these people or their cultures as meaningful. Questions about local cultures, and some national ones, like why Spaniards say *"comer"* instead of *"almorzar"* for a midday meal—is this linguistic Christian-centrism, like *judías verdes*, *duelos y quebrantos*, *Matamoros* and *Matajudíos*?—were crowded out by the celebration of Díaz de Vivar, Cervantes, Velázquez, Picasso, and Almodóvar—men (not women) of genius to be sure: to say nothing of them is one thing, but to say too much is another.

Mayagüez, Puerto Rico, March 22, 2022

ACKNOWLEDGMENTS

A Joanna, Santiago (Tan-tan), Alejandro (Bíbu),
Nana, Bib, Bill, Fran,
Donna, Nelly, Michael, Arturo,
Jennifer, Katherine, Amy, Paola, María Augusta,
Martina, Rose, Duda, Jay, Faith, Coques, Grace, Sebastián, Sofia,
Pablo y Juan Pablo, Ed y Bill,
Vamsi, LT, Gary, Andrea, los Mikes (x4), Stelios, Sholko, Tim, Luis, Héctor y Enrique,
Pere Gifra Adroher, María Antonia Oliver Rotger, Rafael Argullol y Miguel Berga,
Jókay Károly, Alfred Hornung, Heidi Landecker, Miguel de Santiago y Rafael Salas, Amarilis dos Santos Melo, Carlos Santos, Daniel Abdalla, Miss Kelly y Miss Gompert,
Suzanne, Susan, hj, Kurt, Carl, Peter, Josh, Leo, Jenny, Raúl Villarreal y René Villarreal,
Juan José, Carlo, Dimaris, Mariam, Rafael, Sara, David, Jason, Lily y Lissette y Yazmín, Alex, Cora, Dana, Iliaris, Baruch, Ana, Noemí, Lester, Alfredo, Stephane, Rosa y Gergő, Christopher, Emilia, Karla, Lydia, Frances, Claudia, Jerry, Annette, Ramón y Michael, Yvette, Sandra, Anderson, Nelson, Heriberto, Anthony, Fernando, Marcel, Matías y JAL, Lissette, Carmitas (2), Ahmed, Rabéb, Endah, Orsi, Katy, Jacqueline, Janet y Mulhizzle,

Gloria, Sandra, Milena, Flor, Cristal, Oswaldo, Pablo (el otro), Mario, Gabriel y Carlos,
A mis estudiantes en Mayagüez, Budapest, Reading, Cuenca, Everett, Barcelona, Quito y Sioux City,
Con agradecimiento.

This book grew out of an article titled "After Hispanic Studies: On the Democratization of Spanish-Language Cultural Study," which appeared in *Comparative American Studies* 13, no. 3 (2015): 177–93. Sections also appeared in the *minnesota review* ("Academic Imperialism; or, Replacing Nonrepresentative Elites: Democratizing English Departments at Top-Ranked US Institutions," *minnesota review* 85 [2015]: 80–106); *US Studies* ("The Transnational as Civil Obedience," *US Studies*, January 15, 2018); *Voces del Caribe* ("Latinx Multilingualism in Modern American Writing: Colonized Diasporic Writing and the Concealed Transcultural Depths in Williams's English," *Voces del Caribe* 11 [2019]); *The Hemingway Review* ("Cuba in Hemingway," *The Hemingway Review* 36 [2017]: 8–41); *Inside Higher Ed* ("A New Future for Humanities Funding?" *Inside Higher Ed*, May 14, 2021, and "A Case for Multilingual Universities," *Insider Higher Ed*, May 19, 2022) and *The Chronicle of Higher Education* ("Colonialism in US Spanish Departments," *The Chronicle of Higher Education*, June 23, 2016; "Christopher Columbus's Catalan-Inflected Language," *The Chronicle of Higher Education*, October 8, 2017, "The Cross-Lingual Interse(x)tionality of 'Latinx,'" *The Chronicle of Higher Education*, May 1, 2018, and "Hemingway's Cuban English," *The Chronicle of Higher Education*, July 20, 2017). I am indebted to those editors and reviewers, for their insights and encouragement.

This work would not have been possible without the support of the Universidad de Puerto Rico-Mayagüez, where I have been a faculty member since 2009; Eötvös Loránd University, where I served as Fulbright Distinguished Chair of American Studies (László Országh Chair) in 2019; or the Obama Institute for Transnational American Studies, where I completed the manuscript as Obama Fellow in 2022. I am especially indebted to Fernando Gilbes, Matías Cafaro, Jókay Károly, Mita Banerjee, Axel Schäfer and Alfred Hornung, who have been supportive of my work and provided me with the time to develop it. No one has been more important than my family. I thank my parents, whose love is with me in everything I pursue, and my wonderful wife, Joanna, and *nuestros chiquitos*, Santiago and Alejandro, who translate translations into ungrammatical and restorative inspiration.

DECOLONIZING AMERICAN SPANISH

INTRODUCTION

COLONIALISM IN US SPANISH DEPARTMENTS

Since the 1960s Spanish-language cultural studies in the United States have undergone a profound reformation, from Spain-centrism in all subfields toward a frame that balances Peninsular and Latin American topics. At once a radical and democratizing thrust, the move localized a hemispheric shift in intellectual focus and had profound influences on the central tenets of the disciplines, on the institutions involved (departments, universities, publications, professional associations, and so on), on the structural presumptions that organize knowledge-production, and on the latitude of subjectivities that may be conceptualized and institutionalized. While many of the pre–Latin American studies methodologies remain (including the centrality of literature, foregrounding the national/transnational as a meaningful container of culture, and periodization exigencies[1]), the move toward Latin America localized the themes and subjects that appeared in US classrooms, deconstructing some of the Eurocentric supremacy of the traditional model.

But Spanish-language cultural pedagogies remain mired in theoretical presumptions that underpin (and thus ensure) a widespread Eurocentrism, grounding knowledge-production in US institutions to a specific set of distant objects, periods, figures, narratives, cultural geographies, and variants of Spanish—many of which are incompatible with students' lives and that of their communities. This structural scaffolding enforces the continuing foreignization of Spanish where it is a domestic (and in many regions *dominant*) language; it provides the conditions of an encounter in which local memory-making (of Latinx students and communities specifically) is explicitly omitted from institutionalization.[2]

Colonial pedagogy produces absence (silence, not words). Its presumptions conceal sacrifices of those who suffer from such logics (Quijano 2000; Ortega 2017; Mignolo 2000, 2011), functioning on epistemological levels (modern ways of knowing have precedence over all others, including local knowledge, restricting *what can be known*) and ontological/sociobiological planes: coloniality is a lived experience that shapes not only the cultures but also the minds and bodies of those subordinated to it. The Hispanic studies project is a Eurocentric knowledge framework for organizing, scaling, and classifying communities, cultures, and language varieties that is interlinked with political entities and neoliberal programs: my argument in this book suggests options to detach power from Eurocentric prescriptions as applied in hiring, course design, departmental organization, the stated and implicit missions of professional organizations, among other intellectual activity—and to apply local forms of knowledge-creation in ways that delegitimize contemporary best practices (in the enormous range of intellectual activity that Spain-centric knowledge patterns influence). Upon a base of statistical data regarding faculty appointments and courses in Spanish-language cultural topics, my argument aims to unlink knowledge production from Eurocentric certainties, to retreat from epistemological conditions that make Spain-centrism to a degree inevitable, and to engage domains of knowledge that are marginalized in the transnational turn. (Some of the conceptual implications in a shift from a traditional universe to a decolonial pluriverse can be seen in the following list.)

From Universe to Pluriverse

TRADITIONAL UNIVERSE	DECOLONIAL PLURIVERSE
Spanish as "foreign"	Spanish as "domestic"
convey historical certainties	*produce* localized knowledges
Spain / Latin America–centric	local materials
Geographic prescription	de-territorialized (critical territorialization)
transnational views	deconceptualize trans/nation as exceptional bearer of culture

this, that (and/or both)	"Decolonial Potential of NEITHER" (F. White 2018)
monocultural or hybrid	post-prescriptive conditionality
"worlded" views dominate	local community as cultural locus
Area studies epistemes	Post-area knowledges
periodized, epoch-based	situational, conditional, heterogeneous perceptions of time
monolingual priority (standard)	nonstandard, cross/multi/translingual enunciations
Peninsular language ordinary	subgroup-focused, local as ordinary (Peninsular as dialect)
learned, received	cultivated, reflective reinvention
reasoned and rational	lived and performed
a priori cultural prescriptions	situational descriptive analyses
literary canons	various performative iterations
literacy-based culture	plurality of experiential and participatory acts
text as exceptional culture	multiple performative materials
gendered	post-gendered
class hierarchies	unstratified
essentialized	performative, provisional, situated
positioned	ephemeral (situational, circumstantial, conditional, migrational)
analogue	digital (multiple performance, community, emotion codification)
pre-analysis categorization	begin with a performance; work toward categorization

Stressing the exceptional importance of local knowledges and expanding the notion of "local," this book considers methods that would undo the Spain exceptionalism that (with a few notable exceptions) characterizes the contemporary academy. The argument intends to add to what the hemispheric, Latin American studies move achieved: once the collective epistemic threshold situates Peninsular topics as nonexceptional, tenure lines in other topics could appear: How might new lines conceptualize culture, language, performance, and the Peninsula? What are the cultural capitals of US Spanish? What about provincial centers, rural arenas, and zones of transience? How might such material become foci of PhD programs and tenure-line appointments? Aside from traditional takes on geography, notions like "Latin American culture in the US," and city-state/regional views, what are additional layers of "local" culture?

Conceptualizing "local" in city / town / village / provincial senses *as well as* across a series of oft-neglected axes of the human condition (including colonization, [il]literacy, class, migration, and multilingualism), the argument develops methods of study, reflection, and teaching that disengage the intellectual environment from Eurocentric rationalities. A focus on scholarly appointments—a profound long-term institutional expression of mission—allows the suggestions to function within existing structural exigencies and to complement traditional knowledge bases by integrating (and thus making inevitable) spheres of intellectual activity that are unreachable within existing structures. The approach aims to domesticate Spanish in the United States and to institutionalize local memory-making (in Spanish) through critical, cultivative, and co-creative pedagogy; using higher education as a node of entanglement, a principal thrust of this book addresses the creation and maintenance of unequal relationships between Spanish-language communities (mainly Spain/local senses but also extra-US-Latin America / local) that characterize US institutions.

COLONIALISM IN US SPANISH DEPARTMENTS

Eurocentric pedagogies are an exercise in distortion. Despite the radical opening of Latin American studies decades ago,[3] today there is roughly a one-to-one ratio of faculty specialists in Iberian study to those in Latin American topics across the academy: Latin America has approximately ten times more Spanish-speakers than Spain, but the cultures and languages of each receive comparative attention in US classrooms. While Mexico has nearly three times more inhabitants than Spain, many departments in the dataset compiled in chapter 1 did not have a *single* Mexico specialist—but 97.7 percent of departments surveyed had *multiple* specialists on Spain. Spanish-speakers in the United States have outnumbered those in Spain for years, but local cultures receive *far* less curricular focus than Spain, Mexico, and every other region.

The Eurocentric hiring practice vastly overrepresents Spain not only in pedagogy and publications but also in critical attention to cultural material like art, texts, film, and spoken accents in the Spanish language. These faculty demographics privilege specific ways to use the language orally and in writing, including accents (like *distinción*'s "th" sound for "z" and "c" when followed by an "e" or "i"),[4] grammar and syntax (the use of the perfect tense rather than preterit for a recent event, completed or not), articles (like *leísmo*, or the use of *le* as a direct-object pronoun instead of *lo/la*), vocabulary (*ordenador* for computer, *coche* for car, *zumo* for juice, and so on), verbs (like *conducir* for to drive and *ponerse de pie* for to stand up), and the second-person plural (the use of *vosotros* as informal you plural). The tendency also overloads class time and assignments with material from Iberian cultures and histories, ignoring their unstudied local / Latin American parallels. In the same way that unwalkable city layouts have forced people into automobile usage, the Eurocentric pedagogical framework forces Spain into the academic experience of all scholars. As a corrective measure, this book suggests transitioning from *multiple* Peninsular specialists across effectively all US departments (the received "best practice") to a model that has *at most* a single Spain specialist per department: the lines transitioned away from Iberian-foci could engage cultures more local to each institution.[5]

The existing faculties have been organized so that Cervantes's Mozarabic wordplay matters but not Sandra de la Loza's Spanglish or Titu Cusi's *quechueñol*; we see ourselves in Velázquez's mirror but not Guillermo Gómez-Peña's plate glass or Tezcatlipoca's volcanic rock; and Picasso is neither "Jay Michael Jaramillo of the Left Bank" nor "Guayasamín of the North"—such examples could go on ad infinitum. But they are not natural hierarchies. Even the most passionate Iberian studies apologist cannot maintain that the material is more aesthetically engaging, historically meaningful, or relevant to students' lives. Perhaps the way we present the work (or don't present it—or label it "folklore" rather than "culture") makes this pedagogical Spanish exceptionalism appear normal to some, if not appropriate.[6]

Such practices rely on several myths: The colonizer is the "root" of the cultural system (a hierarchy that continues after political independence); the language, art, text, and aesthetics of the subaltern have been profoundly influenced by imperial directives; and the existence of European languages and cultures in the Americas is generally positive. Our faculties are designed to reproduce that reality: Spanish cultures, languages, and accents are more important, and thus, our curricula and faculty demographics must reflect that idea. Myths like these are a language, one that must be repeated and presented as fact by faculty and other authority figures, lest the system fall apart. A decolonial move would shift the curricular emphases toward local cultures and traditions, while decoupling the institutional fetishization from a Eurocentric axis. Overloading faculties, canons, and curricula toward Spain has occurred for five hundred years—transitioning our professoriate toward local realities is an ethical imperative that is long overdue.

DECOLONIAL PARADIGMS

The presence of Spanish and other European languages in the Americas is part of an ongoing intellectual project that dehumanizes non-European peoples. The implementation of language and the reduction of colonized populations to nonhuman status "referencia a supuestas estructuras biológicas diferenciales entre colonizadores y colonizados" (Quijano 2014, 777), the concepts from which modernity verticalizes people and the cultures that ostensibly codify their emotion and agencies. As Ramón Grosfoguel, Nelson Maldonado-Torres, and José David Saldívar have noted, this phenomenon has shifted to a degree "from biological to cultural forms of racism" in which "culture" is weaponized, becoming "a marker of inferiority and superiority, reinstalling again the same colonial/racial hierarchy" (2015, 12, 13). Since Donald Trump's inauguration, however, traditional racism has been comprehensively re-institutionalized in the United States and elsewhere: "The decolonial turn consists of the shift from the acceptance of inferiority," notes Maldonado-Torres, "to the assumption of the position of a questioner" (2017, 118). In this process, "the colonized subject emerges not only as a questioner but also as an embodied being who seeks to become an agent" (Maldonado-Torres 2017, 118).

As Maldonado-Torres situates "the *primacy of ethics*" as a response and "an antidote to problems with Western conceptions of freedom, autonomy, and equality" (2008, 7; my emphasis), *Decolonizing American Spanish* revisits and critiques the ethical conditions that maintain Eurodomination across the US academy.[7] Maldonado-Torres deftly observes that many recent educational initiatives "seek to socialize youth into a reality where *the continued patterns of exclusion are justified*."[8] This book envisions decolonial frameworks as emancipating epistemes from the modern/colonial exigencies of Eurocentric ontologies, using Spanish-language cultural studies as a site of entanglement: the analyses revisit the colonial modalities of the Eurocentric university; reflect on the outcomes of its curricular, linguistic, and cultural prescriptions; and consider multiple modes of undoing (including cultural jamming through activist pedagogy, hiring, and curricular design) toward localized forms of intellectual solidarity and social resistance.[9] Engaging shades of Gloria Anzaldúa's border epistemes, I argue that Eurocentrism—i.e., Hispanic studies—is a key site for denaturalizing the ways students and educators discover, conceive, perceive, and act in their worlds. Since traditional pedagogy silences local knowledges and cultures,[10] this denaturalizing requires a two-pronged move: 1) the annulment of Spain exceptionalism (a core component of Hispanic studies), and 2) the emergence of activist apparatuses that foreground local Spanish-languages and cultures as domestic (not foreign), constituent components of belonging and agency. Exploring such a move from within contemporary institutional exigencies, this book examines critical and conceptual lenses that may complement (if not be antidotes to) traditional Eurocentric prescriptions, delving into the potential of the university as an emancipating institution.

Eurocentric Spanish-language cultural studies implicitly maintain that cultures and texts distant in time and geography, produced in European communities, are more important to students' lives than their own languages, cultures, and experiences. At many universities in regions claimed by the US political body, such programs elicit (and in fact require) the institutional foreignization of local performances. Critical and decolonial pedagogies understand learning as a cultivative, political act and reject the objectivity of culture and knowledge; they maintain that questions of social justice and democracy are embedded in teaching and learning. Critical and decolonial pedagogy also strives to emancipate classroom narratives from already-power by engaging the students' critical consciousnesses in ways that encourage effecting change in their worlds through cultural critique and political action that grow from their scholarly preparation. Decolonial pedagogies strive to *produce* localized knowledges rather than *convey* canonic and Eurocentric certainties.

What conditions could make such a move possible? The statistics in this book make clear that Eurocentrism is a (perhaps *the*) defining metaphor in how knowledge is conceptualized and organized in many US Spanish departments. This situation has grown from generations of implementing and institutionalizing imperial culture over local ones, by foregrounding the biases and distortions of the conventional foreign-domestic ideology. This book encourages modes to unlearn—and thus denaturalize—the traditional positions that characterize US higher education and the social and cultural maps upon which it exerts influence. Such shifts hinge on Latinx knowledges and leverage student experiences: when students enunciate their own voices in their own languages, decolonial Spanish-language cultural studies engage, as a feature of knowledge, the extra-imperial experiences that individuals and communities have and have had throughout history. Institutionalizing the voices that students use to recognize themselves and give meaning to their communities, the foundations of Spanish-language cultural studies (in a decolonial mode) pivot toward unlearning the biases of Eurocentrism and "foreign" status, toward an imaginary that centers on the local ways of being that are concealed in Spain-centric institutions.

Decolonial approaches replace Eurocentric recitation with students speaking from their own voices, knowledges, and histories, cultivating their own experiences, while challenging the certainties in which representation, pleasure, codification, comparison, and other dimensions of cultural studies occur. Such an approach strives to enlarge the range of identities that students may study, perform, experience, and develop knowledge about. While decolonial Spanish-language cultural studies authorize student and local voices, they cultivate awareness and critique of the Eurocentric conditions of their articulation. Grounded in a commitment to social transformation, decolonial strategies aim to reconcile higher education with the inequality it generates.

Such a move is a formidable challenge, as the preexisting educational structure (and the student outcomes designed in correlation therewith) is anchored in conditions that are largely determined outside the university. The institutions are embedded within the US political body, an entity that forces a Eurocentric cultural and linguistic canon upon each campus, and thus upon each student and instructor, in ways that far transcend education. If Eurocentrism is the de facto structural entanglement and institutional architecture of each classroom, curriculum, and campus, these "foreign language" topics participate in the allegedly unassailable and putatively de facto foreign/domestic map. We form knowledge and cultivate learning in conditions that preexist our entrance in the academy—these conditions foreignize some communication and cultural activity while domesticating others; since participation in the broader cultural, political, economic, and civic realities often requires credentialization (a university degree), the institutions in question wield immense power.

But a classroom is a unique space: it is one in which material may be released to a degree from the external pressures and prescriptions in ways that recognize voices, accents, spiritualities, and migrations that are silent (and impossible to hear) in the Eurocentric tradition. While scholars cultivate knowledges (and the courses, degrees, publications, and other material codify them), we do not make them autonomously, in surroundings that we design. The decolonial initiatives described here aim to unlink the student experience from Eurocentric modernity, as iterated in university settings, by nuancing the design of how knowledge is cultivated, nourished, performed, and shared. Such ambitions have seemingly insurmountable restrictions, confined and pre-channeled into ideological interpellations (of student, faculty, and cultural demographics) that are conceived and structured to repeat the foreignness/domesticity of the material itself (and thus of the people who practice it). But students are perhaps those best situated to enunciate futures, pluralities, ideas, and forms of local autonomy not yet perceived or described by cultural institutions. Their ideas, feelings, emotions, and intellectual interventions are prime resources from which decolonial options will grow and develop, democratically nuancing the conditions in which we are now entangled.

A main thrust of such institutional transitions could come from hiring student-scholars who situate the Eurocentric tradition as nonexceptional—and who in fact perceive the *local* as exceptional. Resistance to the Eurocentric, worlded, transnational and national, and other relational and communal logics that are the center of the contemporary Spain-centric praxis would grow from such appointments: students who train in these conditions would bring their experience with them out into the empire. Can such a shift reorient the knowledge production of a field, unlinking its core components from the stifling hierarchies of patriarchal colonial modernity? Can attention to new spheres of intellectual activity, new notions of "US" and "Latin America" and "the Spanish language" and "Spain," generate modes of acting, knowing, and being that are unrecognizable in the Eurocentric tradition? Does decolonial pedagogy reappropriate agency of subaltern communities, recognize their struggles and collective action, in appropriate ways? How can decolonial networks be located, recognized, voiced, studied, and organized *after* pedagogy— and *outside* classrooms? What dimensions of pluriversal pedagogy reach into communities? Where does Spain fit in a decolonized field? Which Spanishes will be recognized? How will multilingualism, nonverbal performances, and the cultural mores of illiterate peoples be treated? Among others, these are some of the overarching inquiries undertaken in this book.

FROM *WORLD* TO *WORLDS*, STRUCTURAL SHIFTS IN DECOLONIAL PEDAGOGIES

Decolonial understandings of cultural material maintain that "different worlds can coexist without an imposed assimilation ethos into a dominant culture" (Veronelli 2016, 406). The ways knowledge is formed in Spanish-language cultural pedagogies could refocus, engaging pluriversal views that hinge on *non-European ways of being, living, and creating knowledge*. In an applied sense, Robert McKee Irwin and Mónica Szurmuk argue in favor of:

1) a pronounced move from a literary to a cultural studies focus;
2) a displacement of Spain in departmental hierarchies, accompanied by an increased focus on Mexico (and Latin America in general); and
3) a prominent role for local culture (modified from 2009, 49).

In concert with these suggestions, this book builds on Irwin and Szurmuk's work by engaging additional spheres of "local" through post-area (denationalized, post-cultural, and to a degree post-geographic) conceptualizations of "location":[11]

4) localized area (non-transnational views: region, town/city-inflected);
5) multilingual cognition (multi-language thinking as a "location");
6) Spain as an Arabized "location" in Latin America (i.e., Islamic/Arabic performance as "Spanish"); and
7) modes developed at the Universidad de Puerto Rico as "exceptional" (UPR as an educational "location" to emulate in the United States).

The case studies in this book aim to bring these strands of cultural studies into meaningful relation with cognitive linguistics, neuroaesthetics, and cultural psychology, among other fields, organizing these mergences into localized intellectual emphases with potential to be developed into disciplines not unlike "Southern Cone" or "golden age Peninsular poetry." Applying those dimensions of knowledge production toward pedagogies aims to push the boundaries of what forms of thought, feelings, and cultures the institution can support. As Ramón Grosfoguel notes, the idea is to "start imagining alternative worlds beyond Eurocentrism and fundamentalism" (Grosfoguel 2011, 27) and thus to provide a platform external to the hierarchies of Euro-modern certainties through attention to now-silenced axes of cultural performance. The data in chapter 1 demonstrate that Eurocentrism is yet the "home" of the discipline, the sphere of knowledge through which all other inquiry must pass: "We must leave home," notes Caren Kaplan, "since our homes are often sites of racism, sexism, and other damaging social practices" (1987, 187–88). Away from home we can recognize other nodes of being—and if we perceive "coloniality as a process of inventing identifications," as Walter Mignolo notes, "then for identification to be decolonial it needs to be articulated as 'des-identification' and 're-identification,' which means it is a process of delinking" (qtd. in Gaztambide-Fernández 2014, 198). How might new identities be studied, described, and investigated? How (or in what ways) does material culture "represent" emotion? Mignolo continues, "'Representation' is a keyword in the rhetoric of modernity, that is, in Western mainstream epistemology. In this regard, thinking decolonially (that is, thinking within the frame of the decolonial option) means to start from 'enunciation' and not from 'representation.' When you start from the enunciation and think decolonially, you shall run away from representation, for representation presupposes that there is a world out there that someone is representing. This is a basic assumption of modern epistemology. There is not a world that is represented, but a world that is constantly invented in the enunciation" (qtd. in Gaztambide-Fernández 2014, 198).

Throughout this book the term "represent" *re-present* (and its derivatives) is used in a transitive sense, perhaps more similar to *plasmar* than *representar*; that is, it refers to making physical the internal dimensions of the enunciative process (i.e., making thought physical—into sounds, texts, visual material, etc.) in ways that are accessible and may become praxes in educational settings. In relation to this concept, the case-study chapters engage an important shift away from the critical presumptions embedded in traditional critique and regarding the nature of cultural entanglement, *from received to conditional*.

CONDITIONAL ENTANGLEMENT AND THE SITUATIONAL NATURE OF CULTURAL EXPERIENCE

While entanglement is often an a priori, received circumstance, it is also conditional: thus, a move to analyze a performance *then* move toward categorization (rather than the other way around) would examine culture in ways that gesture toward more atomized, de-territorialized (de[trans] nationalized) sensibilities. The relational entanglement structure, if it exists, is presumed to be fluid; when it can be known, it is presumed to be conditional to surroundings and fleeting: if performances may be linked to a priori categories (e.g., woman/man, "Mexican" or "American," and so on) these are understood as conditional, transitory, and ephemeral conditions.[12] This approach to cultural categorizations and social relationships has many links to queer theory, and in particular to the work of Judith Butler: "At a lesbian feminist rally," as Eboo Patel notes, Butler "opened her remarks by saying that she was fine appearing as a lesbian feminist as long as she was free to define what that meant for herself, and change her definition depending on the time, place, situation and stage of her life" (2019, 1). Indeed, the notions of cultural individuality, inevitability, performance, and their supposed relation to (always a priori) umbrella groupings to be discussed here follow similar sensibilities, based on *conditions* of performance, rather than the *permanence* of received and external categorization.[13]

NATIONAL AND TRANSNATIONAL AND OTHER COLONIALIZED HYBRID CONTAINERS

Much of the curricular Eurocentric "home" stems from the reliance on the nation and transnational myths as methodological containers—and to a further degree, on the notion that geography of residency (if not origins) is *always* a reliable identity proxy. The functional inertia of transnational and national knowledge subordinates other realms of study in destructive ways. The nation-based myth also stipulates untenable positions, like: *Spain is an exceptional nation; all others are inferior and for that appear less frequently as themes of study, publication, and specialization.* The notion that nations and transnations are meaningful loci culture and history exerts a silent Eurocentric hegemony in all facets of disciplinary logic, grammar, vocabulary, and reasoning, one that prescribes a homogeneity centered on the national and transnational timeframes, geographies, and assertions of belonging.

Indeed, the transnational and national approaches are obedient to some of the principal myths of this age: that people believe in or identify (in a direct, hybrid, multi, worlded, temporalized, or dialectical sense) with national or transnational material. Rather than transcending the slippery folklores of national idolatry and its cultures, the transnational theories reengage them in ways that do not intend to annul their relevance. In this way, the myth that national stories, narratives, and feelings inform people's lives and cultures in a hybrid or direct way is a (if not *the*) fundamental presumption in the transnational turn, and it is also a fundamental weakness. National exceptionalisms are reinforced, albeit with new nuance, by transnationalizing the base of inquiry. Donald Pease has observed that the transcultural and transnational approach represents "a change in mentality but not in institutions or structures," one that leaves "power intact" (2011, 16). Constrained by these grammars of inquiry, nonconforming voices are situated within the transnational exigencies: their critique is restricted to objecting to such orders of community and identity instead of entirely displacing them.[14]

LINGERING TWILIGHT OF IDOLS

> I think the nation is here to stay; it's not going to vanish for a long time as an analytic unit, and certainly not as an organizing unit.
>
> **Wai Chee Dimock, qtd. in Jeffrey J. Williams,**
> **"American Literature in the World" (2016, 174)**

For some, the transnational offers a map of the hybrid, fluid spaces between cultural/national groups. Rather than inquiring if these discrete groups exist in the ways imagined, the transnational fluidity presumes they do in an a priori sense, and that blending of these vessels are always and everywhere markers of meaningful culture, history, community, and individual and communitive performances. The transnational assigns a person, community, or piece of material culture a categorization with two or more of these pre-apportioned (allegedly existent and supposedly) disconnected groups, makes associative observations, and uses the inferences to form ostensibly new and stable modes of knowledge.

The transnational does not question the self-evidence of the a priori mythos but rather remobilizes it by insisting that people engage with myths in traditional and hybrid ways. Wai Chee Dimock's explanation could be understood as typical of the influence of these traditional approaches when she invites "us to see the nation not as a closed chapter but as one endlessly in flux, endlessly in relation": Dimock argues that these views make "each [trans/nation] less a foregone conclusion as a heuristic occasion," but instead of engaging this uncertainty to tease out the potential non-transnational (or any meaning system external to a nationalized qualifier), her analyses return to the traditional "center and peripheries" containers, thus maintaining a critical vocabulary that explicitly avoids ontologies external to transnational exigencies. The terms of the comparison remain tied to the supposedly discrete groups, thereby rehashing the traditional understanding of "interconnectedness" as a key feature of cultural performance (qtd. in Williams 2016, 2–3).

Whether the transnational imagines A + B = C, or D, A/B, B/A, A/B/C, A–Z, or another arrangement, A and B are not variables in the equation, and C cannot be articulated outside the confines of A and B. A fundamental flaw is that studies in social psychology and cultural neurology refute that discrete cultural groups (A and B) or their hybrid blends (C), so embraced by the trans/national, exist in people's lives in these ways (Glatzeder 2011, 242; Blaser 2014, 1). The trans/national lacks extra-disciplinary affirmations of its constituent components, but despite these serious theoretical miscues, the transnational turn has an increasingly axiomatic grip on scholarship.

It's an old form of thinking to assert that what surrounds a person (cultural geographies of residence and life experiences, familial and social backgrounds, etc.) fully informs their being. But that is precisely what transnational lines of inquiry require. Such exigencies lay the groundwork to continue ad infinitum, "endlessly" as per Dimock's description, a form of cultural inquiry that excludes any recognition or institutionalization of other webs of being, which have little or nothing to do with transnational ties. In relation to the existing grammars and their exigencies, as Grosfoguel notes, "We need to find new concepts and a new decolonial language" (2011, 19).[15] As Gabriela Veronelli deftly observes, this task is at once destructive and creative, as "decolonial futures don't have words yet" (2016, 405).[16]

DECOLONIAL ONTOLOGIES THAT SUPPLANT WORLDVIEWS WITH WORLDS

The decolonial, ontological turn in Spanish-language cultural studies has largely yet to occur. The single-world logics of colonial modernity (one world, many worldviews) obfuscate attention to alternative worlds and the material cultures that codify them.[17] The plural ontological approach (multiple world) has relevancies that the modern approaches (sole-truth and sole-world, which has been perhaps trans/nationalized or transcultured) deem illogical and irrational. Drawing from research in cultural geography, neuroaesthetics, and behavioral psychology, my arguments in chapters 1 and 2 locate pluriversal and localized sensibilities as loci of nuance to the colonial (one-world) universe. Bringing these findings to bear on Spanish-language cultural pedagogies refutes the dominant view of Spanish-language cultural reality as a unified, amalgamated world with subsets of worldviews: constellative and pluriversal narratives subvert the essentialization of sole-truth views and thus fragment a Eurocentric modernity that totalizes all down into territorialized and periodized units (these are codified in curricular foci and tenure-line appointments); once this shift (one-world toward multiple worlds) is in place, localizing praxes may arise in emancipative pedagogies.[18]

Modern Eurocentric pedagogies do not remain in theoretical or academic domains. The imperial worldviews that saturate classrooms shape the ways students interact with others, perceive and create cultures, construct reality, effect political orientation, and mobilize metaphoric and symbolic barriers. These worldviews also have a significant influence on the public health and mental wellbeing of students immersed in them. The formation and preservation of hierarchies among Spanish-language communities occur in classrooms much the same way that they do in political and economic centers of power: individuals and groups (and the cultural materials that codify their emotions, sensibilities, communities, and identities) are embedded in a longue durée institutionalized inequality that pivots on relational "truths" that organize these curricular disparities. The standard pedagogical praxes command that some groups and individuals be treated with deference and others with disregard; these longstanding socialized judgements (codified in mission statements, departmental and scholarly association nomenclatures, weighting of curricula, courses, appointment practices, cultural prizes, and publications, among many other arenas) have consequences that far transcend the pedagogical materials seen or unseen in a classroom setting.

While the Eurocentric structure may be self-evident, many Peninsular specialists understand disciplinary reform as long overdue.[19] As Ann Abbott, director of Undergraduate Studies at the University of Illinois, writes, "Many of us have been saying [the field needs decolonization] for a long time," and goes on, there is a: "dismal representation of Spanish in the US in Spanish programs. From our department's curriculum, you would get the impression that 'Spanish' is 50% Spain and 50% Latin America because that is the logic of the courses—which reflects the logic of the graduate programs. Furthermore, you would have the impression that 'Spanish' is 50% literature and 50% language/linguistics—which again represents the logic of the graduate programs. It is unbelievably frustrating to see post-colonial critics (some) reinforce a colonial curriculum."[20] In response to Abbott's remarks, Francesco D'Introno comments: "El problema también reside en la inercia/falta de voluntad intelectual de los latinoamericanistas en discutir este muy importante tema e injusticia, y en resolverlo" (qtd. in Abbott 2016). Some reflections on the topic concern specific language structures: "We never learn *vos*," observes Caitlin Archer-Helke. "As far as I know, it doesn't even appear in textbooks. But everybody learns *vosotros*" (qtd. in Abbott 2016). Jason Jolley adds, "Teaching *vosotros* to anyone other than students heading to Spain is a very, very odd proposition" (qtd. in Abbott 2016). Iván Fernández Peláez prefaces his remarks, "I say this as a Peninsularist," and goes on to note, there is an "almost total absence of US Spanish language and culture. Unfortunately, a sense of cultural superiority is not exclusive to European scholars" (qtd. in Abbott 2016). Others perceive additional dimensions of colonialism in the academy, as Richard John File-Muriel comments in an email to the author (Sept. 2, 2016): "Here in New Mexico [at the University of New Mexico], we deal with ongoing colonialism of all sorts," and continues:

> I see colonialism in structures like the TOEFL (English proficiency exam) in UNM, and Spanish Proficiency Exams in Latin America. In both reside large indigenous communities who don't speak Spanish and are shameful-

ly excluded from participation in intellectual exchanges, are not admitted into Universities, and are marginalized in almost all aspects of our societies. Why not have proficiency exams in Spanish, Navajo, Nahuatl, Tiwa, etc.? Why require language proficiency exams at all? Well, the answer is obvious, it's to ensure that the "right" kind of people are admitted; that is, people who speak English (or Spanish, in Latin America) fluently.

As many scholars perceive Spain-centrism and as an inappropriate epistemic condition, why does it continue? There is some misunderstanding about what constitutes Eurocentrism or Spain-centrism. If themes of study are divided up into area studies terms (as they largely are now),[21] Eurocentric means *beyond 10 percent of the content, intellectual activity, and/or appointments relating to Spain*—and thus, almost every department and curriculum in the United States falls in such a category. There are arguments that the Spain-centrism has benefits, specifically with respect to enrollments, and that any shift to a decolonial model risks losing matriculants and thus funding and, ultimately, the existence of departments.

INCUMBENCY BIAS, TRADITION, NEOLIBERALISM, ADJUNCTIFICATION, ENROLLMENTS, AND APOLOGY

Once a tool is in place, it is extremely difficult to displace that tool. It's like a dam on a lake. Without the dam, the water would flow downhill and find its way to the ocean. With a dam in place, the water must reach a much higher level before it overflows and continues on its way. The incumbency bias is the dam—it prevents change.
Known set of tools
Avoid disruption
Avoiding uncertainty and stress
Little or no training needed because [faculty] have expertise with the toolset
In other words, calm waters.
Modified from Sarah O'Keefe, "The True Cost of Incumbency Bias" (2012, 1)

For some, Spain-centrism means calm disciplinary waters, institutional stability, and the enrolment constancy that neoliberal and corporate universities command. Robert McKee Irwin and Mónica Szurmuk argue that "with rising and sometimes overwhelming enrollments has been that there is no time to think about curricular reform" (2009, 45).

Tied to the incumbency bias, the non-tenure-track labor status of the supermajority of faculty likely contributes to maintenance of intellectual frameworks that benefit conservative/traditional modes. While tenured scholars enjoy a degree of disciplinary autonomy, the corporate nature of the US university involves adjunctification as a preeminent labor status, a circumstance that severely constrains academic freedom and the abilities to pursue knowledge creation in lesser-established fields (local Spanishes, for instance). This precarious situation also tacitly maintains existing standards of Eurocentrism even for those hired onto the tenure stream: unemployment is a looming *nonacademic* factor in what is studied, taught, published, and disseminated throughout the US academy. And for the tiny cohort of individuals who reach the tenure stream, each scholar must endure a probational period including teaching, publishing, and service, all of which must fall within "acceptable" forms of inquiry, so as to validate oneself in an already-institutionalized situation. Since Spanish language and cultural studies have enjoyed enrollment success in Spain-centric modes, and given that career options for PhDs are severely limited, the labor environment facilitates a Eurocentric repetition of one-to-one balance across disciplines.[22]

SHOULD SPAIN MAINTAIN 50 PERCENT OF APPOINTMENTS, COURSES, AND DEGREES?

> In most situations, promoting Spain and its culture, promoting the status of one's own field, and promoting one's own career have amounted to much the same thing.
>
> **Sebastiaan Faber, "Economies of Prestige" (2008, 13)**

Even with a one-to-one balance in which Spain-specialists have five times more appointments than any equivalent cohort, some opine that Iberian and Hispanic studies are not overweighted but *marginalized*. If one yields to traditional terminology, the notion of "marginalization" for Peninsular topics should be conceptualized as any number below 10 percent (not 50 percent). Peninsular material/faculty/texts/publications may be understood as "underrepresented" only when a scholar submits to the tradition of overwhelming Eurocentrism that pushes the notion of *appropriate* up to 50 percent Spain-related or more, despite the enormous demographic imbalances involved. Jonathan Mayhew, a professor of

Peninsular topics who "didn't go to any Spanish speaking country aside from Spain until I was in my 50s" (Mayhew 2017, 1), argues that "a lot of people" in every department specializing in Spanish literature is appropriate if not beneficial: "I begin every seminar with a quiz. This week, I had . . . six or seven texts and had them see if you could tell whether the author was peninsular or Spanish American. The result was that nobody could tell the difference between the lyrical language of Spain and that of Latin America. . . . This leads me to reflect on that idiot [Jeffrey Herlihy-Mera] in CHE a while back who wrote that the teaching of peninsular Spanish in US universities was so colonialist, that having a lot of people with peninsular Spanish on the faculty was such a bad thing" (2016b). The students evidence some of the reasons why excessive material on Spain (i.e., more than 10 percent of hires, courses, conferences, publications, etc.) is unethical: the presumed natural exceptionalism in texts written by Spaniards or any other demographic is a myth. Since there is no aesthetic or "quality" variance among texts in Spanish per national or regional origin of the author, why continue such a disproportionate role of Spain in pedagogy? As Peninsular cultures, languages, histories, and traditions are *nonexceptional*, why should they be treated as exceptional in hires, courses, and the gamut of scholarly activities? While Mayhew does not address such uncertainties, he argues that Spain centrism vis-à-vis Latin American themes is: "Not an apples to apples comparison, since most Latin Americanists do not study a single country, except in the case, precisely, of Mexico. People study Latin American literature generally, or are specialists in a period, a genre, or a region, less often a single nation state" (2016a). As Mayhew clarifies, the Spain-centric discriminations result in the following structural marginalization of US and Latin American communities: "If you were hiring Latin Americanists by region, you would say Mexico, América central, caribeño, cono sur . . . Andes" (2016a). The received, presumed, and prescribed (and farcical) exceptionalism of Spain and Spaniards created and now maintains this hierarchy.[23] This Eurocentric privilege means Spain receives *multiple* "nation-centric" appointments in every department (shaping courses, degrees, publications, prizes, etc.) while other ostensibly equal units (nations) *must* be grouped across regions—except Mexico, which is nearly *three times larger* than Spain in terms of population and unquestionably more local to US classrooms. According to these institutions, Spain and Mexico and the rest of the nations involved are not equal, a myth that legitimizes the disproportionate intellectual activity dedicated to Spain:[24] "Only Spain seems to have the right to teach its literature as a national literature," observes Nicolas Shumway, and the "lumping" together of all non-Spanish communities "hides vital" elements and experiences from the students' potential knowledge base (Shumway 2005, 296).

This Eurocentric model also frames the possible topics in which one must specialize to receive an academic appointment: "I think if I were a Latin Americanist," Mayhew continues, "I would have many more job opportunities" (2016a). If this reflection were true, the additional opportunities would be marginal in number: there are *not* tenfold more jobs in Latin American / US topics (as there should be) or even two-to-one more positions, precisely because of the Eurocentric exigencies around which the field is structured. Indeed, any piece of culture realized today (or any time throughout history) on the Peninsula is *far* more likely to appear in US classrooms due to the structural exigencies that this book critiques.

Malcolm Alan Compitello also believes moving away from Peninsular centrism "represents the kind of wrongheaded thinking and lack of knowledge about how departments form curricular decisions and what actually goes on in them that is dangerous to our discipline as a whole."[25] While complacent or "wrongheaded" thinking may have informed curricular and hiring decisions for some time, and has detrimental health and wellbeing consequences for our students, nuancing Eurocentrism is perhaps a dangerous concept for those who perceive the status quo as a utopia. Such shifts could also be perilous in a neoliberal sense, potentially lowering enrollments in the near term, as some students likely look to confirm their preexisting biases through Spain-centric studies. "My department," notes an unidentified scholar at an MLA panel, "hires the very best people we can, regardless of the research area because we need talent and good teachers." When there are disproportionately more (over 10 percent more) Peninsular-specialist PhDs than US / Latin American–specialist PhDs, the results of hiring the "best" can only recite Eurocentrism, which underscores the urgency of restructuring knowledge production away from traditional centers; when the structural exigencies preserve Eurocentrism, whatever the enrollment or tradition, this requires deconstruction (or destruction) in preference to nuance. Many scholars have noted that this is indeed inevitable: "Herlihy-Mera's prediction about one statistic is hard to deny," notes Maureen Russo Rodríguez. "The amount of faculty appointments for Peninsular specialists vs. Latin Americanists will not continue to maintain its present ratio . . . 'roughly one-to-one' . . . amidst the changing currents in success of Spanish programs in general" (2016, 1).

CLAIMS OF CAUSALITY

Pedagogical and institutional norms encode power. These traditions and values in the United States often legitimize exclusion and create realities in which ignorance and Euro-superiority have been so broadly internalized that putatively democratic leaders support construction of walls, ending birthright citizenship, and enhancing Western cultural dominance in all sociopolitical arenas. The rise of a dark and seemingly impenetrable ignorance is due in part (perhaps largely) to the failures in the US education system at all levels. The patterns of exclusion formed in these arenas result in grisly physical and police violence on people of color, including Latinx communities (as will be discussed in chapter 6), and since 2016 this has accelerated: George Floyd's murder and the terrorist shooting targeting Spanish-speakers in El Paso are horrific symptoms of this trend. The fundamental conditions that make such violence possible are cultivated in classrooms by passivity before enormous obstacles (Eurocentrism) and their toxic traditions (Spanish-language cultures are "foreign"), a verity that facilitates the walls (metaphoric and physical) and laws ("Juan Crow") that codify the self-evidence of nonhuman status of those below the colonial masters.[26]

Remaining within Eurocentric frames relies on linguistic, historical, social, and cultural interpellations that limit attention to local subjectivities in destructive ways. The dissolution of the Eurocentric present requires, as Joan Ramon Resina describes, "a change in cognitive structures," as "mere methodological revision is not an adequate response to a discipline's crisis. It is also necessary to acknowledge the radical nature of the crisis and in our case, it is incumbent on us to face up to the possibility that Hispanism no longer has a future in the university" (2009, 36). The arguments here are grounded in the decolonial accountabilities that critical scholars must assume: the responsibility to contemplate what subject positions arise from current paradigms; to reflect on the confines of present theorical approaches (and, more broadly, to take on the complexities of Eurocentrism as nexuses of social and cultural meanings for Spanish-language performances in all places); and to address the residual coloniality embedded in contemporary cultural institutions in ways that endeavor to undo these charged hierarchies.

EUROCENTRISM AND THE INSTITUTIONAL FOREIGNIZATION OF LATINX PERFORMANCE

[Eurocentric pedagogy] communicates the inferiority of any persons belonging to a narrative outside of the dominant. . . . *This affects students.*
Ariana Hernández, "Identidad rasgado y la lengua perdida" (2015, 15)

Somos todos americanos. We are all Americans. Now, I have to make a small confession: I'm lost. Somewhere in my peregrinations on the continent, I lost my way. . . . Maps have been of no use because I always forget that maps are metaphors and not the territory.
Guillermo Verdecchia, *Fronteras Americanas* **(2013, 28)**

[Hispanism] must be rethought and exploded.
Carlos Alonso, "Spanish" (2007, 227)

The key issue that departments of Spanish are currently facing is their change in status from a department of foreign language.
Carlos Alonso, "Spanish" (2007, 220)

Euro-colonized cultural and social canons cause psychological and physical ailments for the demographics they disenfranchise.[27] The broad parameters of Spanish-language cultural studies in US universities (as well as many other US cultural institutions) function on several myths:

1) Spanish is a "foreign language" that is in all cases subordinate in relation to English, the dominant tongue;
2) Spanish-language cultures are "foreign" and therefore secondary, ancillary, heritage, and may exist but only in a sub-relational sense to "American" cultures and to the cultures of "origin" (this "origin" is *always geographically external* to the spaces claimed by the US political body);
3) Spanish-language cultures of the United States do not signify sovereign, independent, natural, autonomous, or self-sufficient (or defining) performances or communities, and occur in sub-relation to the colonial exigencies that external institutions

(including universities and departments that focus on Spanish-language cultures) codify;
4) The occurrence of these languages and cultures in the minds of those using them is an aberration: English and English-language cultures are the primary—and in many cases only possible and only *legal*—maps of meaningful performance and thus memory-making.

While saturating educational realities of Latinx students with the US-mandated Eurocentric canons relegates Latinx cultures, languages, and traditions, it also makes proficiency in Euro norms an academic necessity: "We must learn the Eurocentric canon," writes Miguel de la Torre, "if we hope to obtain PhDs and be considered learned" (2017, 1).[28] Beneath the umbrella of English-centric institutions, Spanish-language cultures local to each university are hyphenated and *always* subordinated to un-hyphenated "American" myths. The pedagogies realized within these imperial designs disenfranchise any non-Eurocentric and Latinx worlds, relegating them to folkloric (or heritage iterations of "authentic" culture) and otherwise irrational and useless, impractical and unrealistic. English is to be understood as the preeminent language: proficiency in Spanish cannot be required—and if that tongue appears on institutional paperwork, it must be *italicized*. In the colonial education project, extra-colonial worlds are acceptable if they have been foreignized into diversity narratives (let's recognize but not move the margin) that are institutionalized as non-domestic languages, knowledges, societies, and cultures.[29] Such a university culture distorts conceptualizations of knowledge, culture, community, and agency, through students' minds. As Marie Battiste has noted:

> Cognitive imperialism is a form of cognitive manipulation used to disclaim other knowledge bases and values. Validated through one's knowledge base and empowered through public education, it has been the means by which whole groups of people have been denied existence and have had their wealth confiscated. Cognitive imperialism denies people their language and cultural integrity. . . .
>
> As a result of cognitive imperialism, cultural minorities have been led to believe that their poverty and impotence is a result of their race. The modern solution to their despair has been to describe this causal connec-

tion in numerous reports. *The gift of modern knowledge has been the ideology of oppression*, which negates the process of knowledge as a process of inquiry to explore new solutions. (2011, 198; emphasis added)

Battiste's deft reflections require an important clarification: the "cultural minorities" she describes cease to be conceptual "minorities" once the nation and trans-nation cease to be understood as the only recognizable and institutionalized containers of knowledge, culture, and community. They are only "minority" if and when interpellated into the umbrella-colonial-transnational whole: uncoupled from that dimension of the imperial design, resituated and re-centered locally, these voices no longer involve *minority* agency but just *agency*.

Unbridled from the myths and prescriptions of the imperial program, local voices and agencies—and the self-determination that accompanies them—may emerge and enunciate new narratives, histories, and cultures. The de-interpellation process is key as it legitimizes local consciousnesses *and* undoes part of the imperial cognitive prescription. While in spaces dominated by Latinx realities, the localization turn *foreignizes* traditional US myths and the English language, such a democratizing and emancipative move would undo, as Battiste observes, colonialized educational institutions that seek "to change the consciousness of the oppressed, not change the situation that oppressed them" (2011, 198).[30]

DECOLONIAL JAMMING AND UNKNOWING

Any move toward domesticating Spanish jams conservative structures in decolonial ways. Even "failed" jamming can open spaces of emancipation, as Ernesto Cuba makes clear: "Si no me nombras, no existo" (2017). Insisting that institutions *name as they reject* is a move that confronts universities and their communities with decolonial avenues of thought—and thus, eliciting a *rejection* (voicing a concern knowing that it will be rejected) can be a source of change. Following the prohibition of a Mexican American studies class in Tucson in 2010, the resistance movement "has spread . . . at a rate no one could have imagined before Arizona banned the class" (Phippen 2015, 1). Jamming the system uncovered an ethical dilemma that accelerated collective action: "It sped up the evolution by about 25 years," said Tony Diaz, editor of the *Mexican American Studies Toolkit*. "It's clear to me that our intellectual advancement is a threat to some people, because they tried to make it illegal" (qtd. in Phippen 2015, 1). Insisting that Spanish in the United States be *named* and *rejected* as illegal (and if not "illegal," non-domestic and therefore "foreign") is a method that satirizes, mocks, and disrupts the stability of the received US knowledges. Culture jamming forces those who control the status quo *to uphold and defend its ironies*. Sometimes using specific figures of prohibition as memes, parodies, and caricatures at once questions the assumptions that cause marginalization and brings attention to the abuses. Like the prohibition of Spanish as a domestic language, the ban of Mexican American studies merits attention not only because Latinx students enrolled in local-focused cultural studies have lower truancy rates, higher grade-point averages and graduation rates, and better mental and physical health (see Dee and Penner 2016), but also because local-focused cultural studies are precisely what many communities desire: "I feel like Mexican-American studies is making me more aware and not me embarrassed of who I am," comments Modesta Bocanegra (qtd. in Paquian 2018, 1).

Mariana Ortega calls epistemological jamming a process of "not-knowing *and* un-knowing" (2017, 514). Applying such a map for studies (elementary to doctoral level) in local Spanish-language cultures is one with many legends, scales, and measures of implementation. Peninsular themes should be *not known* on this map, and they may be *unknown* within existing institutional constraints, just as local Spanishes are largely absent now. Ortega continues: "We not only need an epistemology of ignorance in terms of practices of not-knowing (practices that thinkers from dominant social identities and locations engage in for whatever reason—in the service of empire, colonialism, gatekeeping, etc.); we also need an epistemology of ignorance in terms of practices of un-knowing, or practices that erase the knowledge and hard work already carried out, through a critical assessment and disclosure of hegemonic practices" (2017, 513). The institutional architecture that situates Peninsular Spanish as exceptional explicitly marginalizes local Spanish-language cultures and restates—subtly but with implicit force—that Spanish-language cultural production by non-Spaniards is unworthy of attention due to the inability to compose valid thought. These violent colonialities and their anachronistic pedagogical relics yet characterize the academic structure, but they are notions nearly all faculty expressly oppose. While high enrollments are wonderful and the neoliberal university is a powerful obstacle, the responsibility of critical scholars is to examine the outcomes of these structural exigencies and to act: what a decolonized field might look like is a plural inquiry map with varied iterations in each institution, but it would mean Latinx students and their communities, languages, and cultures would have a domestic place at the university.

ARGUMENT STRUCTURE

Upon a backdrop of statistical data concerning current trends in Spanish-language cultural pedagogy, the first two chapters of this book consider strategies to shift the center of the field toward contexts more local to each institution. Later chapters combine methodological interventions with material examples; those chapters are not intended to be comprehensive or all-encompassing but rather to demonstrate the latitude of inquiry that each structural turn would provide. Chapter 5 argues that Universidad de Puerto Rico could be a model for US higher ed, as the institutional organization allows cross-lingual and multicultural competencies that are inaccessible in monolingual US universities. The conclusion critiques how institutions of US higher ed participate in foreignizing Spanish, foregrounding the ways that domesticizing Spanish would benefit the universities, the communities they serve, and the academy.

CHAPTER PRÉCIS

Chapter 1: After Hispanic Studies

This chapter examines faculty specialties (by self-described "interests") and the themes of courses under the umbrella of Spanish-language cultures at several cohorts of US universities. The data illustrate some of the structural exigencies of Spain-centrism across the academy, including student behavior (study away tendencies, in particular). A principal argument in this section maintains that if area studies grammars are to maintain a privileged status in the standard departmental and disciplinary organization (faculty specializations, course themes, degree program topics, conference themes, publication subjects, disciplinary associations, and so on), appointments in Peninsular topics should be reduced as a method to diminish the overwhelming saturation of European material from all periods (which crowds out other topics) in all subdisciplines.

Chapter 2: Vetting the Decolonial Turn

Engaging epistemes of the posthegemonic turn in relation to institutional genealogies and their internal logics, this chapter situates the decolonial turn within a base of studies in geographic psychology and cultural neurology, so as to assess the latitudes of emancipatory educational programs. The focus on institutionalization of local themes offers a context of inquiry that will be developed in the later chapters. The discussion suggests engagement of localized centers of emphasis across subdisciplines as a method to undo part of the myth that asserts US / Latin American Spanish-speakers (if those demographies are to be understood as separate) are incapable of valid thought *and therefore* their actions (histories, cultural production, and so on) are pedagogically inferior in comparison to the Spain equivalents (a thesis central to the one-to-one weighting parity between Spain and Latin America).

Chapter 3: Multilingual Cognition and Ethno-Lingual Relativity

Taking on a broad definition of a "Spanish language," this chapter considers multilingual inflections of Spanish on other languages (largely Spanish-speaking authors who write in French and English), and multilingual inflections from other languages onto Spanish. Framed through cognitive studies in multilingualism, the argument considers how use of multiple languages influences the mind (and thus behavior) and asks questions about how multilingualism modulates notions of community, emotion, identity, and the aesthetic performances that codify them. A focus on Spanish-speaking writers who publish in languages other than Spanish, as well as those who live in Spanish but write in other languages, reveals many new ways to organize knowledge production in ways that interrogate the limits of traditional "language" (as "a"—singular—discrete, regulated, established form of verbal communication) and its institutionalization in the academy. The arguments also revisit the depths in a "language" (singular) when perceived as a core component of the cultural fabric often used to describe community and identity limits.

Chapter 4: Spain—The Arabized Province of Latin America

This chapter asks questions about the futures of Spain-related cultural studies within the constraints of contemporary area studies. If pedagogies remain tied to national and transnational models, how should traditional Hispanic/Iberian studies paradigms shift toward non-exceptionalist narratives? Understanding Spain as perhaps the most Arabized province of Latin America (in concert with Joseba Gabilondo's suggestion), the argument refocuses attention on how works like *Poema del mío Cid* and *Don Quijote*, when examined through Islamic and Arabic contexts (and the apparent Islamophilia of Cervantes and Díaz de Vivar), open new avenues to engage canons of "Spanish" material that has been programmatically elided in traditional studies—that is: recognition of Islam and Arabic as infrastructural, rather than provisional/ephemeral/superficial/convivence dimensions of "Spanish" realities. Nuancing the Castilla/*castellano*/Latinate/Catholic biases that inform all facets of the way "Spain" is (mis)understood and institutionalized, the discussion gestures toward more descriptive axes to reflect on the communities, cultures, and languages in question.

Chapter 5: On the Puertoricanization of US Higher Education

As an antidote to some of the structural exclusions in the US academy, this chapter brings attention to the Universidad de Puerto Rico, an institution where students develop cultural sensibilities that are to a degree inaccessible in traditional monolingual universities (i.e., the US model). While speaking Puerto Rican Spanish or Puerto Rican English (or their mixes) often breaks conventional norms and rules in both English and Spanish, the profound intellectual competencies UPR students demonstrate pose serious challenges to the monolingual university as a social institution, especially in Spanish-dominant areas. If conventional US universities were more like the Universidad de Puerto Rico, the student-learning maps would expand in ways that traditional institutional systems cannot measure. (The fact that the UPR is so poorly ranked across all measures evidences only the failures of those ranking systems.)

Chapter 6: Conclusion—Overcoming the Tradition of Silence

The social engineering of Spanish into a foreign status facilitates discrimination, oppression, and poverty, among other ills, and binds literacy itself to English and away from Spanish, which has profound effects that far transcend education. The conclusion of this book examines how the foreign status of Spanish has been weaponized into Juan Crow laws, and critiques the subtle but important role of the university as an imperial apparatus that upholds this foreign/domestic linguistic architecture. The discussion examines the positions of political and educational figures who defend Eurocentrism and considers the renewed importance of the humanities after and during COVID-19.

1

AFTER HISPANIC STUDIES

ON THE DEMOCRATIZATION OF SPANISH-LANGUAGE CULTURAL STUDY

In a field as wide-ranging as Spanish-language cultural study, a disproportionately large presence of one subfield in the professoriate can have unintended consequences that are damaging to the communities served.[1] After being dominated by Peninsular and what was generally termed "Spanish-American" or "Las Españas" study, a generation ago the field underwent a paradigm shift that opened a separate Latin American register. This period of transition (in which we are yet engaged) has resulted in a reduction of Peninsular specialists as a percentage of all hires in Spanish-language cultural studies, as Latin American societies were reimagined with cultural sovereignty. However, this hiring trend leveled off before a demographic balance; that is, a faculty ratio that is descriptive in terms of number of specialists per population of the cultural regions present within the passim area studies mold.[2] This chapter argues that if contemporary area-studies exigencies are to remain in place, "best practices" in hiring should transition toward a model that appoints fewer Spain specialists in favor of faculty with specializations in topics more local to each campus. Using existing area studies grammars (largely dependent upon nations and transnations), the ideas presented here should be understood as conceptual rather than binding (or even necessarily implementable); the interest is to illustrate the contemporary slant toward Eurocentric pedagogy through quantitative data sets and to foment a scholarly dialogue on how the field might reorganize in ways that lessen the overwhelming Eurocentric demands that characterize contemporary faculty appointments, curricula, degree programs, study-away tendencies, and the myriad of activities realized in the academy.

After examining the development of Latin American studies as a field, my argument will scrutinize the professional demographics (by subfield specialization) and course offerings (by listed thematic emphasis) at several cohorts of US universities with two principal ends: first, to demonstrate the overwhelming overrepresentation of Peninsular themes (and thus, a Eurocentric register) in the field of Spanish-language cultural studies as a whole; and second, to pose an argument in favor of changes in faculty appointment practices that would ensure a more balanced approach to the scholarly treatment of Spanish-language cultures. The questions posed are not solely pedagogical; the cultural axes that favor European Spanish language and culture have a colonial character, one that has restabilized within the inclusion initiatives that have become common in US higher education since the civil rights movement. The present hegemonic model of cultural power enforces a presupposed Euro-colonial superiority,[3] and classrooms are thus forums of distorted and hierarchical engagements with cultural goods, such as texts, film, art, and spoken accents in the Spanish language.[4] The outcomes of the Eurocentric academic fetishization are evident when we examine the behavior of students immersed academic surroundings that are dominated by Peninsular Spanish language and culture: while less than 10 percent of Spanish-speakers worldwide reside in Iberia, US undergraduates who study away in Spanish-speaking institutions are around five times more likely to choose Spain over Latin America—a figure that roughly corresponds to faculty specializations and course themes.

Eurocentrism is the cultural residue of colonialism. In 1492, when Queen Isabella misunderstood the purpose of Antonio de Nebrija's *Gramática castellana*,[5] Hernando de Talavera explained, "Your Majesty, language is the perfect instrument of empire."[6] In the first paragraph of the prologue, Nebrija defines the purpose of the Spanish language in America as a colonial one: "Siempre la lengua fue compañera del imperio" (1492, 1). And continues: "Después de que Su Alteza haya sometido a bárbaros pueblos y naciones de diversas lenguas, con la conquista vendrá la necesidad de aceptar las leyes que el conquistador impone a los conquistados, y entre ellos nuestro idioma; con esta obra mía, serán capaces de aprenderlo" (qtd. in Pons 2018, 1). In order to control resources, place communities in bondage, levy taxes and realize military conscriptions, among other objectives, the politicization of conquered peoples stigmatized Indigenous social tendencies, cultures, and languages. This process disseminated the myth that the cultural systems of the Spanish crown (and later, of Creole leaders during the republican period) replaced or overtook any non-Eurocentric sociocultural realities:[7] Spanish has existed as a central dimension of this colonial matrix since it first appeared in the hemisphere.

In correspondence with civil rights movements, a new mapping reframed the discipline of Spanish-language cultural studies in the US academy: reimagining Latin America as a set of culturally sovereign entities radically reshaped the composition of the professoriate; over several decades this democratization (reducing number of specialists in Peninsular themes as a percentage of the faculty) granted perennially oppressed communities localized spheres of academic focus. However, the contraction of Peninsular appointments has ceased: across the US academy there is approximately a one-to-one ratio of cultural specialists in Peninsular-study to specialists in Latin American themes.[8] While there are ten-times more speakers of Spanish in Latin America than Spain, the cultures and languages of these imagined communities appear roughly equally in US classrooms, in continual deliverance of the colonial demands: while some notable departments have resisted this trend, the percentage of faculty who specialize in US Spanish hovers near zero, despite the number of Spanish-speakers in the United States being greater than that of Spain.[9]

The data in the below survey were taken from departmental websites. (The "Perceived Elite" cohort departments are in the *US News and World Reports* "Top 25 Modern Language Programs in the World" and/or National Research Council's Top 25 institutions in Spanish in the "viewed by faculty as top-notch" category.) The survey includes tenured or tenure-line faculty members; the subfield statistics are based on departmental or self-reported "interests," "field," "specialty," "discipline," or other related expression of academic concentration. Specialists in subnational Peninsular topics (Catalan, Basque, Galician, and others) are included in "Peninsular" cultural cohort; the "Latin American" cultural cohort includes specialists in Pre-Columbian, and indigenous (and other non-European disciplines). Faculty members whose listed specialization is in a non-area subject (such as second-language acquisition or business Spanish) were not included in these data.[10]

The figures confirm that, with very few exceptions, US departments hire faculty in Spanish-language cultural fields through a framework that is overwhelmingly Eurocentric. A silent internal system structures Latin American and Peninsular study with approximately equal weight, thus allotting Spain five times more specialists in cultural fields than would a number proportionate to its share of speakers, a model that largely neglects languages and cultures local to each institution. While the faculty bodies vary slightly from cohort to cohort, just one institution—Pittsburgh—has a faculty demographic that could be described as characteristic of the target subject.[11] These appointment norms have profound consequences on how departments structure curricula (number of seminars offered in each cultural topic) and on how the disciplinary canon is organized (amount of material tracts studied from each region).[12]

Since faculty design and teach courses that correspond with their personal interests and specialization, the Eurocentric hiring program has a substantial implication on the themes of courses and degree programs. The following table has been compiled from the course offerings, by cultural emphasis, listed on departmental websites. Each department chair was contacted for feedback concerning these data and for input on any possible changes and discrepancies; their contributions have been included in the table.[13] The thematic divisions are: Peninsular, Latin American, transatlantic, and US.

As Nicolas Shumway notes, the academy is "still organized with Spain at the center and everyone else in a marginalized amalgamation that recalls terms like *las colonias*" (2005, 296). While glimpsing at a department's online course listings may be misleading, the responses from department chairs shed some light on the administrative circumstances that produce these statistics. Several noted that it is very likely catalogues contain offerings that exist on paper but not in practice; the official description of a seminar may vary drastically from what is covered; the catalogue represents administrative and bureaucratic exigencies that may not align with departmental missions; the listings are like time capsules from decades ago, the remnants of degrees and minors that have since changed in focus in practice if not on paper. As Jo Labanyi, at New York University, notes, their catalogue contains "previously accumulated courses taught since the beginning of time" (email to the author, March 8, 2018).[14] The titles of courses can also be misleading: "Almost all of my classes combine regions despite the course titles," comments Ruth Hill

Table 1. Faculty Specialties

Cohort I: Perceived Elite Institutions
(*US News and World Report* top 25; National Research Council top 25 "top notch")
Harvard, Yale, Princeton, Chicago, Stanford, NYU, Pennsylvania, Duke, Indiana, Illinois, Cornell, Georgetown, Columbia, Virginia, Texas at Austin, Brown, Penn State, Purdue, Berkeley, Vanderbilt, UNC Chapel Hill, Minnesota, Ohio State, UC Irvine, UCLA, Kansas, Tulane, Indiana, UC Boulder, Pittsburgh, Wisconsin, UC Santa Barbara

Peninsular (153 faculty members)	47%
Latin American (174 faculty members)	53%
Most weighted to Peninsular:	66% Chicago, Vanderbilt, UVA, Columbia, Boulder
Most weighted to Latin America:	90% University of Pittsburgh
Equal (1–1) or within one faculty member:	47% of departments
Average Peninsular overrepresentation:	470% of democratic balance

Cohort II: Flagship Public Institutions in Southern Border States
UC Berkeley, University of Arizona, University of New Mexico, University of Texas–Austin

Peninsular (18 faculty members)	39%
Latin American (28 faculty members)	61%
Most weighted to Peninsular:	50% Berkeley
Most weighted to Latin America:	66% New Mexico
Equal (1–1) or within one faculty member:	40% of departments
Average Peninsular overrepresentation:	390% of democratic balance

Cohort III: Schools over 50% Latinx and Enrollments of 5000+
U. Puerto Rico–Mayagüez, U. Puerto Rico–Río Piedras, Florida International, U. Texas–El Paso, U. Texas–Pan American*

Peninsular (17 faculty members)	37%
Latin American (28 faculty members)	63%
Most weighted to Peninsular:	50% Florida International
Most weighted to Latin America:	74% U. Puerto Rico–Mayagüez
Equal (1–1) or within one faculty member:	20% of departments
Average Peninsular overrepresentation:	370% of democratic balance

(*continued on next page*)

Cohort IV: 10 Largest US Universities by Enrollment
(online institutions excluded)
Arizona State, Central Florida, Ohio State, Minnesota, Texas–Austin, Texas A&M, Florida, Michigan State, Penn State, Florida International

Peninsular (44 faculty members)	46%
Latin American (50 faculty members)	54%
Most weighted to Peninsular:	55% Minnesota
Most weighted to Latin America:	61% Texas–Austin
Equal (1–1) or within one faculty member:	70% of departments
Average Peninsular overrepresentation:	460% of democratic balance

Total Cohort: 44 Departments

Peninsular (198 faculty members)	44%
Latin American (254 faculty members)	56%
Most weighted to Peninsular:	66% Chicago, Vanderbilt, UVA, Columbia, Boulder
Most weighted to Latin America:	90% University of Pittsburgh
Equal (1–1) or within one faculty member:	45% of departments
Average Peninsular overrepresentation:	440% of democratic balance

Note: *No data: Universidad del Este (PR), East Los Angeles College, Hartnell College (CA), Imperial Valley College (CA), Southwestern College (CA), Miami Dade College, Richard J. Daley (IL), Del Mar College (TX), South Texas College, University of Texas–Brownsville.

from Vanderbilt, "simply because the process of proposing new courses is so onerous. Many of us face this reality" (email to the author, March 1, 2018).

Many faculty, including chairs, emphasized the subtle but vital role of "Topics" courses, many of which are used as an administrative loophole to avoid the bureaucracy of creating a new course, a process that often lasts years. "What we actually teach," comments Jo Labanya, "[including] a large proportion of our undergrad and almost all our grad courses—are taught under the rubric 'Topics course,' which allows faculty to teach courses of their own choosing without a formal process of approval at university level" (email to the author). Berkeley has a similar circumstance, as M. Iarocci comments: "Most faculty prefer to teach upper division topic courses as 135s ('Topics in Hispanic Literature'), where

Table 2. Course Themes
Cohort I: Perceived Elite Institutions
(US News and World Report top 25; National Research Council top 25 "top notch")

	Peninsular	Latin Am.	Trans-atl.	US	Total	Peninsular (%)	Latin Am. (%)	Trans-atl. (%)	US (%)
Texas–Austin	13	34	10	12	69	19	49	14	25
Duke	9	8	9	9	35	26	23	26	25
Illinois	9	9	7	5	30	30	30	23	17
Ohio State	24	31	4	10	69	35	45	6	16
UC Irvine	12	12	5	5	34	35	35	15	15
Penn State	8	12	4	3	27	30	44	15	13
Indiana	9	7	9	4	29	31	24	31	13
Minnesota	22	11	2	6	41	54	27	5	12
UNC–Chapel Hill	13	16	6	4	39	33	41	15	11
UC–Santa Barbara	23	20	10	6	59	39	34	17	10
Purdue	8	10	7	2	27	30	37	26	8
UCLA	35	20	12	7	74	47	27	16	8
Wisconsin	10	11	4	2	27	37	41	15	8
Harvard	11	17	11	2	41	27	41	27	6
Columbia	20	18	15	3	56	36	32	27	5
Stanford University	7	10	6	1	24	29	42	25	5
Pittsburgh	6	22	10	1	39	15	56	26	4
Brown	8	9	8	1	26	31	35	31	4
Cornell	16	9	4	1	30	53	30	13	3
Vanderbilt	18	14	3	1	36	50	39	8	3
Tulane	25	31	11	1	68	37	46	16	2
Princeton	25	30	24	1	80	31	38	30	1
Kansas	39	26	8	1	74	53	35	11	1
Virginia	44	25	10	1	80	55	31	13	1
Georgetown	26	26	10	0	62	42	42	16	0
University of Chicago	30	25	8	0	63	48	40	13	0
New York University	13	10	8	0	31	42	32	26	0
U. Pennsylvania	20	16	18	0	54	37	30	33	0
Yale University	35	18	9	0	62	56	29	15	0
UC–Boulder	21	10	5	0	36	58	28	14	0
Berkeley	16	6	4	0	26	62	23	15	0
Total	575	523	261	89	1448	40	36	18	6

(continued on next page)

Cohort II: Flagship Public Institutions in Southern Border States

	Peninsular	Latin Am.	Trans-atl.	US	Total	Peninsular (%)	Latin Am. (%)	Trans-atl. (%)	US (%)
Texas–Austin	13	34	10	12	69	19	49	14	25
New Mexico	10	18	3	6	37	27	49	8	21
University of Arizona	10	15	7	1	33	30	45	21	4
Berkeley	16	6	4	0	26	62	23	15	0
Total	49	73	24	19	165	30	44	15	13

Cohort III: 10 Largest US Universities by Enrollment
(online institutions excluded)

	Peninsular	Latin Am.	Trans-atl.	US	Total	Peninsular (%)	Latin Am. (%)	Trans-atl. (%)	US (%)
Arizona State	13	23	4	13	53	25	43	8	30
Texas–Austin	13	34	10	12	69	19	49	14	25
Ohio State	24	31	4	10	69	35	45	6	16
Penn State	8	12	4	3	27	30	44	15	13
Texas A&M	4	5	19	4	32	13	16	59	13
Minnesota	22	11	2	6	41	54	27	5	12
Florida	22	17	5	2	46	48	37	11	4
Florida International	33	35	17	2	87	38	40	20	2
Michigan State	6	5	3	0	14	43	36	21	0
Central Florida	3	3	3	0	9	33	33	33	0
Total	148	176	71	52	447	33	39	16	12

Total Nationwide Cohort

	Peninsular	Latin Am.	Trans-atl.	US	Total	Peninsular (%)	Latin Am. (%)	Trans-atl. (%)	US (%)
Arizona State	13	23	4	13	53	25	43	8	30
Texas Austin	13	34	10	12	69	19	49	14	25
Duke	9	8	9	9	35	26	23	26	25
New Mexico	10	18	3	6	37	27	49	8	21
Illinois	9	9	7	5	30	30	30	23	17
Ohio State	24	31	4	10	69	35	45	6	16
UC–Irvine	12	12	5	5	34	35	35	15	15

Penn State	8	12	4	3	27	30	44	15	13
Indiana	9	7	9	4	29	31	24	31	13
Texas A&M	4	5	19	4	32	13	16	59	13
Minnesota	22	11	2	6	41	54	27	5	12
UNC–Chapel Hill	13	16	6	4	39	33	41	15	11
UC–Santa Barbara	23	20	10	6	59	39	34	17	10
Purdue	8	10	7	2	27	30	37	26	8
UCLA	35	20	12	7	74	47	27	16	8
Wisconsin	10	11	4	2	27	37	41	15	8
Harvard	11	17	11	2	41	27	41	27	6
Columbia	20	18	15	3	56	36	32	27	5
Stanford University	7	10	6	1	24	29	42	25	5
Pittsburgh	6	22	10	1	39	15	56	26	4
Brown	8	9	8	1	26	31	35	31	4
Florida	22	17	5	2	46	48	37	11	4
University of Arizona	10	15	7	1	33	30	45	21	4
Cornell	16	9	4	1	30	53	30	13	3
Vanderbilt	18	14	3	1	36	50	39	8	3
Florida International	33	35	17	2	87	38	40	20	2
Tulane	25	31	11	1	68	37	46	16	2
Princeton	25	30	24	1	80	31	38	30	1
Kansas	39	26	8	1	74	53	35	11	1
Virginia	44	25	10	1	80	55	31	13	1
Georgetown	26	26	10	0	62	42	42	16	0
University of Chicago	30	25	8	0	63	48	40	13	0
Michigan State	6	5	3	0	14	43	36	21	0
New York University	13	10	8	0	31	42	32	26	0
Central Florida	3	3	3	0	9	33	33	33	0
U. Pennsylvania	20	16	18	0	54	37	30	33	0
Yale University	35	18	9	0	62	56	29	15	0
UC–Boulder	21	10	5	0	36	58	28	14	0
Berkeley	16	6	4	0	26	62	23	15	0
Total	676	644	322	117	1759	38	37	18	7

the topic varies. A 135 can be Latin American, Peninsular, US Spanish, or Hybrid. The same is true for the 200-level courses: 285 for peninsular and 280 for Latin American are 'Topics' graduate seminars that include all of the traditional subfields (colonial Latam, Modern Latam/Latino, Medieval/Early Modern Spanish, Modern Spanish)" (email to the author, March 1, 2018). While Topics courses cannot be included in the course catalogues (and consequently in these figures), they have a significant presence across undergraduate and graduate programs. In many cases, they are even *more important* than the listed courses. The themes of Topics courses, however, are implicitly tied to faculty specialization data: professors trained in Peninsular themes may teach Latin American or US topics, but what occurs in the classroom is largely correlated to faculty preparation and specialization. As nearly all tenure-stream job announcements use area-studies language (with a national or regional specialization explicitly required) these Topics courses may be varied, but they are directly related to the structural concerns in the hiring and appointment process. *Faculty are selected for tenure-line positions in order to develop knowledge in their specializations.* While the Topics courses may remap or explore new material, it is unlikely that there is a great deal of thematic distance from the United States / Latin America vis-à-vis Peninsular tendencies found in the listed specializations and interests of faculty (table 1).

There are some commonalities across the course dataset that deserve attention. While the Spanish-languages of the United States are the most common variant on the campuses of every institution surveyed, with a few noteworthy exceptions, that material is largely ignored: local topics amount to just 7 percent of all courses—and are limited to 1 percent or 0 percent of the material offered in 28 percent of departments surveyed. Trans/hybrid themes appear to be increasing in importance, though that category has a significant Eurocentric weight that reiterates many of the Peninsular–Latin American / US mythic inequalities in new ways. Pittsburgh, Duke, New Mexico, Texas, Arizona State, and Texas A&M merit specific attention, as these departments have moved beyond the Eurocentric traditions by restructuring course themes and faculty appointments toward more localized emphases. Like the University of Puerto Rico, their example represents an institutional approach with many relevancies for universities across the United States: the looming revision of Peninsular-centric missions toward Latin American and US Spanishes and cultures, at least in their institutional mechanisms (among them: hiring and course/degree design), has these departments as precedents to resituate the center of the discipline.

CURRICULAR CRITICISM

While this examination of faculty demographics and course offerings is without an apparent precedent, several scholars have analyzed curricular formation in recent years. There appears to be no unified concept about an appropriate method to restructure (if indeed restructuring is necessary) the topics to be studied, and in what weighting.[15] A generation ago James Fernández of New York University noted that "Spanish is simultaneously an American and a European language. The discipline of Hispanic studies must confront head on—both intellectually, in its scholarship, and institutionally, in its departmental configurations—the history and the current implications of this double identity" (Fernández 2000, 1964). The terms "double identity" and "American" are left unclear: should American / European Spanish-language cultures be treated with equal weight, 50–50, as they essentially are now? Does "American" mean local to each university or Latin American? Are US traditions Latin American? While a shift toward Latin American themes has occurred at NYU since the 1970s, the present faculty demographic is 60 percent Latin American and 40 percent Peninsular.[16]

In "Hispanism in an Imperfect Past and an Uncertain Future," Nicolas Shumway notes that when he was a junior faculty member several decades ago at Yale and Indiana University Northwest, the new faculty members were obliged to include "sufficient material from Spain" (2005, 285). Shumway comments that the "appropriate" weight in the 1980s was 60–40 for Spain over other Spanish-speaking regions. He goes on to note that "this notion of Hispanism also meant a majority of faculty appointments in Peninsular literature" (2005, 285). Shumway mentions his general "disagreement" with such an approach and concludes with this reflection: "[Hispanism itself] is an outmoded idea based on an essentialist, ideologically driven, and Spain-centric, notions" (2005, 297).

Among the most comprehensive reports on curricular development is Joan Brown's *Confronting our Canons*, a study that examines the Spanish-language material taught across the US academy. She argues in favor of a shared graduate canon that would organize scholarship upon a common platform. What is most striking about her data is how profoundly literature-based and Eurocentric the Spanish-language cultural canon is: "Works on 90–99% of graduate reading lists, what I call the core canon . . . [included] nine works, all but one from Spain" ("What do Graduate Students in Spanish Need to Learn?" 2010, ix). Brown advocates for an increased presence of traditionally excluded genres but says little about moving focus away from the traditionalist Eurocentric model. In particular, she envisions a canon that incorporates more work from women and non-heterosexuals, nonprint tracts, texts in non-Castilian languages, anything from the eighteenth century, and work from those whom she terms "exiled patriots, or residents from most of the Hispanic world" (2010, 171). The reader is left to presume here that "exiled patriots" means Spaniards, though exiled Latin Americans significantly outnumber those from the Peninsula.

Brown is a specialist in Peninsular topics and perhaps her study should be understood through that lens. Indeed, the discussion of whom she terms "residents of most of the Hispanic world" is infrequent, which gives the impression that her recommendations are geared more generally toward how *Peninsular* studies could be restructured—not the field as a whole (despite the several instances in her monograph that allude to the contrary). A shortcoming of *Confronting Our Canons* is Brown's focus on a very tiny sector of the target subject—Peninsular topics. Cultural tracts from 90 percent of the Spanish-speaking world are treated perfunctorily. Even if the problems that Brown cites were remedied through application of her model, which is perhaps acceptable within a Peninsular studies frame, if the slant is not democratized toward US / Latin America, the supermajority of the target subject (which includes local cultures) would continue to be ignored.[17]

The field itself is often termed "Hispanist," "Hispanism," and "Iberian-American," each of which attempt to maintain a supposed US / Latin American relation to a Spanish center. The nomenclatures have a radial implication which both initiates and sanctions the flawed concept that all cultural materials under this heading emanate from a singular source: the Peninsula. The terms also exoticize (and therefore marginalize) speakers of Spanish in the United States into a subordinate category, one that has been institutionalized through terms such as "heritage speaker," which construct a foreignness for the tongue (and related cultural traditions)—and interpellates speakers of Spanish in the United States with being "foreign in a domestic sense" (Burnett et al. 2001). While Spanish and English are "heritage" languages in the United States, the received exceptionalism myths prohibit courses in English topics receiving the label "heritage."

OVERWEIGHING FACULTIES TOWARD SPAIN

The conventional one-to-one Peninsular to Latin American faculty configuration prohibits a localized pedagogy. Spanish authors, playwrights, artists, peasants, royalty, Caudillos, and so on, from Cid through Ruiz Zafón, receive more critical and pedagogical treatment than they should, a circumstance which concomitantly subordinates the work of the unstudied demographics and enhances the perceived importance of Peninsular work in all disciplines. Peninsular-centrism also penetrates publication outlets: while *Project Muse* has a "Latin American and Caribbean Studies" subheading with twenty journals (five of which have "Hispanic" in the title), there are thirty-one periodicals under "Spanish and Portuguese Literature" and "Iberian Studies" subheadings. The MLA organizes study groups under "Romance" topics, and the Spanish-language subgroup is termed "Hispanic Literatures," a category that includes three groups with a Latin American focus and four concerning peninsular culture.[18]

Eurocentric departments are particularly misguided for US institutions and associations, as Latin American cultures, performances, languages, texts, histories and family dynamics, inform local cultures in any number of ways (that is, if one identifies the United States as an entity external to Latin America). But even if the United States were institutionalized and categorized as a Latin American nation, or group of Latin American regions (perhaps several distinct nations), or some other characterization that situates Spanish as a domestic language, the bulk of academic attention being misdirected toward an absent European Spanish-speaking community (and the histories, cultures, literatures, and languages of those societies) in these departments might best be described as a case of cultural lag.

Study away trends demonstrate the same problem in other terms: Spain receives approximately the same number of US students as all Latin American nations combined ("US Study Abroad: Leading Destination" 2007, 1). What causes students to esteem Spain so profoundly for study away? The Spain / Latin America inequality in study away corresponds very closely to the course topics and the professor-specialization imbalance ratio: it would appear, students are interested most in the regions that they study. The idealization of Spain in the minds of undergraduates is a product of a broad Eurocentric aesthetic in the United States that is codified in the existing faculty demographics and the courses they teach. As many, and perhaps most, students have not been to Latin America or Spain before choosing their studying away destination, the lopsided numbers going to Iberia (including the author of this book) stem to a significant degree from what students read, study, hear and see in their Spanish language and Spanish-language culture classes.

Some may maintain that an important component of study away is visiting the neighboring countries, and for that, part of the draw to Spain (instead of a country in Latin America) is its proximity to the rich and distinct cultures of Europe. However, one could make the same case for any Latin American nation: that region is as culturally and linguistically diverse as Europe, if not significantly more so. Such is the force of the Eurocentric fetishization constructed and celebrated through formal education and other social institutions. The conceptual ideas of Spain and Latin America are constructed in classrooms (through Eurocentric scholarly approaches) and the results are clear: overweighting pedagogy with Peninsular themes has significant influence on what students imagine to be the "best" experience in Spanish-language culture. To study a text or a painting in a classroom setting is to commemorate a cultural artifact, and the first-hand experiences in Spanish-language culture that undergraduates seek are an important signifier of how the disproportionate presence of Peninsular topics in classrooms influences student behavior.

ON PENINSULAR APOLOGY

There are many reasons that current faculty and course paradigms could be portrayed as ostensibly beneficial to students and the discipline: Spain is the "home" of the language; the "classic" texts, seminal to the culture itself like *Poema del mío Cid* and *Lazarillo de Tormes* derive from that imagined community; there is a canon of important work—from Cervantes through the post-Franco period—that is foundational to Western culture and these command a close focus on Peninsular themes; and this is not to mention the transcendental work in visual arts of Velázquez, Goya, and

Picasso; Buñuel and Almodóvar. Our current faculty demographics are structured to reflect that supposed reality: that these works are so significant, so essential to comprehending the culture of Spanish language and cultures that it is appropriate and, it seems, perhaps necessary to overweigh our curricula and our faculty appointments toward these topics.

An apologist for nondemocratic faculties might also argue that Peninsular themes form one conceptual "unit" with several dimensions (often understood as medieval, golden age, twentieth century, and so on). The focus in that context should be on how to weigh respective conceptual units and sub-units. Is it appropriate to have a department with three peninsular specialists but one (or none) who study Southern Cone, Andean, or Mexican topics? In the case of Mexico and many other regions, we could form similar Spanish-language cultural sub-units: Colonial, Independence, Contemporary, Migratory; Mexico has more Spanish-speakers than any other and approximately three times more inhabitants than Spain, but does not have a single specialist in the majority of departments surveyed in this study; meanwhile 97.7 percent of departments have *multiple* specialists in Peninsular topics.[19] The Mexican community—despite being three times as populous as Spain—and US communities—which have a larger population than Spain—are victims of the Eurocentric norm: Spain triumphs due to the traditional myths of cultural "value" and "history," if not "talent" and "beauty," along with other mechanisms of colonial apology.[20]

NEOLIBERAL DEMANDS AND WHY SPAIN REMAINS CENTRAL

Strong enrollments in conventional departments is a serious obstacle to any dissolution of the Eurocentric celebration. As neoliberal demands often supersede the ostensible—and *stated*—mission of a university or department, financial solvency is increasingly exigent: this neoliberal condition paints Spain-centrism with glowing highlights. Students arrive on campus with already-Eurocentric sensibilities which they seek to cultivate further by learning new ways to pronounce *vosotros* or to appreciate Queen Isabel, Miguel de Cervantes, or Pilar Miró, to learn the high-speed rail routes around the Peninsula, and to gain experience in a European Spanish that is celebrated both inside and outside the classroom. Many carry with them the intention to study away in Spain before arriving on campus. A Spanish classroom, a Spanish minor or major, and eventually a PhD, are a path for students to realize those Eurocentric dreams.

While these are reasons to maintain Eurocentrism, in a larger view such legitimizations only redouble the urgency for decolonization of doctoral studies specifically. Those who educate future teachers are university faculty with PhD credentials: at all levels of instruction, from pre-k to graduate courses, instructors teach in relation to their interests and experience. If a conceptual shift were to occur on a large scale, localizing the centers of the disciplines (composition and rhetoric, linguistics, performance, media, DH, cultural studies, including *literature* and so on), faculty would teach and develop their interests in the same ways they do now. In primary, middle and high schools, and then at the undergraduate levels, students would develop non-Eurocentric interests in study and study away, continuing research, specialization, in ways that cannot occur in the contemporary model. Using some of the same structures that privilege Spain now, in a long view, would re-center student attention (and therefore students' knowledge-system and knowledge-production, interests and curiosity, intellectual development, and scholarly participation) toward local cultures with similar outcomes.

DECOLONIAL OBSTACLES IN SECULAR MONOTHEISM, INCUMBENCY BIAS, AND ENROLLMENTS

Secular monotheism has an important influence in the social and cultural institutions in spaces claimed by the US political body—as well as in the political body itself. When knowledge is developed in such a frame, formations tend to unify all under a single prescribed center: tacit declarations of one-beauty, one-perfection, one-language, one-certainty, one-experience-of-the-world, one-world (perhaps many worldviews), one-right / wrong, one-ethics, and so on, to which all others cannot be *worlds* but mere *worldviews* in relation. This trend appears in a pure form in Spanish language cultural studies, with Spain as the received center, the primordial, the generative force from which all other culture subordinately derives. The academy is structured in such a way that one cannot graduate without proficiency in histories, literatures, and knowledge of Spain in the way one may graduate without similar knowledge of the United States, Mexico, or any other equivalent grouping.

This monotheistic fetishization of one-ness allows the "secular" university to rely on "competition" as a (in fact *the*) standard hiring/admissions mechanism. It also has significant weight in precisely what occurs in classrooms. All this prescribed one-ness is present in the ways languages and cultures are studied and institutionalized: each are to be understood as one homogenous unit, scaled by one-"value" and one-"aesthetics" and one-"epoch" and one-"grammar" and one-"vocabulary" that either approach or distantiate from the presumed center and its prescriptions of one-beauty, one-correctness, one-grammaticality and so on. What is overriding in secular monotheism is the myth that mono-centers unify: the myth tells us that the "center" maps and reproduces reality in appropriate ways. While these one-informed cartographies may have evolving boundaries, they are enforced by the sole-knowledge inevitabilities of the secular monotheistic tradition. It is an organizational unit that evokes perspectives that link "us" to "them," as "they" like "us" share one-truth understandings of reality that oppose "ours." These myths legitimize the divisions of people, communities, cultures and societies into the channels that characterize Eurocentric critique. Decolonial sensibilities are anathema to secular monotheistic traditions and their institutions. They recognize and give voice to marginalized knowledges of meaning; they form new and multiple centers that are ephemeral and contingent; they undo the certainties that hold up secular monotheistic institutions, their pedagogies, and the stratified worldviews which they imagine as self-evident.

"SPANISH"-AMERICAN CULTURAL ESSENCES?

Another argument in favor of overrepresenting Peninsular topics focuses on the supposed role that Spanish culture has had in the development of Latin American authors and artists. Several significant Latin American writers, including Gómez Suárez de Figueroa (El Inca), Rosa María Britton, Gabriel García Márquez, Elena Poniatowska, Gloria Guardia, and José Martí, among many others, spent significant periods in Spain. Moreover, as these figures almost certainly were exposed to canonic Peninsular culture during their formative years, we should—according to the traditional model—address this in our curricular approach. A proponent of such a concept would argue that due to the importance of these outstanding and seminal Spanish cultural figures, and their influence on Latin America creation, we should place special attention on Peninsular material in order to aptly interpret and contextualize Latin American work. To this end, for instance, Brad Epps has characterized the field of Latin American studies itself as a "mode of Hispanism" (2005, 233). In such approaches, Spain must remain—today and for all time—at the center of our Latin American studies.

The supposed cultural mimicry of Peninsular norms—a concept at the center of such Eurocentric approaches to Latin American tracts—could be delinked from these myths by reframing curricula away from these historical axes of inquiry. Gabriel García Márquez lived in Spain in the 1960s and 1970s, wrote there, and returned often for visits over the years. He was the principal author of a plea to the Spanish government to reject the Schengen Agreement, which requires Latin Americans to have visas to enter Spain:

> Al entrar a España no tengo la impresión de llegar, sino la de volver. Quizás a muchos españoles les resulte extraño este sentimiento, pero les aseguramos que esa sensación es la típica del criollo, la del indiano, la del colono o del colonizado nacido en esos territorios de lo que fue el antiguo imperio de España. Si nos atrevemos a hacerle un reclamo a esa gran nación que nos enseñaron a considerar, con razón o sin ella, como nuestra Madre Patria, es por el hondo convencimiento que tenemos de no ser ajenos a España.
> . . . sabemos que es cierto, que nuestra imaginación, nuestra lengua mayoritaria, nuestros referentes culturales más importantes provienen de España. Aquí nos mezclamos con otros riquísimos aportes de la humanidad, en especial con el indígena y el negro, pero nunca hemos renegado, ni podríamos hacerlo, de nuestro pasado español. Nuestros clásicos son los clásicos de España, nuestros nombres y apellidos se originaron allí casi todos, nuestros sueños de justicia, y hasta algunas de nuestras furias de sangre y fanatismo, por no hablar de nuestros anticuados pundonores de hidalgo, son una herencia española. ("Protesta de intelectuales por visa a España" 1989)

García Márquez's description of what has been termed "roots tourism" forms a troubling discourse of long-distance imagined postcolonial nationalism that should be situated in the framework of what it is: a subaltern plea for independence.[21] The Schengen Agreement (like the US Visa Waiver Program) blocks European visitation rights to all but the wealthiest Latin Americans—it is a postcolonial form of political, social, cultural, and economic imperialism.²² In the face of the repression that is the visa system, there is desperation; and these are not issues that ceased to exist at some point in the distant past—Schengen was approved in 1989 and is currently active. The letter is symbolic of a subjugated and yet colonized group attempting to win favor through feigning union. Part of the decolonial process forges localized aesthetics through literature, art, and thought; and the material in the above letter is a chapter in that process: the oppressed intending to maintain a vestige of autonomy—the ability to move from place to place unencumbered.²³

The García Márquez letter recognizes the power of states. Another of his reports on these laws focuses on individual agency—in a second declaration, García Márquez dropped the cultural subordinate tone (el hijo perdido de España, la "Madre Patria") saying: "The first Spaniards who came to America did so without visas and firing in all directions. They joined up with our women and took our gold." He also said in remonstration of the law that he would never again return to Spain (qtd. in Riding 1989, 1). Indeed, many Latin American intellectuals and authors over the centuries have been generally ambivalent toward Spain, if not openly hostile. As Nicolas Shumway points out: "Even well into the twentieth century, the obligatory youthful journey for all Spanish American elites was to France, not Spain" (2005, 288).

Conceiving "Latin America" as an entity is an attempt to connect, on an immense scale, disparate peoples through assumed cultural resemblances. The post-colonial plight unifies, and the language does somewhat—but should we insist on re-conceiving and reiterating this imagined unity? Carlos Fuentes notes that since the initial European incursions, Latin Americans have identified not with Spain but with the cultures "de sus lugares de nacimiento, con sus naciones, con su geografía, con su historia . . . distintas de la historia de España" (1997, part 3). Fuentes describes the subordinate relationship Latin Americans have had with Spain as the catalyst of a shared identity, one that derives from oppression and colonialism, and results in "una identitdad . . . común" (1997, part 4). Fuentes goes on to underscore that these are not concepts from the past; the struggle for cultural and social representation and autonomy is one that "aun no termina" (1997, part 4).

Post-national studies and post-area studies imagine their tracts to be a critical leap forward driven by the need to disentangle traditional hegemonies, particularly those related to trans/national imperialisms. But we are yet in a polarized colonial period due to the controlling and imperialist power imbalance that has been codified in the Schengen Agreement and US Visa Waiver Program—and through the curricular preferences that exist at US universities, which openly treat Latin American (and US, if understood as external to Latin America) culture as less important than Peninsular.[24] If "Latin America" and "Spain" and "the United States" are to exist as conceptual units, treating Spanish-language communities through demographically stable pedagogy (moving away from one-to-one Eurocentrism) gestures toward undoing a degree of the ongoing economic, political, and cultural erasure.

TRANSATLANTIC APPROACHES

Engaging prefixes like multi- and trans- as a method to shift attention toward intellectual duality—that is, imagined connections between imagined communities—often repeats the marginalization of traditionally silenced peoples. We might describe the field of African, American, and European tracts as dedicated to a horizontalized cultural history—its fertilizations, exchanges, translations, contacts, and mixtures—but there is a looming danger of the subfields merging into an approach that results in the same dilemmas as other hyphens and prefixes. Indeed, for a "transatlantic" appointment in a Spanish-language department to be stable with respect to the cultures in question, her or his interests/studies must be 90 percent weighted in the direction of Latin America[25]—a reality that Joan Ramon Resina questions: "What else is the 'transatlantic' jargon that is currently in vogue but a recycled or merely rebaptized Hispanism" (2009, 209)?

The Spanish government finances many pan-Spanish-language initiatives that offer economic capital (often for cultural programs) in exchange for expressions of cultural unity from Latin American nations—for this reason, each of these initiatives involves the prefix "Ibero-" which, possibly indirectly, alludes to a core component of the movements: entrenching, or at the very least expressing, a desired Eurocentric identity dimension in these Spanish-speaking societies:

> Iberoamérica Organización de Estados Iberoamericanos para la Educación, la Ciencia y la Cultura
> Espacio Cultural Iberoamericano

Organización de Televisión Iberoamericana
Secretaría General Iberoamericana
Carta Cultural Iberoamericana
Asociación de Estados Iberoamericanos para el Desarrollo de las Bibliotecas Nacionales de Iberoamérica
Juegos Iberoamericanos
Cumbre Iberoamericana

The perceived union between Latin America and Spain, constructed often through capitalist and neoliberal/colonial—not democratic—interventions, is part of what authorizes the Eurocentric fetishization across US academic faculties. This concept should be closely examined as there are many cases in which this cultural amalgam is openly rejected in Latin America, and the reception of Latin American migrants in Spain in many ways doubly contradicts the concept of one sociocultural community.[26] The supposed union benefits the capitalist interventions for Spain, which dominates much of the banking, publishing, and media in Latin America; but the cultural reality does not correspond to what is implied in the Ibero- prefix.

A PARADIGM SHIFT

Mi corazón está en Latinoamérica . . . o sea, aquí [en Oregon].
Liliana Darwin López, "Liliana Darwin López" (2019, 1)

Using existing structural restrictions, in a new approach to the formation of a Spanish language and cultures department, 10 percent of the professoriate would be specialists in Peninsular themes. However, as Denijal Jegić argues, such "structural presumptions of equality" can often be used to mask and protect colonial power (2019, 119). In order to reorganize the arrangement of departmental disciplines, the perception of a specialist (for the case of the Peninsularist) could change—in the same way that some departments of ten faculty have one "Mexicanist" who is expected to touch all realms of that literary and cultural history—the same could be the case for Spain.[27] Such a transition would require restructuring BA, MA, and PhD programs—and this transition could occur seamlessly within the other paradigm shifts accompanying a democratization and decolonization of the field.

While universities and departments ostensibly design classroom, curricular, and cultural dynamics toward the best interests of student and local populations, the Eurocentric paradigms from decades and centuries ago are fossilized in place—and they yet characterize some central dimensions of the encounter. This study adds to the growing calls for a shift in institutional stance, one that would recognize, hear, and give voice to students in non-imperial languages and ways of being. As the coming chapters develop, such a transition would allow traditional labels assigned to students (terms often weaponized to minoritize them) to be interpreted, critiqued, and at times abandoned. As the distinctions between "educational" and "home" settings dilute, and the materials of study shift away from far-off languages, cultures and histories, students will engage their own experience and voices in ways that cause their institutions to relinquish parts of the imperial narrative, and with it, conceptualizations like "native" and "standard" and "foreign" may receive new contextualization and critique. As Idelber Avelar comments, "democratization of cultural capital in the discipline not only lies in the canon and its expansion" (2005, 279), it also relies on new emphases, new sources, new voices—each of which can emerge from pedagogies imbued with critical integration of non-imperial sensibilities cultivated by students' in their own languages, communities and cultures. The analysis in this book and the solutions put forth would be a part of a complex whole, and while the Eurocentric discrimination in Spanish-language departments is reinforced by tradition, high enrollments, "beautiful" texts and a rich body of critique thereon, a new direction will be a significant gain for our students.

2

VETTING THE DECOLONIAL TURN

> Decolonial movements tend to approach ideas and change in a way that do not isolate knowledge from action. They combine knowledge, practice, and creative expressions, among other areas in their efforts to change the world. For them, colonization and dehumanization demand a holistic movement that involves reaching out to others, communicating, and organizing. A new kind of knowledge and critique are produced as part of that process. That is, decolonial knowledge production and critique are part of an entirely different paradigm of being, acting, and knowing in the world.
>
> Nelson Maldonado-Torres,
> *Outline of Ten Theses on Coloniality and Decoloniality* (2016, 7)

Decolonial thinking endeavors to disrupt the Eurocentric prescriptions regarding who counts as human and thus who is considered possible of producing a valid thought.[1] When applied to critical pedagogy, this praxis often deals with whose cultural manifestations of thought (be them textual, performative, visual, ceremonial, or another gauge) are meaningful to examine in an educational setting, in what proportion and with what context, and why. The data in chapter 1 suggest that the colonial nature of Spanish-language pedagogies attempts to channel student experiences and thus their critical reflections into specific horizons of inquiry: by overweighting some (European) over (all) others, the institution makes a collective commentary regarding which humans have valid thought (and thus culture). Vetting decolonial approaches as a series of alternative praxes will offer a comprehensive context of inquiry on the applications discussed in the next chapters.² This section examines the failure of modern epistemes that celebrate competitions; the psychology of the decolonial pluriverse; and some of the uncertainties surrounding alterity, legitimacy, organization, and other topics implied in the language of decolonial adjectives.

Viewed from within the worlded, scaled, gendered, transnationalized/ transatlanticized, amalgamated nature of contemporary Spanish-language cultural studies, the circumstances that produced each text become distant and irrelevant: information is contracted; events are distorted by Eurocentric explanations and the nonlocal contextualizations imposed on them; textual meanings are adjusted into imperial norms, and standards result in the deliverance of cultural debris—a textureless residue reinterpreted down into pedagogical certainties that hinge on the threads of Eurocentric narratives.³ In this turn toward globalized metanarratives, "Spain has found a unexpected re-entry of sorts," notes Ramón de la Campa (2006, 25), and thus the traditional center has been re-asserted "by the renewed role of Spain in transnational Hispanic culture" (2006, 24). Robert Newcomb observes Hispanism has "guiding principles [which remythologize] (Spain's cultural cohesiveness, Spanish cultural transplantation to Latin America, and Spain's primacy within the Hispanic World)," while scholars have "moved to identify its academic, if not more broadly cultural or political sins" (2018, 196). A principal result of reliance on these epistemic prefabrications is that thought and culture produced in Spanish in spaces claimed by the US political body are understood as secondary to English and Spanish in all other regions, while Latin American tracts are scaled in subordination to Spain. A significant slice of the colonial scaling is based on the myth of "competition" (always against a presumed center) for selection.⁴

SILENCE EMBEDDED IN PEDAGOGICAL SELECTION

Walter Mignolo notes, "Coloniality [is often] covered up by the rhetorical narrative of modernity" (2013, 1). The modernity thesis generally maintains that competition is not only the most suitable but sometimes *the only acceptable* method for human engagement and interaction. The myth that competitions are "won" by some and "lost" by others is a legitimizing apparatus in many economic (capitalism/neoliberalism), political (democracy), and social and cultural institutions (prizes, awards), including the academy (admissions, appointments, publication):[5] in the same way that the "best / most appropriate" material is taught (because the "most talented" become successful artists/writers with the "best" work), the "best" candidates are appointed as tenure-line faculty. When there are more Peninsular PhDs than from other fields, "best" has a specific meaning, and when applied to pedagogy, these structural controls can only repeat the myth that only *some* people who produce cultural material in Spanish have valid thought.

In the webs of imperial relevance, "US culture" is far more likely than any other variation of Spanish-language text and performance to be omitted: it becomes part of no educational curricula, public-interest program, compilation, survey, anthology, discussion, prize, study, criticism, reading, or presentation.[6] The Spain-centric exceptionalism is legitimized in part because the texts chosen to be read, viewed, studied, performed, or heard in a classroom setting have been *selected* by faculty—and thus inflect the institutional authority that cultivated and sanctioned them. Once the Eurocentric, worlded mythologies are situated as the center of the cultural system, there is but one path in an academy already saturated with Peninsular specialists: repetition. The exceptionalist worldviews are reproduced in pedagogy, criticism, and practiced in community outreach—and what is specifically dangerous about such Eurocentrism is that it is not destroyed after use: Spain-centrism cultivates ignorance toward local contexts (Spanish-language cultures of the United States and Mexico) and results not only in cultural but physical barriers. If the colonial worlding may be de-worlded by demystification of categories that presume exceptionality on behalf of imperial interests, such interpellative processes would undo binaries of Latin America / United States, East-West, North-South, reinscribing meanings into the spaces through localized foci that cultivate worlds as strategies of resistance against epistemic violence characterized in colonialist pedagogical imperialism.[7]

LOCALIZING INTELLECTUAL ACTIVITY AND CURRICULA AND CONSIDERING A PLURIVERSAL STATUS QUO

An important decolonial strategy involves jamming colonized institutions. In localized sensibilities, terms like "Spain," "Mexico," "Latin America," or the "United States" become incoherent, representing charged maps of exclusion, membership, and cultural and social hierarchies and their prohibitions. Decolonial approaches offer knowledge domains that are unattainable and ungrammatical within Eurocentric logic, even those that inform the transnational turn. When "local" is engaged as a regional, multilingual, and conditional status—in addition to geographical—it promises to enunciate immediacies of interaction and contact without the fantasy narrative dimensions so intrinsic to larger imaginaries, including area studies grammars of many stripes. Denationalizing sensibilities allows the fields to develop avenues of study that Eurocentric exigencies cannot perceive. As outlined by Enrique Drussel, the institutionalization of such a process often involves two moments:

> a *negative struggle*, deconstructive of a given . . . and a *positive moment of outlet*, of the construction of the new. Insofar as this "liberates"—as in the act by which the slave is emancipated from slavery—its creative potential is opposed to and finally triumphs over the structures of domination, exploitation, and exclusion that weigh heavy on the people. The power of the people—hyperpotentia, the new power of those "from below"—becomes present from the beginning, in its extreme vulnerability and poverty, but it is in the end the invincible force of life "that desires-to-live." This Will-to-Live is more powerful than death, injustice, and corruption. (Dussel 2008, 94)

In line with the notion of threshold moments and the actions that succeed them, there are three interrelated principles in decolonial theory when engaged as an applied praxis:

1) "Decolonial thinking," notes Sara Castro-Klarén, "shows that all epistemes need to be localized" (2016, 4). Once the focus has shifted from external to local,
2) as Walter Mignolo notes, "Decoloniality starts from *other* sources" (2007b, 452; emphasis added).[8] While engaging other (local and non-Eurocentric) intellectual activity in ordinary ways, decolonial approaches engage:
3) *desprendimiento* (or delinking) from the European discourses of power and modernity.

The purpose of delinking is to cultivate multiplicities of *localized* (now-marginalized) knowledge centers, toward a system of entangled (and flat) ontologies that circumvent the universalization of any sole umbrella metanarrative, discourse iteration, or knowledge system.

While giving voice to (and recognizing) marginalized, silenced knowledges and worlds can unlink them to a degree from Eurocentric biases, they are wedded to a system that transcends classrooms: the rise of Christianity, modernity, trans/nations and nation-states, official languages and their literacy programs, twelve-month years / seven-day weeks / 9–5 labor plans, among many other social edifices, construct *a specific reality* that is implemented upon others often by force. The shift toward applied pluriversal epistemes engages democratized and more localized forms of cultural engineering. These develop collective systems intended to promote sustainable and ethical activity in cultural life. Encouraging institutionalization of localized and plural ways of conceptualizing reality that are delinked from Eurocentric narratives of power requires intellectual design principles not unlike those that normalized complex Eurocentric practices (naturalized or internalized, in some minds) in the *longue durée*.

Decolonial nuance provides a framework from which "new" (presently existent but silent) realities may emerge and become institutionalized. Such an epistemic move does not concern specific material (that is, a list of specific books, poems, tweets to be taught, or any faculty demographics to be selected over others) but rather an intellectual process that gestures toward the validation of non-Eurocentric intellectual activities that enunciate community and individual sensibilities in localized ways.[9] When applied to Spanish-language cultural study, a central emphasis of such a turn in consciousness posits that localized group action can reorganize the discriminatory pedagogical mechanisms by exposing oppressive devices, largely (but not exclusively) deconstructing the Spain-centric prescriptions that expressly devaluate what are traditionally labeled US and Mexican (and Mexican American), Latin American, as well as other Spanish-language cultures.

At an institutional level, nuancing the educational models toward local cultures and languages opens the pedagogy, professional practices, and theoretical patterns toward the attuned voices of nondominant groups who are largely absent in the contemporary structures (Swartz 1992, 344).[10] While decolonial sensibilities have many institutional applications at the university level, they also offer possibilities across secondary and primary schools, popular and academic publishing, cultural prizes, and study away programs, among many spheres of intellectual life. A shift to such mechanisms would not have to disrupt existing structures, as the institutional scaffolding could remain largely intact (that is, degree programs, classes, activities, and knowledge-production in the traditional university), but it would shift toward a localized epistemological paradigm.

What is a local context? What conditions enunciate discrete human experiences? How are they embodied in the mind and manifest in cultural materials? How are creativity, group sentiment, and emotions malleable and what influences them? What situational factors (migration, multilingual surroundings, institutional structures) inflect how we conceptualize culture, distance, identity, and community? How might social and cultural distance (that are not geographic) enter the intellectual domain? What dimensions of the human experience are marginalized in Eurocentric pedagogies and institutions? The subjectivities experienced and objects produced in each iterative circumstance may imagine different things, express contradictory sentiments, identify with or unlink from groups and their hybridizations; attention to these situational nudges understands new realms of transformation in which many structures multiply as conditions of possibility. Lowering modern structures that intend to restrict latitudes of possibility—decolonizing the intellectual thrust—is a move that has the potential to facilitate an epistemic emergence from the spaces of control (time and space) that dominate Eurocentric (and trans/national) categories like Spain or Latin America, Mexican-American or unhyphenated-American, and so forth, as well as "Spanish" as a unified (pure) communication system, gesturing toward ways of knowing, being, performing, and realizing culture that require ontologies and epistemes from which institutions of education can form more horizontal and democratized conceptions of culture and other human activity.

WHAT CAN PLURIVERSES KNOW?

Decolonial thinking can be burdened by some implications of the ontological turn in cultural theory, including the complicated metrics of alterity, exigencies surrounding autonomous legitimacy, romanticization of the local, and lack of attention to the situational nature of cultural and social experience. Vetting decolonial narratives in the context of these quandaries will provide nuanced dimensions to such critique and afford some applied relevancies concerning how these modes of thinking influence the study of cultures, communities, and individuals in question.[11] Unlinked from contemporary Eurocentric shadows, such approaches to knowledge creation provide new maps of collective consciousness and memory making, as well as illuminate how each localization possesses cultural experience. More atomized views that derive from techniques like these have the potential to delineate sensibilities in additional contexts, some of which are contingent to the specific conditions in which they arise—a form of "conditional consciousness," only accessible to local constituents, which produces many layers of cultural responsiveness that would be unreachable otherwise (Bautista 2017, chapters 1–2).

Once a decolonial approach to knowledge creation becomes an ethical imperative, a critical issue becomes *how to restructure pedagogical practices in ways that make these worlds and ways of being familiar*. The displacement of Spain-centric takes on the past, present, and future promises to open precisely what faculty and students require: time and institutional support to think, read, write, and study the intellectual activity of local communities. This could occur in relation to appointments focused on local topics, who would (as faculty do now) create classes and degree programs in correspondence to their specialty and interests. Since the colonial exigencies of one-to-one hiring jams European topics into curricula (violently reinforcing "Spain" as the inevitable central point in the field), a decolonial jam could supplant the existing Eurocentric one, shifting appointments toward scholars with expertise on Spanish-language cultural matters local to each campus, recentering the field imaginary away from Europe.[12]

Understanding local sensibilities as autonomous *worlds* rather than independent *worldviews* inaugurates an important inquiry: What is an appropriate method to group the terms? What are the terms? How do worlds interact? Are there contact zones? While a Eurocentric world is replete with worldviews (heteropatriarchal, racist, sexist, classist; ethics and norms scaled by demographics; various spheres of acceptable feeling; multiple demographic-dependent arenas of understanding, and different ways of functioning, of behaving, of performing in relation to each), their plurality is limited to an implicit relational measure, always against the Eurocentric base (the one and only *world*).

By disconnecting the interpretative base from the colonized center, new maps of possibility emerge, but how accurate are decolonialized cultural geographies? Does the emancipatory heterogeneity map with studies of human behavior? Do social psychology and cultural neuroscience examine (colonized) *worldviews* or (pluriversal) *worlds* as conditioning agents in behavior? Examining pluriverses within these cross-disciplinary competencies will provide a backdrop of reasoning toward the praxes of decolonial options and their possibilities in cultural pedagogy. As ontologies of being and realities (that is, distinct *worlds*) have their own autonomous historical genealogies, they offer little trans-contextual stability. Eduardo Viveiros de Castro identified a central purpose of rethinking scholarly axes in these ways, calling it a process that is "working to create the conceptual, I mean ontological, self-determination of people[s]" (2003, 4, 18). This approach works expressly in contrast to modern (colonized) realities, which rest on two columns:

1) the myth of a universal *world* whose supposed purity permits other *worldviews*; any departure from colonial purity norms may represent only contamination, and therefore inferiority; and
2) translation or negotiation between *worldviews* that occurs within the standards of the pure *world*.

A principal problem when working from these modern certainties is the intrinsic inconsistency: as Jodi Melamed notes, there is (and can be) no cross-group equality (2011, chapter 1). This discrimination legitimizes the colonial projects: at moment of contact, two (or more) are scaled, one is inferior, and thus characterized by its irrelevancy in the comparison. It is precisely this irrelevance that is codified in the norms and professional practices in Spanish-language cultural pedagogies at US universities, that which maintains the discriminatory one-to-one Spain-to-Latin-America practice is the institutional application of the purity-contamination myth.

Thus, the pluriversal turn aims to nuance (and eventually annul) the charged hierarchy, allowing plural pedagogies to replenish the codified irrelevance of Latin American (and US) Spanish tracts with localized maps of knowledge and being. Moving into decolonial pluriverses demotes hierarchical views in ways that make codified irrelevance anarchistic. As Michael Carrithers notes, "Any hegemonic view, any single and single-minded truth, [that] always had some kind of answer" is anathematic to ontological / pluriverse-multi-centered views, which enunciate "some means of escape; there [is] some way of healing the kinds of injuries that occur when people say, 'This is the way it is and I'm telling you how it is'" (2008, 8).[13] Applying such a model to cultural pedagogy turns toward specificities that appreciate autonomous emotional and social activity (and the material cultures there produced) and requires a renewed look at how human beings interact with their environments.[14]

THE PSYCHOLOGY AND NEUROSCIENCE OF PLURIVERSES

Situated in the ontological turn, culture does not indicate (i.e., enunciate) a *worldview* but imitates (intangibly materializes) a *world*.[15] An important query in relation to this shift is: Does psychology as a field examine *worlds* or *worldviews* as conditioning agents in behavior? The subfield of geographical psychology demonstrates that some social patterns, including "personality [characteristics], individualism/collectivism, cultural tightness-looseness, and well-being," and the "behaviors, thoughts, and emotions experienced" (Chen et al. 2020, 1) exist among peoples to a degree in relation to their physical surroundings. This emerging realm of inquiry has shown the ways that the immediate geographic environment contributes to frequency and variance of behavioral tendencies. Peter Renfrow's *Geographical Psychology* evidences the ways surroundings influence "personality traits, value systems, and human behavior" (2013, 51). Among the mechanisms that "guide group processing" are proximate physical and social circumstances, including climate, terrain, pathogens, and circumstances like migration; these can influence a person's sense of individualism or communal tendencies, propensity for depression, inclination for nomadism, and political tendencies, as well as personality traits and value—each has been linked to regional specificities (Renfrow 2013, 5).

As Renfrow details in the section "Geographic Differences in Personality," the ways "traits interact with environmental forces" have an influences that "shape[s] people's thoughts, feelings, and behaviors" (2013, 115). Emotions, desires, and thus the cultures that stem from them are localized and to a degree common to geographic context. As he explains: "Environment influence[s] behavior. Climate, terrain, public health, and ethnic diversity can have profound effects on the activities people pursue, their lifestyles, and how they relate to each other" (Renfrow 2013, 130). Since people are to a degree "conditioned by environments" and act under "unconsciously activated norms" (Renfrow 2013, 242, 243), pluriverse-framed views of local cultures can apply such findings in ways that nuance the purity of the (one) worlding imaginaries that inform colonized, worlded, and transnational theories. In an applied sense, Spanish as a communicative tool is not universally received, (mis)understood, performed, or engaged linguistically but experienced locally in concert with other physical and environmental factors, which supports an increasing critical focus on localized views. As our region affects "individuals' life goals, well-being, and [other] . . . views" and "one's city of residence is . . . sometimes [more important] than state, region, or nation" (Renfrow 2013, 115, 180), it would appear that decolonial analyses are perhaps attuned to the human condition in ways that align more closely with how place and region shape behavior than traditional critical imaginaries. Renfrow emphasizes that geography should be at the forefront of reflective analyses because "people do sometimes remove frontiers by cutting down forests and building cities, but they do not frequently build mountains or create oceans" (2013, 46).

In a similar vein, Lawrence White has argued that the uneven environmental distribution of behavior, values, traits, and attitudes can be characterized by three mechanisms:[16]

> Social Influence. People who live in different countries, different regions, or even different neighborhoods usually follow different customs and norms, and these affect attitudes and behaviors. In Montana, for example, local norms encourage owning a gun and being emotionally reserved, two factors which appear to be partly responsible for the high suicide rate among Montanans.
>
> Ecological Factors. Features like climate, the prevalence of disease, and urban crowding can affect the psychological processes of individuals. For example, studies have found that people in countries with a long history of pathogen prevalence tend to be more cautious and less willing to take risks than people in other countries.
>
> Selective Migration. People who choose to migrate to a new region or country are often psychologically different from their counterparts who choose to stay behind. Studies have found, for example, that immigrants tend to be more intelligent, more open, and more extraverted, whereas people who don't emigrate tend to be slightly more agreeable. (2018, 1)

These data offer scaffolding to the conceptualization of decolonial communities as *worlds*: while region of residence has been shown to shape behavior, health, propensity for disease, and brain function, other local—instead of world-containing—factors also appear to be primary agents in cultural activity. As Mignolo has argued, the "biology of cognition, praxis of living, languaging, lifeworld, coloniality, modernity/coloniality, decoloniality. Your sensing changes with your knowing; and your knowing reifies or modifies your sensing" (2018, 362).[17]

QUESTIONING DECOLONIAL ONTOLOGIES

How distinct are local sensibilities? Can a person experience multiple localities at the same time? What are the boundaries between them? Are they irreducibly plural? In what ways are they not geographic? To what degree are they perspectival? In what domains are they permeable, flexible, negatable, or absent? How does technology mediate emotion, community, and performance? As Arturo Escobar queries, "Which 'world'? What 'design'? What 'Real'?" (2018, 23). A critical examination of the heuristic continuity between decolonial conceptualizations must assume the substantial burden of recognizing difference, distance, isolation, separation, and combination. Pluriverse-engaged thinking also revives the conundrum of how difference and autonomy are located, performed, situated, delimited, articulated, expressed, and examined.

The essentialization logics that ontological and pluriversal approaches empower have received serious critique: Eduardo Viveiros de Castro has noted that situating ontology away from "people" toward "a people" is a tactical and political change, one that mobilizes strategic essentialism: "I think the language of ontology is important for one specific and, let's say, tactical reason. It acts as a counter-measure to a derealizing trick frequently played against the native's thinking, which turns this thought into a kind of sustained phantasy, by reducing it to the dimensions of a form of knowledge or representation, that is to an 'epistemology' or a 'worldview.' . . . I shall conclude by once more claiming that anthropology is the science of the ontological self-determination of the world's peoples, and that it is thus a political science in the fullest sense" (2003, 18). The circular plurality of such methods has also brought confusion: "There are as many ontologies as there are things to think through" (Henare et al. 2006, 27). Such a radical new conception of difference is rebellious to coherent cultural associations between communities. "It's more than about bounded units," notes Amy Pollard. "It's about whether or not we can talk of concepts as emanating from societies, emanating from cultures, and I think that if you would entertain the idea of not making the exotic the index of how interesting an ontological discussion can be, then we might be able to explore the dissonance in conceptual planes in societies as well—that's my problem with this actually: it doesn't allow enough for dissonances in concepts, dissonance of discussion" (2008, 41). In a sense, a pluriverse-framed project focused on an axis of the human experience like language could be understood as contradictory to the grammar of its own critical model: applying pluriversal sensibilities to Spanish-language cultures inverses the plural base by reducing it to "one" language experience. But many reports in cognitive linguistics (to be discussed in greater detail in chapter 3) maintain that language—like geographic and social surroundings—informs brain function in specific ways, and the structure of a language (in regard to gender, nouns, communities, colors, and directions, among many other competencies) influences how the brain conceptualizes reality, and thus can be considered to a degree as a register of meta-geographic community and linkage. Inasmuch as language—like geography—has been shown to influence emotion, cognition, and spatial awareness, among other capacities, members of a language community cannot share brain matter:

> Even though groups share socially constructed assumptions and values that organize memory into roughly similar patterns, individuals cannot share another's memory any more than they can share another's cortex. They share instead the forms of memory, even the meanings in memory generated by these forms, but an individual's memory remains hers alone. By maintaining a sense of collected memories, we remain aware of their disparate sources, of every individual's unique relation to a lived life, and of the ways our traditions and cultural forms continuously assign common meaning to disparate memories. It is the difference between unified memory and the unified meaning for many different kinds of memory. (Young 1993, xi)

Language-based decolonial projects have significant overlap with cultural memory initiatives, sharing similar uncertainties and posing comparable questions: they localize focus onto understanding the world of which one is a part; they interrogate what can be known about it—how surroundings and community can influence emotions, and how its events may be recorded physically (into text).[18]

NEO-SITUATIONAL VIEWS OF CULTURAL PERFORMANCE

Many studies in sociolinguistics and neuroaesthetics demonstrate that the ways cultural and linguistic identities are performed, experienced, embodied, enunciated, and codified are neither universal nor permanent but malleable, temporal, conditional, transitory, and ephemeral. As William McNeill has noted, this circumstance complicates cultural study, as people "are able to inhabit two worlds simultaneously . . . human communities, in other words, are becoming at least partially detachable from geography" (1986, 77). Annemarie Mol and John Law maintain, "Where 'we' end and 'they' begin is at least partially detached from geography. The category of 'we' is widened. Or—perhaps the crucial point—it keeps jumping about" (2005, 639). The fluidity of linguistic and cultural character complicates the stability often presumed in categorizing adjectives (like "Ecuadorian," "Spanish," or "Mexican American"). This predisposition is carried over into a criticism and pedagogy, as performative and biographical analyses (even those with a localized tenor) can be restricted to the prescriptive cataloging: the fluid nature of poly-cultural reality is thus relegated in favor of these preconceived myths that posit a *static* nature of being, regardless of surroundings.

What is complicated about conventional critical labels, which are often binding signifiers, is that they describe performances—not essences. Recent studies in multicultural psychology and cultural neuroscience stress that social affiliations, collective emotions, and sentiments of relationships are explicitly conditional upon the circumstances in which they arise: the identities that someone may perform—and the comparative importance which might be attached to them—are in perpetual unsettledness. Collective identities have inconsistent and even fluctuating meanings depending on the context, a circumstance that destabilizes some of the basic tenets of group-based considerations of individual action (such as interpreting a text or person in reference to terms like "American" or "Spanish," but less so in the case of "local"). The cultural nature of the self, moreover, is regenerated, restated, and reconstructed over time—and some scopes of that negotiation are only available amid specific conditions. A close look at what is termed "local" as per pluriversal logic—whether it be biographical, performative, migratory-based, or linguistic—may engage conventional critical lenses but derive from a complex sense of collective and cultural orientation.

LEGITIMACY IN THE PLURIVERSE VIA A MOVE TOWARD TEMPORAL ADJECTIVES

One solution to these quandaries has been to reconsider the use of qualifiers that allude to permanence. In pluriverse-framed logic, qualifying characterizations could shift toward *temporal* adjectives, provisional to the conditions in which they arise. In Spanish this is perhaps an easier task than in English as there are two verbs, *to be*: the linguistic shift would be toward *estar* and away from *ser*. Since in English "to be" is used for the temporal (e.g., illness: "she is/was sick") and permanent (e.g., origin: "she is/was American"), pluriverse-framed sensibilities might engage a qualified, contextual use of "to be" as a characterizing adjective—such as the *ser/estar* distinction in Spanish. Thus, a phrase like "She is/was Mexican/American/Spanish, etc." has a conditional (*estar*) rather than perpetual value (*ser*), not unlike what is understood in in the phrase "She was sick"; both are reliant on upon conditions and change over time. It is worthwhile to note that, as some illnesses are temporary, others are chronic—pluriversally understood identities may "be" similar (Herlihy-Mera 2018a, 2020). While cultural study grammar often presumes self-sameness across contexts, "the guiding mantra of modern academic social psychology is *the power of the situation*," as Renfrow notes. The contexts "exert considerably more influence on behavior than [scholars] generally think they do" (2013, 241).

TRADITIONAL HIERARCHY, DECOLONIAL PRAXES

While examining new loci of intellectual activity will unravel networks and ways that community, culture, autonomy, and emancipations are performed in Spanish, and potentially are institutionalized, the decolonial school has received serious critique about its own exclusions. Mariana Ortega wonders: "How is it that decolonial work that gets uptake is produced in English by scholars in major research universities in the United States? What narrative of knowledge dissemination is at work here?" (2017, 509–10). She continues: "Even among practitioners of decolonial methodology, the work of some scholars is regarded as more important than that of others—while other work is not regarded and becomes or is made invisible. Unfortunately, the intellectual production of U.S. women of color is part of the work not getting appropriate attention" (2017, 506).

Ortega deftly describes a situation in which "even epistemic attempts to counter control of the macronarratives used to support and reproduce empire also get caught up in these narratives" (2017, 505). The results of this circumstance can scale who can publish, teach, and study, and, specifically: "Women's activities as unseen and unthought can also become the shadow in the background of a decolonial imaginary, especially when these women are Chicanas, Chicanas who, in fact, have already said much and have more to say about decoloniality. The question, then, is, Why isn't much being said about their work in our current discussions of decoloniality? *Has decoloniality become the domain of Latin American thinkers and Latin American exiles living in the United States, especially when they are part of elite institutions?*" (2017, 508; emphasis added). Silvia Rivera Cusicanqui has also levied some scathing critiques, arguing that the community of scholars has:

> construido un pequeño imperio dentro de un imperio, apropiándose estratégicamente de los aportes de la escuela de estudios subalternos de la India y las diversas variantes latinoamericanas de reflexión crítica sobre colonización y descolonización. . . . Neologismos como decolonial, transmodernidad y eco-si-mía proliferan, y ese lenguaje enreda y paraliza sus objetos de estudio: los indígenas y afrodescendientes con quienes estos académicos creen dialogar. Pero también crean un nuevo canon académico, utilizando un mundo de referencias y contrareferencias que establecen jerarquías y adoptan nuevos gurús: Mignolo, Walsh, Enrique Dussel, Javier Sanjinés. (2012, 98, 102)

Similar exclusions appear across disciplines and are codified not only in hiring, but also in publication, scholarly prizes, external funding, and the gamut of academic activity.[19]

DOCTORAL STUDIES AFTER PERIODIZATION, TERRITORIALIZATION, AND EUROCENTRIC FETISHIZATION

A reformation of doctoral studies, engaging localized emphases across all subdisciplines, is a key site of liberation[20] that may reform cultural perspectives toward "a prelude for a politics of democratization" (Fujino et al. 2018, 69). Foregrounding the transnation as an unassailable conceptual unit (as appears in hiring announcements and stated faculty interests) prohibits logics and vocabularies that would develop avenues of critique on many human conditions, including migrant performances, city-state-town-village-cultures, age as a metric of being, multilingualism as meaningful, as well as many other containers of being. The traditional Eurocentric (and largely transnational, elite institution–centric) academy pushes grand narratives into local histories, cultures, narratives, languages, and performances, presenting them as subordinates: if, in this model, local traditions are non-sovereign and corrupted versions of distant cultures, a shift away will be "exciting, challenging, and deeply meaningful" (Fujino et al. 2018, 69).

The process of collective and institutional unlearning, delinking pedagogies from received structures tends to occur gradually and locally, and then abruptly on larger scales.[21] A transition away from Eurocentric certainties, as Enrique Dussel notes, would require "un siglo o dos" (2016, 1). Many options suggested in this section relate to doctoral programs: if the PhD is to remain the unassailable credential of professional existence (the *only* means of faculty appointment), rethinking the structural exigencies (Spain-centrism and top-ranked institutional fetishization) that produce the colonized superstructure would support the cultivation of forms of consciousness and knowledge creation that have the potential to undo Eurocentric curricula / degree programs, appointment practices, study-away tendencies, publication themes, departmental nomenclatures, and so on, by reframing toward views and domains of knowledge *already present* (and marginalized) in classrooms.[22]

These emphases are also important beyond the tertiary (professorial) level: as primary- and secondary-school faculty are trained by professors with doctoral credentials, and because instructors teach in relation to their preparation, over time the shift away from Eurocentrism as the unifying intonation of the intellectual domain would have cascading effects that refigure many power relations at many levels across communities in spaces claimed by the US political body. Localizing the thrust of inquiry gestures toward forms of intellectual participation that are untenable in the existent academic structures. It is important to clarify that suggestions posed here do not gesture toward specific components of the superstructure—that is, lists of "texts" or the scholarly material that presently draws students physically (study away) and intellectually toward Spain (specializing in Peninsular topics). But rather the decolonial move is a *process*, one that queries and destabilizes the grand-story narratives repeated in the contemporary intellectual tradition: these methodological pillars represent the self-evident and unquestioned (and unquestionable) certainties that maintain and re-inaugurate some of the Eurocentric stratifications of the academy. The epistemic shift would address some of the "prescriptive incongruence" (Castro Klarén 2016, 5) of the pedagogical doxa through elision of specific, central spheres of the imperial grammars.

As Sara Castro Klarén has noted, the unlinking techniques developed by decolonial scholars in recent years *"need* to inform the curriculum in a more direct and incisive way" (2016, 4; emphasis added). And in order to achieve that end, the preparation of the faculty who write the curricula is a fundamental factor. By engaging modes of study and pedagogy that abandon forms of power conservation at the doctoral level, the resulting epistemological reordering would fragment the Eurocentric certainties and endeavor to annul what Antonia Carcelén-Estrada has called a process that channels "colonized subjects into the grammar of empire" (2016, 59). While there are many dimensions of pedagogical consistency that reiterate Eurocentric knowledge, there are two primary centers, as noted by Danilyz Arroyo, "Hay que desarmar ambas cosas: tiempo y espacio" (2018). Some conventional epistemic centers involve:

- Periodization
- Territorialization
- Confidence in geography of residence as irrefutable identity-proxy
- Perceiving the trans/nation as exceptional bearer of culture
- Maintaining literature as exceptional holder of culture (often transnational)
- Rhetorical confidence in transatlantic and hybrid presumptions
- Epistemic dependence on area studies suppositions
- Conceptualizing distant, national, transnational, or worlded views that dominate local ones
- Assertion that textual and other highbrow performance is superior to that of nonliterate cultures
- Priority of ostensibly monolingual Spanish over multilingual inflections
- Emphasis of sole and hybrid-cultural views over conditional interpretations
- Essentialized cultural mythos over performative, situational ephemerality
- Top-ranked PhD (instead of local) fetishization

What constitutes valid knowledge? One must master the traditional centers (iterations vary from the above list but repeat in primary and secondary schooling, and undergraduate and graduate levels) in order to receive a PhD: the knowledges promoted "impose agendas" that tacitly link the academy to colonized student learning outcomes (Ramos and Daly 2016, xv). Central to decolonial consciousnesses, notes Walter Mignolo, is "delinking from the already-made entities such as the ideas of 'literature' and of geohistorical entities like 'Europe,' 'Euroasia,' or 'America'" (2013b, 117). While the attention on doctoral specialization is the specific aim here, the received knowledges saturate educational, public, cultural, and social institutions that reach into all dimensions of life—as the doctoral program is a part of an immense colonial ecosystem.

ESSENTIALIZED PRESCRIPTIONS—
HERE OR THERE, NOW OR THEN

In relation to the existent grammars, logics, vocabularies, and sensibilities, decolonial knowledge production is likely to appear utopian if not frivolous (a verity important to the maintenance of the Eurocentric system). Each strategy of knowledge production in the traditional model relies on prescriptions brought to the material analysis in an a priori sense: these presumptions are subsequently unpacked in pedagogy that relies on those certainties to create knowledge and to define communities, languages, and cultures and their relations to one another and to the languages themselves. In the traditional views, the critic inscribes external meanings onto a work, relating it into these conventional—supposedly existent—often essentialized channels (female/male, national/transnational, epoch/period, and so on) in ways that reiterate the already-power of states, nations, transnations, religious groups, corporations, neoliberal machinations, ostensibly democratic social entities, and so on. The role of geographic-based cultural prescriptions in traditional critique is worthy to single out: that a person of a certain background who is born in, a resident of, and writing in Spanish in Districto Federal "is Mexican" is received knowledge; their dominant relational identity sphere (through which all interpretation and pedagogy must pass) is beyond question, self-evident, and outside the terms of critique (as is the status of "Mexican[-]American," once the same person is positioned in an area claimed by the US political body). The theoretical miscues embedded in traditional critique produce these rigid categories; the critic or pedagogue engaging them re-authors new dimensions of the presumptive relational links *and* their binding relations—as well as the forceful consequences that such catalogues command.

But in fact what is self-evident is something resembling the opposite of that traditional certainty: geographic residence combined with an externally assigned cultural demography (presumptions almost universally used to slot authors and their work into a priori classes of relation) may have influence but they do not absolutely determine emotions, sentiments, identity, community membership, or the other grouping mechanisms used to prescribe and categorize. Performances relate to such categories *conditionally*, provisionally, and circumstantially, and codify only the fleetingness of moments—not the broad-brushed absoluteness of the abstractions unpacked in Eurocentric and trans/national studies (among other scales of traditional critique). As data in neuroaesthetics and cultural psychology illustrate, the fabric of cultural being is significantly more malleable, flexible, fluctuating, temporary, transient, and ephemeral than what these critical models permit—such insights throw into question the grouping certainties necessary for geography-, demographic-, period-, cultural- (and other traditional)-based categorizations.

CITY-STATE EPISTEMES

The prescriptive language of nation and transnation—this Eurocentric and Euro-defined period or that one, *this* Euro-historical sense of "importance" or *that* one, and the other abstract grouping measures that engage millions (occasionally hundreds of millions) of human beings—is overdue for revision if not annulment: nuancing these logics makes possible grammars of knowledge creation with the potential to transcend the fixed horizons of study that Eurocentrism prescribes. Many have argued that city-state approaches could replace the slippery claims of homogeneousness and other abstractions characteristic of national and transnational prescription; some see this as an inevitable perspectival shift: "There is a less than a 50% chance that the United States will exist as a nation by the middle of the century," notes Paul Saffo, and "this is . . . a good thing." He continues: "The previous century was shaped by nation-states as the primary actors . . . the central locus of power and economy and control as we move deeper into this century is shifting from the nation-state to the city-state" (2007a, 1). But even using traditional cultural definitions,[23] the United States (i.e., communities resident in spaces claimed by the political body) is/are rebellious to categorization as "a nation" or series of transnational groups. If understood through the dimensions of collective unity articulated by Clifford Geertz (1994)—namely: ethnicity, language, religion, region, and custom—or any other standard "transnational" cultural definition, the "United States" perhaps never met the threshold of such conditions, and appears to be moving away from those parameters. The educational institutions therein, then, instead of relying on the national and transnational theses, should consider moving toward a city-state model that situates local cultures as a priori (and to a degree "exceptional") emphases instead of the standard transnational and Eurocentric abstractions. As Saffo continues: "There are actual city-states like Singapore. But then there are things that we think of as parts of larger national entities but are actually city-states: Silicon Valley and the Bay Area is a virtual city-state. Los Angeles is a different city-state. California in some level is independent" (2007a, 1). Saffo goes on to note that not only culturally but also politically, economically, militarily, and socially, US communities "are getting more and more independent." He uses California as a case example: "The president of the United States says 'we've got to protect our borders'; he says to the republican governor of California, a member of his same party, 'please send your troops to the Mexican border, the national guard, to protect California and the nation against people sneaking across.' And what does the republican governor say to the republican president: 'no'" (2007a, 1). Meanwhile, California has entered in unions with entities including the United Kingdom around climate change; as Saffo makes clear, these moves are "in direct opposition to the explicit policies" of the federal government, and confirms, "This is good news." The shift to localized perspectives are important, Saffo concludes, as "city-states are the center because they are large enough to have impact [in people's lives] but they are small enough that everybody, everybody who lives there, sees the collective consequences of individual action" (2007a, 1). Similarly, as Olga Bezhanova comments, "How do you feel about the feudal system where you were either born a prince or a commoner and could do very little to change your lot? Stupid, right? But this is exactly how people 200 years from now will look at our nation-state system because it's not that different" (2014, 1).[24]

When thinking through and beyond extant structures, toward presently nonexistent scales of being and potential institutionalization, as Paul Saffo notes, it is important to "embrace the things that don't fit" (2007b, 5). For instance, "Spanglish or Spanish in the U.S.," notes Lorgia García Peña, merit specializations, but in the academy, both are almost "inexistente" (email to the author, August 28, 2016). The existing educational practices, policies, and structures are largely based on Peninsular Spanish cultural superiority and associated purity myths (in language, culture, community membership, etc.)—and these envelop the ways both local departments (curricula, programs, nomenclatures, and so on) and US professional organizations (nomenclatures, prizes, publications, among other forms of support) realize and codify their initiatives. Decolonizing these at the doctoral level would require a large-scale *conscientization*, or "the process whereby people become aware of the political, socioeconomic and cultural contradictions" that hinge largely transnational theses and "interact in a hegemonic way" (Ledwith 2011, 97).

Forming the conditions for a different encounter, one that undoes the networks of thematic *distanciation* from and discrimination against local cultures, requires tenure lines in fields that seek to annul conventional logics and the received "best practices" that have defined the fields for generations (centuries). Moving beyond geographic and transnational exceptionalism, rational and temporalized consciousness, among the other epistemic exigencies, if the present structural exigencies from our institutions (requiring a PhD for appointment) remain intact, a doctoral program would begin with *cognitive localism* as a central emphasis, a concept that could be engaged through several key dimensions:

Faculty	shift to local specializations (Replacing Peninsular-themed appointments, these faculty move thematic emphasis in courses/degrees, etc., from one-to-one Spain / Latin America focus to local cultures.)
Curriculum	designed on "local" cultural axes (broadly defined but including US Spanish(es) cultures as central thrust)
Students	perceive, study, and perform local Spanishes as domestic (living and natural—not "foreign" interactions and routines)
Institutions	distinguish, recognize, and enforce Spanishes as domestic (ordinary and commonplace) forms of communication

Such a reappropriation strives to de-world the imperial relations between texts, accents, peoples, and communities, but also to de-connect (and thus de-compare) individuals/communities geographically (in Spain *or not*), politically (citizen *or not*), culturally (literate *or not*), and economically (bourgeois *or not*), and to do so in ways that are outside Euro-prescriptive time scales. Such approaches will allow pedagogy and learning to function as social criticism. Collectively, students and faculty examine and unlink from past norms and rewrite new ones that emancipate organic horizons of being and group membership, and generate sensibilities that are attuned to students, communities, and institutions in ways that are inaccessible within Eurocentric prescriptions.

MASTER SCRIPTING ISOLATED NARRATIVES

Master scripts of Eurocentric knowledge, when engaged as an applied practice in classrooms, attempt to disrupt and distort the memory-making processes of Latinx students and their communities. In many regions, the legitimization of Anglocentric Euro myths (involving exploration, freedom, manifest destiny, and the other dimensions of US grand narratives) coexist with Spain-centric myths (exploration, Christianization, extermination of pre-Columbian peoples and cultures, and comprehensive cultural and linguistic implementation in conquered spaces). The founding myths of both imperial systems (Anglo America and Spanish America) are mutually complemented and further empowered by the reduction of Latinx narratives to single-example cases, such as that of César Chávez, J.Lo, or Sonia Sotomayor: "This practice often separates the events and individuals from the historical struggle of the entire group. Such historically selective education conveys both an implicit and explicit message of isolated heroism rather than courage and resilience as collective group traits" (Novoa et al. 2013, 1). The pedagogical and (US) state-sponsored celebration of single events and of single-person achievements promotes individualism as a character trait and distorts student understanding, presenting history as a decontextualized process in which talented individuals use their superior capacities to achieve success in the Eurocentric world. This approach reiterates "exceptionalism" myths central to the maintenance of traditional center–margin power imbalances. Like much of the US Eurocentric grand narratives, the message is similar: if a person is exceptional, dedicated, hard-working, and perseverant, any individual (indeed any member of a marginalized group) may (if not *should*) achieve success.

This promotion of boot-strap success narratives is a useful tool to inculcate Latinx and other marginalized demographics into the dominant Eurocentric reality. Instead of holistic and contextual framing, boot-strap stories apply the models of Euro-Protestant Horatio Alger fictions that imagine success as a function of hard work and determination, despite social, economic, and cultural capital often necessary for "success." The single-story / person approach could be characterized as margin-targeted codifications of the "American experience" and "American dream" falsehoods, packaged into a material, pedagogical, and plausible fantasy. The application of hard-work and perseverance illusions *always* strives to link "success" to exceptional effort and talent, a circumstance that requires poor and oppressed individuals to understand themselves as responsible for their own poverty and oppression: after all, the example for success is there (be it in the form of J.Lo, Wa-Tho-Huk, Obama, or Oscar de la Hoya, etc.). Howard Zinn has called these narratives "a useful myth for control" (1980, 254).[25]

The ellipsis of context obfuscates the conditions that cause poverty, illiteracy, and poor public health, and, as Alfredo Novoa, Andrew Greene, and Rosa Hwang note, it "disconnects students from their ancestral struggle" and blurs "Latino students' capabilities for critically understanding social circumstances and historical inequalities" (Novoa et al. 2013, 1). In order to have "success" within the exigencies of "American experience" narratives, Latinx students are instructed to assume the dominant worldview and are penalized when they vary therefrom. This a learning circumstance that "hinders them from critiquing and challenging the systems that discourage academic and social progress" (Novoa et al. 2013, 1; Blanchett 2006).

SPANISH AS "SECOND" LANGUAGE

A significant amount of published and unpublished documents from a variety of sources, always aware of the place that Spanish has as a *second*, rather than as *foreign*, language in many communities throughout the US. Precisely because of the distinctive history of Spanish in this country, and its current status as the language of the largest *minority*, [requires] the reevaluation of the structures and curricula.

Alan V. Brown and Gregory L. Thompson, *The Changing Landscape of Spanish Language Curricula* (**2018, x; third emphasis added**)

Many ostensibly progressive reports that express findings like these maintain that Spanish is best understood as a *minority* or a *second* language rather than a "first," "natural," or "ordinary" linguistic system. The ways that academia extra-territorializes communities from standard conceptualizations of the United States and of Latin America intensify these fictions, to the extent that, as Alonso points out, the "field must be rethought and exploded" (2007, 227). The enduring prescription of Spanish as foreign, external, heritage, diverse, minority, and so on, shapes students' experiences in Spanish and English and Spanglish: these have been called "disaffirming language ideologies [that operate] in U.S. schools that efface Latinx experiences, reduce and problematize bilingualism, and demonize U.S. varieties of Spanish and Spanglish" (Carter 2018, 251). The ways such pedagogies have been standardized and institutionalized re-disseminates Eurocentric authority and dogmas that oppress local cultures and curb linguistic attention to local (usually described as "incorrect," "vernacular," or perhaps at best "dialectical") versions of Spanish and English. As Philip Carter notes, among "Miami-born Latinx college students, we have come across language attitudes—without even looking for them—that suggest that English in Miami is not 'real' English, that Spanish in Miami has been contaminated by English or less prestigious varieties of Spanish, and that the presence of Spanglish bespeaks a population that knows neither language well, is unmotivated to learn, is uneducated, is lazy, and so on" (2018, 251). Carter goes on to observe, "for Latinx students at U.S. universities" the Eurocentric thrust of "Spanish language classes may disaffirm the national-origin and local varieties of Spanish students learn in the home . . . and even Heritage Language Spanish classes . . . reproduce colonialist, nationalist, monolingual, and standard language ideologies that *promote the loss of Spanish* rather than its maintenance" (2018, 252; emphasis added). Perhaps most striking about the saturation of coloniality embedded in the educational institutions to which Latinx students have access is the extent to which "individuals blame themselves for the personal and community patterns of Spanish to English language shift" (Carter 2018, 251). This circumstance is redoubled by pedagogies that presume students are monolingual in English or Spanish, the absence of Latinx communication in what is termed "American" language,[26] and the presumption that English is the most appropriate institutional language across all universities. "The default is the positioning," note Leeman and Serafini, of Latinx students is "out-of-place in the Spanish classroom.... This was the case even when [Latinx] students constituted more than 75% of the students" (2020, 2).

FOREGROUNDING LATINX EXPERIENCE

Ariana Hernández's treatise "Identidad rasgado y la lengua perdida: The Impact of a Traditional Literary Canon on Latino Perceptions of Identity" is notable both as intellectual achievement and a cultural document: her perceptive analyses articulate the power and toxicity of Eurocentric education in South Texas, situated from her experiences transitioning from small-town life to the Euro-amalgamated Texas State University in San Marcos. Hernández's work shrewdly reframes some of the foundational assumptions about community, culture, and language; the role of higher education as a social apparatus; and the power of pedagogy to prescribe marginal positions to Latinx peoples.

Upon matriculating at university, Hernández "had not read any texts by Native American or Latino authors" until Sandra Cisneros's *The House on Mango Street* appeared on a syllabus. "[I] had never felt so passionate about a text before because I saw myself in it. I became angry and frustrated that *I had never read a text written by my people before in my education*" (2015, 1; emphasis added). She describes the pedagogical scaffolding as a pan-disciplinary "repetition of values—the same values" (2015, 13) and questions: "What real grounds are the works students read chosen on and whose values do the works represent?" (2015, 8). Hernández critiques her institutional environment and its Eurocentric fetishization: "Limiting the variety of texts students read[,] we limit what they learn to a specific set of events, characters, settings, values, and emotions. And worse, when texts are analyzed with the same perspective repetitively, students learn only one perspective" (2015, 13). Hernández attacks this "tradition and inertia" and describes how the absence of local cultures creates exclusions that shape her reality and manipulate her behavior, causing her to realize "how ignorant I was about my own culture and became more aware of how it is *hidden* in everyday life by the actions of myself and others. From the details of how my name is pronounced without the 'r' rolled, to wanting to marry a white man" (2015, 1).

While Hernández concedes that there is a place for Eurocentric topics the curriculum, she maintains it must be "taught in a way which create[s] a space for students to explore the identities of themselves and their peers" and makes clear "this is not happening" (2015, 13).²⁷ The saturation of colonized pedagogical methods situates Latinx students "in a position of inferiority [and thus] students do not feel capable of success and only few excel past their fears of failure," she writes. "Students who do not see themselves, their cultures, values, beliefs, languages, or ways of speaking in the words of the canon are left with the choice to conform the way they communicate to that of the dominant culture or fail" (2015, 16). In this hierarchical, exclusionary model of education, Hernández "was never allowed to explore who I was" (2015, 2), and the controls situate Latinx students in a context in which they "need to hide their accents with a tendency to need to explain their cultural traditions" (2015, 18), all this in a university categorized as a "Hispanic-Serving Institution."

The elision of Latinx cultures and languages at South Texas universities pressures students to mimic dominant iterations of citizenship in ways that, as an anonymous female in Hernández's study commented, pressures students to "conform to those worlds" and vanquish local identities: "You cannot be the way you were back in your [South Texas] hometown" (qtd. in Hernández 2015, 18). An anonymous male student had similar reflections: "I felt obligated to change my accent" when saying "San Marcos," the name of his university (Hernández 2015, 18–19). Several anonymous comments in "Identidad Rasgado" note that there is a change of sensibility from the hometowns where local identities are performable, to the colonized environment in San Marcos. There, the behavioral, cultural, and linguistic exigency "communicates the inferiority of any persons belonging to a narrative outside of the dominant narrative . . . *this affects students*" (Hernández 2015, 15).

WRITING OVER ERASED LANGUAGE, CULTURE, HISTORY, AND AGENCY

"We are in it, not of it."

Michael Rodríguez (2021)

The institutional devaluation of Latinx experiences Hernández describes distorts regional knowledges and cultures into a perceived parochialism, one that can be a source of embarrassment and shame. The monolingual university participates by forcing English into all facets of existence, thus creating a space in which many are "in" but not "of" the civic body.

Elaborating on this concept, Stockton College professor Michael Rodríguez reflects on his boyhood in South Texas, "The localism I owned was parochial because it felt that it was simply un-recognized by officialdom (mainstream Spanish and mainstream Americanism)." He continues,

> I was convinced that the localism of the Mexican American culture I was immersed in was not something that fell within the gaze of recognition from the broader society—it was, again, in but not of this country. I also mistook that localism for being parochial, not just in relation to the mainstream Spanish language and culture you write about being worlded, but also the American mainstream.
>
> The community I grew up in is called Losoya (named after a Tejano hero) in the outskirts of San Antonio. We all were intimately familiar with La Llorona. Not only do I believe I heard her one evening, I was absolutely convinced the legend (actually, her real-ness) was completely our own—in Losoya, and nowhere else. The hyper-localism of La Llorona—anchored almost exclusively in a specific geography of Losoya and the broader region of San Antonio (perhaps), was not something I thought could be shared with other Mexican Americans from other parts of the country, and certainly not with whites. In my mind she was not trans-local. That conceptual frame was shattered when I read *Bless Me, Ultima* and I was astounded to learn that virtually everyone in the Southwest experienced La Llorona as their own. That was quite emancipatory—to know that my hyper-localism was in fact trans-geographic and trans-local. That made my localism significantly less parochial, by realizing that it had "recognition." Recognition is what bridges being "in" with being "of," albeit the "of" was the broader Mexican American / Chicano experience, not the broader American experience in this case. (2021)

The same deformation, truncated by "American" dominant colonial narratives, reached into language domains, and into private home space, causing indignity on the Spanish and English ends of the imperial design. In the colonial matrix, the imposed and foreign language blurs the intimacy of local tradition:

> The same was true of the Spanglish I grew up with, or what is termed Chicano Caló. I grew up convinced that our Spanglish idioms too were hyper-local—not even Mexican Americans in other parts of the country, much

less Mexicanos, would find them familiar. We called a tostada a *chalupa*, we called a truck a *troca*, we called young rebels (or troublemakers) pachucos, not *cholos*. We referred to each other as *vato*, girls were referred to as *rucas*, beer was called *vironga*. The list goes on. I was very aware that these words were not standard Spanish, and indeed were ridiculed by the older generation (who BTW were born in the US but referred to themselves as Mexicanos) and completely un-recognized even as bastardized Spanish by the broader society. Oh, and BTW, whites were called *bolillos* (yes, like the bread, but I did not know it was bread until my adulthood). I thought it simply meant white people.

The lack of recognition of the Spanglish I grew up with was indeed a source of embarrassment because it felt so local, and so parochial, and hence so outside of mainstream culture (both Spanish and American). As an undergraduate I also began to learn that my local idiomatic expressions were actually part of a broader geography of linguistic localisms. It became less parochial while remaining intimately local. Recognition is a peculiar phenomenon. We can either desire it from the broader society or we can assert it ourselves through self-recognition.

Localisms are indeed intensely intimate, but when one realizes they are not parochial the sense of being not "of" begins to dissipate. But how do we protect that sense of (local) intimacy when we enter the (othered) public sphere of whiteness? (Yes, we are othered by them, but we also other them.) How does the intense intimacy of our localism survive in the othered spaces of whiteness? The fact we were spanked by teachers/principals for speaking Spanish on the playground sent a powerful message—"do not inject your language of intimacy into public spaces"; that intimacy could not be "of" the public space of whiteness.

I recall attending a one-woman play by a Chicana in San Antonio. I don't recall the play or the name of the actress. What I do recall is a point in the performance in which she mimics her father—in a state of rage—yelling at her for some *pendejada* (as my dad was fond of saying) but having to cycle through all the names of her siblings before he blurted out her name. Everyone in the theater broke out in laughter. I was astonished—I thought that only happened in my family! That which I assumed was hyper-local was indeed trans-local. I walked out of that theater with a deep sense of pride in my cultural particularity—it was being recognized as not parochial. (2021)

As Rodríguez deftly describes, while colonial programs caused the disconnection, silence, and ridicule, spaces of local performance and recognition can be loci of the connections necessary for resistance. In relation to the literatures of colonized communities and the relationships forged in private spaces, Rodríguez comments:

> Richard Rodriguez's *Hunger of Memory* ([was] derided by many Chicano intellectuals) who opposed bilingual education[, but Rodríguez] felt that bringing the language of intimacy into the public space of whiteness (he didn't quite call it whiteness, as I do here) destroys that intimacy. He recalls his father's sadness when he and his siblings all spoke English at the dinner table—that silenced his father; intimacy was dying where it should thrive.
>
> English was a public language utterly lacking in intimacy. I have issues with this conceptualization of demarcating separate spheres for intimacy and being "of" the public space, but I can't help but think he has a bit of a point. Perhaps that point is that *the power to de-recognize intruded into the intimacy of the home, the language, the culture.*
>
> There's a powerful scene in the documentary *Children of Giant* (about the filming of the classic movie *Giant* which was filmed in Marfa, Texas). The documentarians revisit the community to highlight the lives of the children (now adults) who were extras in the film. In the documentary the story is told of the public school in Marfa where a—supposedly well-meaning white teacher—had the Mexican American children write on a scrap of paper "I will no longer speak Spanish." The teacher gathered all the slips of paper and inserted them into a tiny, makeshift coffin (yes, I know—kind of weird and sick). She then marched the kids outside to the school grounds by the flagpole where they dug a hole and buried the coffin. In the documentary the children—now adults—disinter the coffin. (2021)

Children of Giant addresses segregation in Texas, classrooms as sites of colonial violence, and the feeble nature of Americanization and Mexicanization theses when the center of focus shifts from imperial centers to local sensibilities. When such transitions occur in institutional settings, they often result in violent colonial reprisals, as has occurred in recent decades to initiatives that situate Spanish, Spanglish, and non-US-imperial cultural experiences as natural and ordinary, and worthy of attention in classrooms.

DIRECTED AGGRESSION—ANTI-CHICANX AND MEXICAN AMERICAN STUDIES

In the early 2000s, the Tucson Mexican American Studies Program "emphasized critical thinking and focused on Mexican-American literature and perspectives"; the initiative resulted in "increased graduation rates, high student achievement and a state-commissioned independent audit that recommended expanding the classes" (Planes 2013, 1). Arizona's then-superintendent of public instruction, John Huppenthal, ordered the program be shuttered or lose $14 million in state funding. Prior to his stint as superintendent of public instruction, state senator Huppenthal coauthored House Bill 2281, which prohibited pedagogies that do not support the cultural and linguistic myths advocated by the US political body. Judge Lewis D. Kowal maintained that any form of teaching that "advocates ethnic solidarity of Latinos" is to be understood as unlawful (qtd. in Peralta 2011, 1). Using this bill and Judge Kowal's opinion to leverage fear, Huppenthal's colonial move caused the initiative to be shuttered.

Like many who wield undue social power in regions recently claimed by the United States, like Arizona, Huppenthal and his family moved to Tucson, bringing their language (English) and certainties regarding the cultural proprietorship of the space (the colonial mandate) and implemented those in their new community upon arrival. The Homestead Act (1862–1986) offered free land to US citizens who relocated to recently conquered and annexed regions; many communities receiving Homestead Act settlers are Latinx-majority and Spanish-speaking areas. While direct governmental aid for resettlement ended in 1986, the economic collapse in the Midwest and elsewhere has brought a new crush of US citizen—culturally immigrant-settlers—to places like Arizona. These cultural soldiers (like Huppenthal and his family) continue to arrive without impediment, with voting rights and working papers, bringing their language and prescriptive ideas about the spaces in which they newly reside. (Due to the ways the US colonial prescriptions have been codified into law, newcomers from elsewhere have none of these rights.) The social power of the settler-US-citizen demographics is recodified in the legislation they write for themselves and the education models they create for Latinx peoples. For instance, in comments posted anonymously (he later admitted authorship), Huppenthal clamors about his new home in Arizona (his errors and spacing included):

> We all need to stomp out balkanization. No spanish radio stations, no spanish billboards,
> no
>   spanish tv
> stations, no spanish newspapers. This is America, speak English.
> I don't mind them selling Mexican food as long as the menus are mostly in English. And, I'm not being humorous or racist. A lot is at stake here. (qtd. in Roberts 2014, 1)

The same notions about foreign/domestic status of the Spanish language informs SB 1070, which *requires* police to establish whether people in their presence have documents when a "reasonable suspicion" exists. What is a "reasonable suspicion"? Speaking Spanish. Nearly all of the public figures who support the colonial linguistic/cultural mandates codified in 1070—including Joseph Arpaio, Janet Ann Napolitano, and Governor Jan Brewer, who signed it into law, like Huppenthal, are English-speaking US citizens who moved to Arizona from elsewhere.[28]

In January 2019, Ana Suda and Martha Hernández were detained in Montana after a Border Patrol agent heard them conversing in Spanish at a grocery store. Instead of saying "hello" back to them when they walked by and greeted him *in English*, agent Paul O'Neill "commented that she had a strong accent and asked where we were both born." When asked if he were serious, he replied: "Dead serious." He arrested them. When queried on the reason they were being held against their will by an officer of the government, O'Neill replied, "You guys are speaking Spanish." When asked if they would have been detained if they were speaking French, O'Neill responded: "No, we don't do that." Suda and Hernández filmed the encounter. The video circulated on national outlets and the women and their families have been "harassed repeatedly" online and in the town where they live. Ana Suda notes that her "8-year-old daughter is *scared to speak Spanish* and has started responding to me in English when I ask her questions." Suda added that other Latinx people where they live have approached them expressing fear "about whether they could also be stopped by Border Patrol just for speaking Spanish or looking differently" (Suda 2019, 1).[29]

Spain-centric pedagogical culture at US universities contributes to the foreignization and obfuscations of US Spanishes, while facilitating police violence against many communities. This scholarly environment has detrimental effects on Latinx students' mental and physical health, and promotes an environment in which speaking Spanish in public is de facto illegal. The almost complete absence of US Spanish in US universities urges reconsideration, but there is very little space available in a crowded curriculum and a priori channels of tenure-track lines. Robert Train has noted that "the foundational coloniality" of Spanish-language and cultural study in US higher education profoundly "shape[s] what we do" (2011, 143). The traditional Eurocentric mandate *determines* the horizon of possibility, the goals of pedagogy, the material to be studied, and the ways cultures and peoples are organized in relation to one another, and these colonize the fabric of the student experience. The tradition supports "ideologies of unity and purity of language . . . notions of speakership [are] grounded in the dynamics of (not) belonging, inclusion, and exclusion" (Train 2011, 147). The application of Lisa Fortuna's felicitous phrase "a bio-psycho-social-cultural model" (Fortuna 2009, 5) would recreate pedagogical and tenure-track expectations around Latinx and Latin American cultures, histories, and languages, unlinking from the already-power that defines contemporary departmental emphases. "To bridge what Spanish programs actually do," notes Ann Abbott, with those goals, "we need to focus much of our curricula on US Latinos, commit to social justice education and engage with our local Latino communities. Few departments do this, though, because few departments have truly seen this as their mission" (2017, 33). Abbott's discerning critique recommends "a more radical—and uncomfortable—shift" (2017, 33). These new centers of pedagogical sensibility would concern local Spanish-language cultures and provide an emancipatory and decolonized model of cultural studies that de-foreignizes Spanish and institutionalizes it as a domestic, community language.

COGNITIVE LOCALISM AND DECOLONIZING THE APPOINTMENT PROCESS

An important principle in this movement shifts teaching toward *facilitation* and learning toward a *generative and creative process* instead of a resuscitative one. Engaging cognitive localism as a primary axis, faculty development, curricular programs, and student experiences could address the traditional lack of US Spanish and Spanglishes through, precisely, "smaller geo-cultural comparative units" (Castro-Klarén 2016, 9). Until institutional shifts could occur in degree paths and hiring, "topics courses" could be useful tools for some initial steps toward:

- engaging content emphasizing local sensibilities, languages, and groups;
- creating opportunities to connect with local communities;
- fostering critical analyses of local custom, tradition, trans-localities, and regional/migrational connections;
- connecting community members to instruction and program development;
- creating and using new resources with local emphases that discontinue Eurocentric myths;
- institutionalizing local Spanishes as living, vibrant sources of cultural expression;
- recreating Spain as a subsidiary, ephemeral, and marginal occurrence in relation to lived sensibilities;
- modifying student-faculty dynamics, encouraging student independence, expertise, and creation; and
- facilitating a shift toward local knowledges as exceptional forms of scholarly preparation.

In addition to thematic and knowledge-based shifts in focus, cognitive localism calls for profound, structural changes to the appointment process. There are several important dimensions of the crisis in Spanish-language cultural studies, as it influences employment practices:

1) the reduction of tenure lines;
2) the one-to-one Spain-centric weighting in contemporary appointments; and
3) a culture of biased evaluation for the existing appointments, which results in a scaling of PhDs by institutional affiliation.

While it would seem that larger applicant pools that accompany a reduction of tenure lines would result in hires from many backgrounds, the opposite has occurred: the available data demonstrate not a broadening but a channeling of appointments toward scholars who studied at top-ranked institutions. This tendency is clear throughout the academy but is particularly severe at doctoral-granting universities in the humanities. Consideration of nuanced or radical changes to the hiring process could be an important component of pedagogical decolonization.

Given the intellectual foci in Spanish-language cultural topics, one may imagine graduates of universities in Spanish-speaking areas of the United States, or with majority Latinx enrollment, would find success, given their proximity to some of the lived experiences of the discipline. But in fields like Puerto Rican and Caribbean studies, the available data demonstrate that hiring competitions prefer doctoral graduates from top-ranked institutions over those from the Universidad de Puerto Rico and its cohort.[30] Data demonstrate that, across the humanities, those who reach the tenure stream tend to be graduates of one tiny sector of PhD-granting institutions (see Colander and Zhou 2015; and Arner 2014); the parameters of the hiring competition exclude many qualified candidates not as a result of their own shortcomings but due to the unethical ways applicants are ranked (often before interviews occur). The selection preferences are scaffolded by procedural issues of enormous applicant pools and a lack of focus on how conventional protocols prioritize some candidates over others.

The myths of academic hierarchy insinuate that scholars with top-ranked affiliation achieved such status through talent and intrinsic potential, factors external to the social, cultural, and economic circumstances that often authorize their selection over other applicants (at both the student and faculty levels). The selection of candidates—in humanistic fields, certainly—should result in a descriptive demographic sample, as no one group (linguistic, regional, ethnic, institutional, cultural, socioeconomic, and so on) should claim authority on the teaching and analysis of the human condition. But faculty bodies are socially engineered through a system that overweighs cultural status (prior affiliation) in the selection process, and the results are clear: in the present system "virtually no one moves up," as Sydni Dunn notes (2015, 1). Thus, scholars from mid- and low-ranked institutions—including UPR applicants for positions in Caribbean studies and Puerto Rican studies—are deemed incompetent to teach on the tenure stream about Puerto Rican topics vis-à-vis their privileged peers. "How did we prune our field from 637 to 27?," notes Lou Marinoff, department chair at CUNY. "An important selection criterion was holding a Ph.D. from a good university. Members of our department earned their Ph.D.s at Columbia, Harvard, Oxford, and University of London" (2009, 1). In light of these "best practices," as Marc Bousquet comments, "further up the food chain, the less merit required for appointment" (2016, 1).

The existing hiring culture has protocols that protect the myth of top-ranked exceptionalism rather than identifying talented scholars from backgrounds presently absent from faculties—and specifically, applicants from Hispanic-Serving Institutions who demonstrate excellence in local sensibilities. If "competition" is to remain the mainstay of appointments, for this process to be "winnable" by mid- and lower-tier scholars, structural changes are required in the hiring process: appointment protocols should be modified so that candidates from lower-ranked universities reach the tenure line. Many studies in psychology, which I will soon discuss, demonstrate that humans cannot adjudicate between supposedly equal candidates and instead rely on proxy values (i.e., affiliation); thus, it is important to clarify that the event horizon for an appointment is the campus interview, not the submission of a dossier—an essential point to distinguish as many announcements receive hundreds of applications.

An important part of this discussion concerns what characteristics determine interviewees. One would assume search committee members read each application. In practice this does not happen. According to Leonard Cassuto, "Most readers don't read a CV carefully. . . . You can't change that fact" (2019, 1). Susan Lord notes, "In almost no time we can reject half our applicant pool just by looking at their cover letters" (qtd. in Reis 2000). Nancy Scott Hanway believes the process is "all about the letter." She continues, "I, like many committee members, don't read [beyond the cover letter] until the stack of applications has been whittled down." While Scott Hanway admits that she "may never get to your [statement of teaching] philosophy," she has seen committee members who "have forgotten to read [the files]" and demonstrate a general "ignorance" about the candidates (2015, 1).

The ethical concerns escalate when letters of recommendation are scrutinized. Zach Bowen points out that "special letters from old boys and old girls are treated with some respect in our department. Since we often write similar letters for our students, I make an effort to order the dossiers of all the recommended candidates."[31] Michèle Lamont cites an anonymous scholar who said this about letters of reference: "I make judgments based on my knowledge of how distinguished the writer [of the letter] is, but I pay very little attention to what the writer actually says" (2009, 165).

Reports from faculty about candidate valuation are similarly disquieting. David Damrosch has participated in searches in humanities fields at Harvard and Columbia, and strives to offer a review that he feels is ethically sound: "I was always on the side of looking instead at applicants, from whatever school, who showed independence of mind, a real voice in their writing sample, and creativity of thought and potential for growth as expressed in their personal statements." Harvard and Columbia's appointment records (Herlihy-Mera 2015, 80–106) demonstrate what Damrosch terms "independence of mind," "a real voice," and "creativity of thought" cannot be articulated by scholars outside top-ranked universities. While Damrosch is generally uncritical of himself and his peers (or this search committee culture in general), he acknowledges, ultimately, his belief that the present valuation model and its scaled labor outcome is appropriate: "Elite programs," he comments, "provide a better environment for students to thrive in, not only in terms of better funding and lower teaching requirements, but also because graduate students learn as much from each other as from the faculty" (email to the author, November 25, 2012).

The myth that "elite" institutions are "a better environment for students to thrive" belies that success in humanistic fields often derives from cultural, pedagogical, and investigative experiences that are not available at top-ranked universities. It disregards that many top students—in particular, the very demographics largely absent from the tenure-track—simply aren't interested in enrolling at such universities (Meraji 2015; Orr 2016; Fain 2016).[32] Damrosch's broad-brush indictment of institutions like mine fails to acknowledge that overcoming a lack of prestige, cultivating pedagogical sensibilities and research questions in settings external to conventional theoretical prescriptions, enjoying a cultural and socioeconomic scholarly environment (one untenable at top-ranked universities), and studying among a cohort of scholars who are outside the privileges and discriminations of the top ranks could be—but are not—understood as conditions ripe for groundbreaking work at the tenure-track level.

The exceptionalism Damrosch defends is not by any means unique to Harvard or Columbia. While it's clear those in positions of power should visit the institutions they deem inferior, and speak with our students and challenge the presumed superiority they maintain those from top-ranked scholarly backgrounds enjoy, such corrective action on a large scale is unthinkable. The incumbent scaling system is too ingrained, too easy to carry on, and there's no incentive to break such patterns. At my institution, 98 percent of students are Latinx and around 75 percent are eligible for Pell Grants. While much of the student work on our campus—on Spanish-language cultures and on comparative and world literatures, among other topics—has sensibilities that transcend the scholarship Damrosch has in print, even if cover letters and writing samples from UPR students *are* seen by his eyes, or that of any search committee member, coming from such an institutional context, the students' preparation in a de facto sense is perceived as substandard due to his perceptions on what he terms "elite programs"; couple such preferences with candidate pools so large that all submitted documents cannot *possibly* be read by humans, the overwhelming reliance on affiliation as proxy value accelerates paperwork from UPR applicants (and those of our cohort) toward the wastebasket.

Many studies diametrically oppose Damrosch's anecdote that affiliation is of minimal importance in hiring. In fact, the available data show prestige bias is a determinative factor in all facets of the appointment procedure: "Faculty hiring follows a common and steeply hierarchical structure that reflects profound social inequality" (Clauset et al. 2015, 1). In line with the labor statistics, reports in behavioral psychology demonstrate group membership is a determining factor in how an individual is perceived in relation to others. In "Defined by Your Category," Adam Alter reports that when faced with a task like comparing the work of hundreds of hypothetically equal PhDs, evaluators are "willing to view the world with guidance of labels." Scholars from Princeton assessed an imaginary female as "smarter when she was wealthier," and considering imaginary students from top-ranked backgrounds, evaluators "emphasized students' strengths and overlooked their weaknesses." The presence of a desirable affiliation "primed [evaluators] to see academic progress" that was unsubstantiated. The inclination toward the top-ranked-affiliations-are-best model influenced the assessments to the point that evaluators "saw exactly *that* pattern of achievement . . . [and ignored] missteps" (Alter 2013, 38). These conditions inform the decisions taken by search committees at all levels.

The exceptionalist myopia results in a general ignorance of the quality of scholarship at institutions like mine, favoring a deliverance of scholars with preparation at top-ranked universities. This situation prohibits appointments of scholars with expertise in local cultures and languages in all fields, and is particularly misguided for Spanish-language cultural studies, as not a single high-Hispanic-enrollment institution (those with arguably more local-cultural sensibilities in the target subject) is considered "top-ranked" or "elite" in any humanistic discipline; moreover, the fact that Spanish-language majority areas of the United States lack "top-ranked" departments of any kind links the faculty of universities in Spanish-dominant communities to scholars whose preparation occurred outside those areas.

LOCALIZING DECOLONIAL MEMORY AND DE-EXCEPTIONALIZING HARVARD AND YALE'S COHORT

> Why are [top institutions in this field] at Yale and Harvard and not in Cuzco, Bahía, Cartagena, or Piura?
>
> **Ricardo Salvatore, "On Knowledge Asymmetries and Cognitive Maps" (2015, 372)**

> No se puede exponer conceptualmente algo *que no se ha vivido*.
>
> **Rafael Bautista, *Del mito del desarrollo al horizonte del "vivir bien" ¿por qué fracasa el socialismo en el largo siglo XX?* (2017, 22)**

Preferences for applicants from top-ranked universities tacitly prescribe an intellectual parochialism throughout the academy through the importation of ontologies to communities with autonomous but unrecognized and noninstitutionalized cultures. When a graduate of a top-ranked university in California or the Northeast arrives in South Florida, Texas, or Puerto Rico (or any other region claimed by the US political body) as a recent-PhD junior faculty member, she, he, or they unpacks a subtle epistemic violence by engaging their surroundings in ontological terms cultivated during their preparation elsewhere. This imported distance-knowledge base requires "not being able to hear, understand" their new surroundings in ways that cultivate localized, decolonial epistemes (Trownsell et al. 2019, 1). While the present exceptionalism myths in academic hiring support the mischaracterization of Spanish as "foreign" and one-to-one Spain-centric thematic exigencies, it is a tradition that enjoys a great deal of support. "At South Texas Universities," queried an interested faculty member, "why not hire South Texans who studied with the best at Harvard and Stanford?" (conversation at "MLA 2017 Convention Panel: Histories of Digital Labor"). This is the general solution: scholars leave their communities and become socialized into the dominant epistemes and cultures during their studies away from their local contexts; this circumstance is sometimes understood as a boon for the local communities, globalizing the educational institutions into the mainstream through such appointments. The scholars return "modernized"—cured of the provincial nature of the local area and with the knowledge, experience, and expertise that top-ranked universities afford.[33] While the existent model (provincial area to "top ranked" elsewhere, and back) has ostensible benefits within "progress" frameworks, the pedagogical outcomes (ontological commitments honed and developed away—nonlocally, with few exceptions) inform a faculty member's primary assumptions about the nature of knowledge, community, culture, performance, and identity, among many other topics. These fundamental dimensions of academic existence—the core assumptions cultivated at a distant institution—operate within a new institutional space, be it a classroom, department meeting, academic conference, journal article, or monograph, and so forth, and pre-map the emphases that the faculty member will develop over the span of a career. The externalization of this pre-mapping prohibits local foci in ways that re-hierarchize knowledge production away from localities in all regions—save in those few communities that have top-ranked universities.

As Ricardo Salvatore notes, "Harvard, Chicago, Stanford, Berkeley, or Yale prepare the future ministers and presidents of the 'southern republics,'" a circumstance that, like appointment practices, is an imperial process: each "brings back from these Meccas of knowledge *an admiration* for US libraries, archives, and museums. This intangible cultural capital circulates . . . in an endless circle of expanded reproduction" (2015, 380; my emphasis). Especially in Latin American studies, Salvatore queries, "Why are [top institutions in this field] at Yale and Harvard and not in Cuzco, Bahía, Cartagena, or Piura?" (2015, 372). In order to decolonize paradigms in ways that localize agency, there is a "need to reverse the gaze implicit in US conceptions of Latin American Studies, offering as alternative a perspective tentatively named 'Critical Hemispherism.'" (Salvatore 2015, 363). Even within the traditionalist grammars of area/geopolitical approaches, Spanish-language cultural studies *is* Latin American studies, and thus, the intellectual paradigm shift Salvatore has coined has important applications here: unlinking the top-down, externalized notions of merit would move toward the antimodern and de-progress thrusts of decolonial and anticolonial epistemes.

At the moment of appointment, it is generally understood that all spheres of professional activity will relate to a scholar's interests, specialization, concentration, and knowledge areas, as vetted in the hiring competition: how a faculty member conceptualizes their reality and their relationship to surroundings, to knowledge, to students, and so on, link to the conditions cultivated, recognized, and credentialized (in the PhD, and thus) exteriorly. The move toward localization in appointment practices recognizes the values, commitments, communities, languages, and cultures marginalized by the present system *and* gestures toward undoing some of the invisible, received controls on knowledge production that are commonsensical in the colonized shared meaning system of the external-preparation model. A local-as-exceptional move would require many more doctoral programs: such reforms and opportunities would be beneficial to each community in concert with institutional missions. (Doing away with the exceptionalism myth for top-ranked universities would allow those departments to turn toward immediate contexts in ways that also undo the Eurocentric certainties that presently characterize the field.)

Privileging local vis-à-vis top-ranked PhDs has recently been voiced in a region claimed by the United States since the Treaty of Guadalupe Hidalgo: "We are not talking about North Dakota," notes Jorge Cañizares-Esguerra. "We are talking about Texas, and an institution that is mostly all white when it comes to power. So we are talking about a civil rights issue" (qtd. in Flaherty 2019, 1). A group of faculty petitioned against the tacit prohibition of local hires, specifically of Latinx scholars from Texas. The existing "best practice" has "disturbed and demoralized faculty, staff, students and members of the community at large" (qtd. in Flaherty 2019, 1).While 7 percent of UT Austin's tenure-line faculty are Latinx, among Texan students aged eighteen to twenty-four, that figure is 46 percent. Among 130 deans (including vice, associate, and assistant), ten are Latinx men (none are female); of ninety-eight department chairs, six are Latinx. "Our critique is aimed not just at UT Austin" but at many other universities that have the same implicit policies (qtd. in Flaherty 2019, 1). The recommendations are clear:

> We mean the following groups: Tejanos, Hispanic Americans, Chicanos, Puerto Ricans, and other Latin Americans, including Brazilians, following the traditional legal designation of "Hispanic" for the category that may well be identified as Latin American. Administrators should prioritize hiring Hispanics who are Tejanos (native Texan Mexican Americans) and who originate from disadvantaged groups and who labor to improve the inclusion and academic advancement of Hispanic students.[34] (Martínez et al. 2019, 5)

The contemporary externalization of faculty preparation (top-ranked affiliation preference, nonlocal institutions) has forming effects on what may be understood as usable forms of knowledge, culture, agency, language, and community—and what is and what isn't local. Engaging multiple ontologies with a local emphasis empowers students and faculty to interpret colonized relationships in ways that undermine the systems that strive to oppress them, and to rewrite performances and histories in ways that source collaborative knowledge from the communities in which institutions are embedded. Local-focused hires and locally prepared hires will provide, as Ylce Irizarry notes, the "agency to tell a new story" (2016, 159). These new forms of memory making, and the institutionalization thereof, privilege the agency of each author or artist in ways that undo the transnational parameters, as well as those homogenizing narratives of difference.[35] An important dimension of this shift in valuation (top-ranked to local PhD) would make possible the denaturalization of "what is allowed to be considered possible or true" (Trownsell et al. 2019, 1). by undoing the prevailing presumptions regarding Spanish-language worlds ("foreign" in the US and rooted to Spain in all cases). Such a shift would allow "living in one's own or a group's terms" which presently is "a struggle [because] they are not aligned with the more predominant logic." The public health and wellbeing improvements underpinned to such shifts would benefit communities in a myriad of ways: "What entities are, therefore," note Trownsell et al., "is not given in advance" (2019, 1). The departure from set scripts that would occur via local hires with localized specialties gestures toward erasure of the categorical lines of traditional Eurocentrism.

This situation is symptomatic of a much larger problem in academic—indeed in contemporary, neoliberal—culture, which has many similar "competitions" that in practice can only be won by certain demographics. The discrimination against mid- and low-tier students (particularly against Latinx scholars—and especially those who come from Spanish-dominant areas *and* study at high-Hispanic-enrollment (HHE) universities on Pell Grants) begins long before they apply for the tenure track, and the same exclusions reappear at every phase, from pre-K to PhD, during faculty hiring, and, once appointed, they re-emerge in competitions for grant funding, scholarly prizes, publications, among others.

Traditional academic competitions do not achieve what they pretend (Bernstein 2015). Despite the entrenched nature of these biases, humanistic disciplines are generally resistant to the concept that one analysis of the human condition (that is, whatever is in a cover letter or writing sample) may be inherently superior to another. Presently, inordinately large numbers of Latinx PhDs (especially women), scholars on Pell grants, graduates of community colleges, and politically undocumented individuals are absent from humanistic faculties—but they are overrepresented at high-Hispanic-enrollment universities: these demographics have perspectives deemed insignificant due to flawed hiring metrics. Such preferences amount to a subtle attack on what it is to be human, what it is to participate in a community, to voice one's ideas, among other topics that are generally central to the disciplines themselves.[36]

A CRISIS IN HUMANISTIC EVALUATION— SEARCH COMMITTEE CULTURE

The solutions to the labor crisis put forward thus far by many scholars are remarkably uncritical of the ways search committees carry out their work. David Colander and Daisy Zhou, National Endowment for the Humanities (NEH), and the Modern Language Association (MLA) task force on doctoral study have pushed for the institutionalization of "alt-ac" (or non-academic) professional preparation for humanistic scholars (Colander and Zhou 2015, 139–56; Herlihy-Mera 2015), a solution that is loaded with tacit preferences for the perpetuation of existing biases. It fails to address the structural problems that produce severe interviewing imbalances, which in part causes the enormous labor stratification of scholars with the same degree. The NEH, MLA, and Colander, among others, do not call for structural changes that would address affiliation-based biases; they do not criticize or recognize the culture of prejudicial applicant evaluation; they do not condemn the contemporary hiring culture in which candidate success is imminently tied to their location in a hierarchy of cultural status (affiliation), a factor *external* to one's application documents. While these reports recognize the institutionalized discrimination against non-top-ranked applicants, their response is to subtly push lower-tier scholars out of the academy (alt-ac).

Such solutions are not unlike Donald Trump's policy for undocumented US citizens (Cornelius 2016). The former president believes life for undocumented peoples should be made so terrible that they "self-deport" from the United States—likewise, the alt-ac promotion strives to create a situation in which low- and mid-tier academics realize their prospects are so bad that they "self-deport" from higher education. What is perhaps most troubling about the implied outcomes of alt-ac is that they present scholars outside top-ranked cohorts as though they have no value or potential contributions to make to the academy, or higher education in general, and for that, they should look elsewhere for a career.

While alt-ac should be a formative part of any doctoral program, one that receives public funding as well, presenting alt-ac as a *permanent* solution is irresponsible. Our academy needs tenure-line faculty who studied outside the top-ranked tiers. While some scholars at top-ranked institutions may select alt-ac careers (and a few forcibly so), the vast majority are de facto from lower-ranked universities, due to the hiring discrimination evidenced in all available data. Resources and energy should be dedicated to securing the possibility of tenure-line positions for *all* scholars, regardless of background—but especially for those demographics largely absent from the academy: that is, those from Spanish-dominant communities who prepare at HHE universities. Humanistic associations including New Faculty Majority (NFM), Latin American Studies Association, American Studies Association (ASA), American Council on the Teaching of Foreign Languages (ACTFL), NEH, American Historical Association (NHA), MLA, American Association of University Professors (AAUP), Humanities Education and Research Association (HERA), Association for Computers and the Humanities (ACH), American Council of Learned Societies, and National Education Association (NEA); as well as presidents, deans, eminent and public scholars; boosters, coaches and athletes; parents, enrolled students, alumni, and donors; among others, should join together and:

1) Pressure public representatives to link accreditation to ratio of non-tenure-line faculty (over 20 percent should be immediate probation).
2) Pressure public representatives to revise US cultural expenditure,[37] raising it from .2 percent of gross domestic product to that of Colombia (1.3 percent), Iceland (3.2 percent), or Hungary (4.1 percent), in order to fund a Cultural Cabinet Department that endows tens of thousands of humanities tenure lines at public universities, particularly those with high enrollments of communities systematically blocked from opportunity; and initiatives that would employ PhDs in other capacities (alt-ac). A rise of 1 percent would equal $185 billion per year.
3) Transition existing Eurocentric lines toward local emphases.
4) In all competitions, HHE graduates should be understood as "exceptional" candidates.
5) Consider blind applications: a letter of interest and writing sample with no letters of reference; or, as an alternative to a traditional writing sample, solicit a response to a rhetorical inquiry or specific disciplinary uncertainty.[38]

Educators in Spanish-language cultures can have a central role in reconstructing the conditions necessary for a different kind of encounter, one that opposes renewed colonization and seeks to overcome colonial history through attention to local languages, cultures, and traditions. It is a circumstance that involves *unknowing* the traditional logics of formal education that have demarcated Spanish-language pedagogy since its inception in US universities. The words of decolonial pedagogies engage silenced local cultures, voiced in ways that rethink the violence and hierarchies of transnationalism and cosmopolitanism and contextualized with sumak kawsay / *buen vivir*, the limits of capitalism, neoliberalism, and activism.

3

MULTILINGUAL COGNITION & ETHNO-LINGUAL RELATIVITY

EXPANDING "SPANISH" MAPS OF MEANING

> So, if you want to really hurt me, talk badly about my language. Ethnic identity is twin skin to linguistic identity—I am my language. Until I can take pride in my language, I cannot take pride in myself. Until I can accept as legitimate Chicano Texas Spanish, Tex Mex, and all the other languages I speak, I cannot accept the legitimacy of myself. Until I am free to write bilingually and to switch codes without having always to translate, while I still have to speak English or Spanish when I would rather speak Spanglish, and as long as I have to accommodate the English speakers rather than having them accommodate me, my tongue will be illegitimate.
>
> I will no longer be made to feel ashamed of existing. I will have my voice. Indian, Spanish, white. I will have my serpent's tongue—my woman's voice, my sexual voice, my poet's voice. I will overcome the tradition of silence.
>
> **Gloria Anzaldúa,** *Borderlands / La Frontera* **(1987, 59)**

> I write in French to tell the French that I am not French.
>
> **Kateb Yacine, qtd. in V. Orlando,**
> **"The True Cost of Incumbency Bias" (2017, 5)**

> Whoever makes the cultural standard makes the cultural hierarchy. The act of making a cultural standard and hierarchy is what makes cultural racism.
>
> **Ibram X. Kendi,** *How to Be an Antiracist* **(2019, 83)**

Traditional lines of inquiry that tell us "Spanish" resonances in languages other than "Spanish" would be contradictory. Spanish is Spanish, other languages are other languages, and never the realms shall meet. But recent studies in multilingual cognition demonstrate that the linguistic-isolate (silo) model that drives disciplinary balkanization should be rethought, as people with more than one language are "not two monolinguals in one body" (Thompson and Lamboy 2012, 33), but rather experience multiple knowledges and communicative bases at the same time. Language acquisition, for instance, influences the mind such that people develop a "different knowledge of their first language" (Cook 2013, 48), and "multilinguals can see the same phenomenon in several different ways and have several perspectives on the same situation" (Kharkhurin 2016, 433). The myth that "clearly separatable languages" exist brushes up against other interpretative miscues, like "a speaker can 'switch' from one language to the other; or that expressions can be analysed and subsequently classified as belonging exclusively to 'one' or 'another' language" (Franceschini 2016, 99). An institutional shift in perspective on this topic gestures toward performance of multiple philosophies within the constraints of one-language codification: that is, "Spanish"-inflected (if not informed) performances in languages other than Spanish.[1]

As the traditional monolingual "Spanish" prescription blurs these depths,[2] there are inquiry maps yet to be drawn in relation the conventional binaries enforced in "Spanish"-language cultural studies: is it possible to speak English with Spanish meanings, or vice versa? How does a multilingual person maintain stable use of a word, emotion, identity, social philosophy and cultural sensibility when it has different meanings in each language? Are multiple linguistic indexes in the mind separate and unconnectable, or complementary? What establishes a division between languages? Does it also link philosophies? Are these linguistic, cultural, and epistemic borders ever crossed? If so, are multiple languages "registers" of one-another in the mind—performed, spoken, written, inflected in harmonizing ways? Are they independent storage units—isolated and discrete cultural and knowledge spheres? Engaging a multi-competence approach to cognitive linguistics, this discussion is mainly in relation to Spanish-French and Spanish-English mergence, and scrutinizes how linguistic conditions inform behavior (perceiving creative activity as behavior) in order to suggest additional ways "Spanish"-language cultural materials may be conceptualized in a post-purist and post-Hispanism model.[3]

When such performances occur, as Stephanie Álvarez deftly observes, "language itself takes on the role of protagonist," while "a seemingly English text uncovers the hidden Spanish" that drives the sensibility of the writing. She continues, "to the monolingual English speaker, the narration may seem ridiculous, but for the Spanish/English bilingual it serves another purpose" (2013, 444, 446). As Roberto G. Fernández comments about his novel, *Raining Backwards*: "The discourse for the monolingual that reads this book is limited. If a bilingual reads it, he can enjoy it on a different level. The other one might find it exotic or whatever and does not understand it. Maybe the Anglo world imposes the language. What we do with the language is play with it, and so we give him the things in English he cannot understand" (qtd. in Binder 1995, 8). While those who use Spanish with other languages outnumber monolinguals, this circumstance is just beginning to emerge in studies of cultural cognition (Krogstad and González-Barrera 2015, 1). Reframed "Spanish" pedagogies that appreciate how translingualism shapes consciousness, identity, emotion, and community sentiments, among other topics, allows access to how and to what degree use of multiple tongues informs different aspects of life that are brought into physical realms (e.g., text) by cultural performance. A shift toward such epistemes emphasizes action and dialogue across and through traditional linguistic units, both institutional and geopolitical—and thus opens knowledge-creation toward what are often concealed sensibilities within the Eurocentrism, language-purity prescriptions, and the transnationalisms of the nation-state system and area studies pedagogies in general. Inquiries like: How do multilingualism and translingualism influence creativity, writing, and performances in languages other than "Spanish"—as well as in "Spanish"?[4]—recomposes scholarly attention onto communities, performances, and potential tracts of meaning in heterogenous ways and mobilizes questions that are hidden in Spanish-only approaches.

LINGUISTIC RELATIVITY AND THE PURITY OF "SPANISH"

While translingualism is often a core dimension of Spanish-language cultural imagination, criticism and pedagogy tend to be organized in ways that limit attention to siloed views that exclude recognition of the contact, intonations, emotions, and philosophies from multiple traditions and sensibilities.[5] Attention to this cross-linguistic component of creativity perceives linguistic identities as plastic, malleable, circumstantial, and fluid in ways that aim to transition the siloed and balkanized knowledge structures toward multi-competence relevancies. These would be situated within numerous centers of meaning and performance at the same time. Linguistic relativity maintains that the components of a language (for instance, gendered nouns) can affect the ways a speaker conceptualizes their world regardless, of the language(s) being used. In this way, language has been shown to influence our most fundamental cognitive processes, such that multilingual people "view the world in different ways depending on the specific language they are operating in," and these factors shape conduct in ways that indicate "distinct behavior [occurs] in bilinguals depending on the language of operation" (Athanasopoulos 2015, 1). Lera Boroditsky notes that these language-specific "ways of talking" shape "the way they think . . . the way they conceptualize things" including time, place, color, community, and "many abstract ideas [including] justice, love compassion or truth" (2015, 1). Vivian Cook has argued that such findings require a "re-valuing of the concept of a native speaker" (2003, 3) as it is clear that multilinguals should not be understood as "native" speakers of any single tongue: "Indeed," notes Cook, "there is little point to counting 'languages' in a single mind—L1, L2, L3, Ln—as they form a single system" (2003, 7). In *Applied Psycholinguistics and Multilingual Cognition in Human Creativity*, Christiansen and Turkina argue that even when using one language, "speakers engage a singular language or lexical system characterised by fluid and dynamic processes" (2018, xv). These fluidities draw largely from "pre-existing schemata" in the brain and mind, as nodes of embodied experience (Tasos and Paschalidou 2018, 68). As multilingual brains offer ranges of experience and perspectives inaccessible to monolingual cohorts, these circumstances represent a "wider range of descriptive choices" that make possible more varied "idea generation and lexical complexity"; thus multilingual creation (even when codified in *one* language) "renegotiates thinking structures and combines a variety of materials, forms patterns of his/her cultural reality and social experience in a novel and at the same time effective manner" (Tasos and Paschalidou 2018, 68). In a multilingual brain, the generation of ideas and their transition from metaphysical to physical domains engages a "multifaceted processing of reality" that draws from experiences and knowledges of a "heterogeneous subject" (Tasos and Paschalidou 2018, 55, 57).

In this sense, when a multilingual person performs Spanish or any tongue in their purview, she or he should not be understood as a speaker of "Spanish" *per se*, because the "Spanish" base is flexible and shaped by its co-relation to other language structures. "The language mode continuum is not then about which language," writes Vivian Cook, "but about how much of each. It is like a mixer tap that merges hot and cold water, but neither tap can be completely turned off" (2003, 10). When applying such insights to cultural inquiry, traditional Spanish-centric biographical and cultural critiques, as well as close readings of texts, could be broadened to encompass the dynamic linguistic condition that occurs in the mind, behavior, speech, and writing. If Spanish-only exigencies are a central part of the theoretical and thus pedagogical base, these findings command a reinterpretation, as "people who know more than one language have a distinct, compound state of mind" (Jarvis and Pavlenko 2008, 17).

Siloed-knowledge presumptions tend to make multi-structural aesthetics appear illogical, making the elusive and often trans- or cross-lingual depths embedded in Spanish-English amalgamative writing "apparent only to readers who know both English and Spanish (or at least some Spanish) and can see the colliding linguistic planes" (Rogers 2015, 238). Gayle Rogers observes that such a "minoritizing of a dominant language" has remarkable outcomes, including a "multiperspectivalism that prompts this effect and its force upon the characters, the dialogue, the narration, and the plot" (2015, 225). In this view, in the case of someone proficient in multiple registers—if we perceive Spanish and English for instance, as a one-language amalgam, not separate linguistic units—texts in Cuban Spanish or American English can perform parallel sensibilities, identities, and affiliations: both may perform *the same sensibilities*—a circumstance that presents many anxieties to traditional systems of critique that have been institutionalized toward one-language and one-country specificities. Using traditional grammar and interpretative logic, Cuban literature in English and American literature in Cuban Spanish, for instance, become not only possible but mutually and simultaneously performable.

The precise effects of this interlingual approach to texts in English—or mainly in English, written by multilingual authors—are often manifest in semantic, aesthetic, and thematic forms. Spanish and English have some fundamental structural differences, which, among other variances, include divergences in uses of time, perception of color, and understanding of gender. "Even basic aspects of time perception can be affected by language,"[6] notes Boroditsky. "English speakers prefer to talk about duration in terms of length (e.g., 'That was a short talk,' 'The meeting didn't take long'), while Spanish . . . speakers prefer to talk about time in terms of amount, relying more on words like 'much' 'big,' and 'little' rather than 'short' and 'long'" (2009, 1). When English-speakers regularly discuss time in Spanish, and in these "Spanish" ways, their "cognitive performance [in English begins] to resemble" those of the other system. This also occurs in the case of gender (nouns and adjectives have gender in Spanish) and, once an English-speaker who learns Spanish is dominant in the new grammatical gender systems (applying femininity to the sea, for example) this process "influences mental representations of objects in the same way it does [for native] . . . Spanish speakers" (Boroditsky 2009, 1).

These effects transcend linguistic spheres and influence how multilingual people experience reality (and, thus, codify ideas in text).[7] Multicompetence performances are manifest in literary themes (gendered objects) and in formation and structure of sentences; in how a person perceives cognate concepts; and in how a person constructs a memory in the mind (Kecskes and Papp 2000, 58–59, 81). Moreover, even further afield language-mediated concepts like space, identity, gender roles, and community-affiliations (i.e., national and transnational identities) are thrown into flux as language acquisition occurs. As Jarvis and Pavlenko point out, "individuals . . . are shaped through their socialization into new discursive communities" (2008, 153). These socialization processes "can result in the modification and transformation of already acquired concepts" (Jarvis and Pavlenko 2008, 153). Such reports gesture toward a transition away from linguistic essences and sole-reality myopias they enact as bases of study. These have cascading spaces of relevancy that reform not only language perception and institutionalization, but also the geopolitical and social institutions that strive to maintain balkanized, sole-language competencies as a central dimension of power. As Javier Zamora notes, writing across languages, "I destroyed fences, jailed kings, invented a replacement for countries" (2019, 1). In *Transnational Battlefield*, Tijuana writer Heriberto Yépez comments that English in this way can be a space for decolonial jamming:

ABOUT ME: IN ENGLISH

I am possessed by the most powerful
Revolutionary force in the world today:
The Anti-American spirit.

But I am written and I write in English
I too sing America's shit.

I am inhabited by imperial feelings
Which arise in my mind as images
Of pre-industrial rivers
Or take some technocratic screen-form.

My hopes are these wounds
Are also weapons. But they may be undead
Scholarly jargon.

I am colonized. I dream of decolonizing
Myself and others. The images of the dream
Do not match up. I am the body
And the archive.

A bomb is ticking in my old soul.
And the life of the bomb
Trembles in the hands of my new voice.

I am a professor in the Third World.
What do I know? Libraries in the North
Do not open their doors. I laugh at myself
Imagining what the newer books state.

Writing is counter
-insurgent. But the counter
-insurgency
     Leaders want our body
Believing writing is freedom.

This is as far as my English goes. (2017)

If the presence of several languages in the mind shapes *both* "verbal and nonverbal tasks" (Jarvis and Pavlenko 2008, 171), the role of multilingualism and translingualism in identity, perception, behavior, culture, and cultural performance are difficult and perhaps impossible to isolate from one another. As Ivan Kecskes has observed, there is a relocation of standards patterns of communication "from one language to another" (2014, 137), blending some of the core blocks of communicative, creative, and therefore cultural practices, which queries some of the certainties of Spanish-only critique of texts in "Spanish." If there are distinct behavioral codes, often unconscious to the speaker, which are engaged depending on the language of the conversation or interaction, an important concept to bear in mind is that "the most used language becomes dominant" (Maitreyee and Goswami 2008, 33), and thus, in an applied sense, if we are to read a Spanish-language performance in an English-language backdrop through any linguistic index, it should be more descriptive of their environment and perhaps less Spanish-centric, despite the language of the words.

CROSSLINGUAL PERFORMANCE IN ONE LANGUAGE

A significant segment of this realm of inquiry re-examines what Spanish "is" in relation to the mental maps that produce it—language often discloses several axes of meaning by:

1) expressing a message to an audience
2) negotiating cultural and social relationships between the speaker and audience
3) navigating links between the mind, words, worlds, codified languages (as well as the communities they ostensibly represent and reproduce), and the individual speaker.
(modified from Goatly 1997; Hoey 2012)[8]

If language functions on these levels, the messages conveyed disclose notions of a self to others, performing expectations in ways that reproduce, reject, or play with *a priori* categorizations embedded in the communicative framework. Glimpsing at other languages and philosophies embedded in "Spanish" provides disclosures on the ways each dimension of the interplay changes conditionally over time, especially in relation to the speaker's (other-than-Spanish) language performance. A central insight is the confessional nature of an interlingual review: looking beyond, through, and across "Spanish" at additional dimensions in the same words, at once acknowledges that which cannot be recognized in conventional (Spanish-only) critique and subtly shifts the a priori expectation (inevitability) that organizes the structure. The script (of self) may not be communicable only in Spanish, though some of its qualities are manifest in multiple layers within "Spanish" words.

Linguistic relativity pluralizes not only the use of "Spanish" words but also the meanings and philosophies embedded in them. Those who change from Spanish to another language—entirely, for publication and/or daily life, or circumstantially—often note a new, idiosyncratic notion of language itself, one that is not easily defined by existing grammars and logics. In relation to the material in first part of this chapter, this is often, though not always, evoked as a factor of migration. As Luisa Futoransky, who departed Argentina for France and later the United States, describes:

> being in a different language, the problem of having two cultures presents many advantages, disadvantages, complexities for or against. You work in a language that isn't the language of your contemporaries. The language has changed, and you're making a sort of centrifugal and centripetal force with your own language which is not the language of others, but it is yours, but others understand it, it's very complex. At the same time, you portray in your language *in misericorde* the others' culture. I'm not the first. It's somewhat the frustrations, the joys that pass through your language in order to speak of the language of others, all rather complex. (qtd. in Weiss 1999a, 1)[9]

For Futoransky, the idiosyncratic process of growth, individualized and specific to a time, place and language, was tied specifically to the cultural displacement/language interplay, allowing her to script her own form of communication (be it in Spanish or another language) that is her own (or its own) autonomous realm. Similarly, Héctor Biancotti, who moved to France from Argentina, comments: "I was trying to keep writing in Spanish . . . but after twenty years living in France I couldn't do it anymore. My Spanish had become uprooted" (qtd. in Weiss 1995, 1). He continues, describing the effects on how living in a language other than Spanish shaped his sense of being: "It's another vision of reality, yes. If I say, for example, the word *oiseau*, in French the word is very soft. We feel the softness of the feathers and a sort of warmth, we'd say that the French bird has never left its nest. And if you say "bird" in Spanish, you say *pájaro*. It takes off like an arrow. Those are two visions of reality! You sense that quite well when you belong to two languages, that the same word does not mean exactly the same thing" (qtd. in Weiss 1995, 1). And this externality, for Biancotti, is a source of stimulation: "I feel best in France," he begins: "I have a strong accent in French. So, the moment I open my mouth, I know that to the other person I'm a foreigner. . . . I find it very pleasant not belonging. I don't want to belong to any group." And Biancotti is conscious of the precise moment when his transition from Spanish to French occurred: "[I] had done a collection of stories, I had ten written in Spanish, I needed one more. I kept turning it over, and then one day I thought I'd found how the characters enter, and five lines were written in French. It had an expression there, a turn of phrase, that was typically French, *"aussi loin qu'il m'en souvient."* I told myself, If that expression came spontaneously, perhaps I should be writing in French. Since it's a short story, I'm going to try. And that was the moment I swung into French" (qtd. in Weiss 1995, 1).[10] The French language, though, is not exceptional in this process: distance and negotiation of absence of Spanish (among other culture) is the realm of stimulation: "That's how I became a writer in French," recalls Silvia Baron Supervielle years after departing Argentina: "For me it was a discovery, which has nothing to do with the idea of the past or the French language tradition. . . . It could have been another country. . . . maybe the same thing would have happened to me with another language and I would have found a terrain that was mine as well" (qtd. in Weiss 1999b, 1).

Among the most prolific Spanish-language writers who transitioned to French is Eduardo Manet, who was raised in Cuba. Like Biancotti, he describes the "spontaneity" of French in his consciousness.[11] When asked, "Why do you write in French?," he responds (in English): "I always say two things. I write in French because French editors and French directors wanted my novels and plays. Nobody ever asks me for them in Spain, Venezuela, Mexico, and of course never in Cuba. So, what shall I do? The second thing: One day I had the blues, because I saw some review talking about Latin American writers in Paris, and at that moment I was, modestly, very well known, but they never mentioned my name. So, I felt sad."[12] If language is a social resource with the depths to transcend external prescription (supposed trans/national belonging, gender, and other dualistic categorial relations), some writers use language assignments in the inverse, as Guillermo Cabrera Infante, raised in Gibara and long-time resident of London, called himself "the only English writer working in Spanish" (qtd. in Weiss 2003, 180).[13] An author who lives, works, and writes across several languages may not be "renouncing his native tongue," writes Julio Ortega, "but rather seeking his own language" (qtd. in Weiss 2003, 184).[14]

In addition to the intersocial stimulation, it is possible that dwelling in another language fuels creativity. As Vamsi Koneru notes, "due to the necessity for higher cognitive engagement and focus, the continual engagement of multiple languages has been shown to have positive consequences for intellectual activity—specifically, writing" (email to the author, October 26, 2018). It has been shown that Spanish-speaking writers, artists, and other figures working in other languages experience higher oxygen levels and blood circulation, as well as neurological activity in lobes that manage complex tasks (Kovelman et al. 2008, abstract). Multi- and translingual brain activity, like cultural displacement with which they are often coupled, require higher cognitive functions including depth of attention, multitasking, and concentration. These conditions enable people to "have better memories and [be] more cognitively creative and mentally flexible than monolinguals" (Mackey 2014, 1). Edgardo Cozarinsky evokes this specific dimension of English, despite—or perhaps because of—his limited knowledge of it: "I write in English sometimes, because I feel that English, which I speak with a certain difficulty, is the language in which my imagination unloosens more easily. . . . But the first step, it's as if by putting some words on paper I was joining a club or entering a room where some of my favorite writers exist" (qtd. in Weiss 2010, 1). While studies in cognitive linguistics have paid less attention to intralanguage outcomes on creativity and identity, it is likely that exposure to and use of several versions of Spanish causes parallel intellectual sensations and conditions. Inter-Spanish transitions would also be an entry for close-reading and interpretation of figures like Remedios Varo, García Márquez, Carlos Fuentes, Gabriela Mistral, among many others. While the transformative weight of this circumstance is rarely addressed in critique, such language shifts also evoke a discrete cognitive condition: "La nevera de España" notes Bryce Echenique, "se convierte en refrigeradora, ahora que he vuelto a Lima, pero era frigo cuando vivía en París, y de pronto se vuelve a llamar frigidaire en la Lima de nuestra infancia"

(1993b, 269). The intra-lingual shifts can evoke nostalgia, and as he notes, the difference in use of something as ostensibly simple as a diminutive became illustrious: "El diminutivo, por ejemplo, que es tan importante en Un mundo. . . . 'Vamos a tomar un cafecito, cinco minutitos,' le dicen a uno en Lima cuando pasa a la carrera en dirección a algo importante. Y cae uno siempre en la trampa, porque esa frase quiere decir en realidad: 'Vamos a zamparnos dos botellas de whisky y amanecer bebiendo.' Es ésta una manera de no comprometerse, de no nombrar las cosas. Ese diminutivo del peruano en el que está su timidez, el esconder su estado de ánimo real, en el fondo prácticamente su 'declaración de principios'" (Bryce Echenique 1993a, 631).[15] The residual shaping effects of European linguistic life, resituated in Peru, remain important in his understanding and use of language after a significant period in his homeland: "Cumplido ya un año de residencia en Lima . . . , la vida que llevé en Europa, principalmente en Francia y España, continúa asomándose por todos los rincones, por todos los pliegues de la realidad cotidiana. ¿Qué es alejarse de algo y qué es acercarse a algo?, me pregunto constantemente, sin lograr encontrar hasta el día de hoy una respuesta satisfactoria" (Bryce Echenique 1993b, 328). While these matters appear of particular relevance to many figures from America, the same circumstance is common among writers, artists, and other cultural figures from Spain from all periods: Picasso's *Sueño y mentira de Franco* was written in frañol and his play, *Les Quatre Petites Filles*, in French.[16] Judah Halevi, Leonor López de Córdoba, Teresa of Ávila Cervantes, Rodrígo Díaz de Vivar, أبو عبد الله محمد الثاني شرع, Abu 'Abdallah Muhammad XII had interactions and knowledges of Arabic, Castilian, Latin, Mozarabic, among other tongues.

One of the salient figures among the Peninsular fray who lived across several languages was Christopher Columbus—or Cristòfor Colom. While conventionally regarded as Genovese, Columbus's language (specifically his Castilian) had resonances of Catalan. Columbus signed documents (and was referred to in state records) as "Colom"—a Catalan last name meaning "dove." There is no record of him writing in the Genoese dialect or Italian, even in letters sent to Genoa. Save one letter in Catalan, his epistles are in Latin or Spanish—some have marginal notes in Hebrew. The conquest chronicler Bartolomé de las Casas noted that Colom "doesn't grasp the entirety of the words in Castilian"—and much of his Spanish was colored by false cognates, idiomatic interference, and cross-lingual appropriations from Catalan:

English	Catalan	Colom (in Spanish)	Spanish
the sunset	el sol post	al sol puesto	la puesta del sol
all at once	tot d'un cop	todo de un golpe	todo a la vez
everywhere	tot arreu	a todo arreo	por todas partes
Antilles	Anti-illes	Antillas	Anti-islas
number	nombre	nombre	número
to say no	dir de no	decir de no	decir que no
seven hundred	setcentes	setcentas	setecientos
virtue	virtut	virtut	virtud
charity	caritat	caritatt	caridad
they died	esmorteíren	escmorecieron	fallecieron/murieron
I didn't care for	no curava	no curaba	no me interesaba
it has rained some	ha plogut poc o gaire	ha llovido poco o mucho	ha llovido algo

Lluís de Yzaguirre, a professor at the Institute of Applied Linguistics at Universitat Pompeu Fabra, studied Colom's Spanish with a forensic linguistics algorithm that applies lexical mistakes to decipher the native language of the writer. He found Colom's hypercorrections of "b" and "v," as well as "o" and "u" in Spanish were typical of a Catalan speaker.[17] Colom's case is likely not unique among those of his era, as languages had fluidities and interchanges in spelling, lexicon, semantics, syntax, and grammar that institutions, trying to maintain them as separate, have since prohibited.

SPANISH IN ENGLISH-LANGUAGE COMMUNITIES

Multilingual literature in English sounds counterintuitive but I can't think of many American writers, at least contemporary or 20th century, who write or wrote in English and were completely monolingual. Vonnegut, Bukowski, Steinbeck, Gertrude Stein, Henry Miller: all spoke other languages on a regular basis, while they were writing. I am sure there are many more writers to list, and not just expats. Maybe not so aesthetically crafted as Hemingway's Spanish-English, there is positively more of this around. It's an interesting subject.
Kendal Owen (2017, 1)

Speakers of different languages pay attention to different aspects of reality.
Goro Murahata, Yoshiko Murahata, and Vivian Cook,
"Research Questions and Methodology of Multi-Competence" (2016, 31)

The myth of the English-domestic, Spanish-foreign mold in the United States sets in place many umbrella scholarly tenets: who and what text can be studied in relation to what center. For instance, the use of the Spanish language among ostensibly English-language communities has a rich and prolific cultural history in the United States—perhaps since these performances are studied largely in an academy with the above-mentioned monolingual exigencies, they receive little scrutiny. They are almost entirely absent from "Spanish" cultural histories as well. The thrusting unhyphenated-American authors into "English-only" categorizations[18] enforces the implicit balkanization that causes serious interpretative flaws that muddle profound depths in the text and performances, and the experiences from which they often derive.

There are many examples that merit attention from both "Spanish" and "English" angles: while John Wayne spoke Spanish at home and wished to have his gravestone inscribed in that language, his experience is—to my knowledge—completely absent from Spanish-language cultural studies. The same is the case of Henry McCarty (aka Billy the Kidd), whose home language was Spanish; he also was nicknamed "el pistolero hispano" (Cervera 2016, 1). These sociolinguistic circumstances inform a great deal of unhyphenated-American literature: the main characters of Cormac McCarthy's "The Border Trilogy" were born and raised in Texas in Anglo-surnamed families and spoke Spanish before English, and Spanish is the dominant language of their homes in Texas (see Herlihy-Mera 2015). But these sensibilities are clouded by an academy that maintains and enforces transnational and linguistic boundaries as prescriptive methodological containers: unhyphenated-American literatures and other disciplines often only recognize English as a qualifier (that is, a necessary component in the grouping) despite the centrality of Spanish and multilingualism in the lives of the authors and that of their characters.

While he wrote largely in English, John Steinbeck spoke Spanish and longed to live in Mexico, which is the setting of some of his most important writing. "Steinbeck's Mexican influences," notes Eric Moore, are the "often-neglected part of Steinbeck's legacy" (qtd. in Ponce 2017, 1). Steinbeck's boyhood experiences in Salinas (California) were ordinary, involving Spanish and English, but "People have this belief that he was a predominately white American author" (qtd. in Ponce 2017, 1). notes Moor. Among other works, *Tortilla Flat*, *The Pearl*, and *The Log from the Sea of Cortez* are colored if not informed by Californian/Mexican languages and influences: these dimensions of his work are lost to the exceptionalist prescriptions of the English / Anglo-American distortion in all Steinbeck affairs. And a result of these critical blinders, his embeddedness in Mexican cultures—that is to say, the cultures of California—may be recognized but only as a contrarian form of reading, not as a structural part of Steinbeck's craft and intellectual achievement. As Rogelio Martínez notes, "Las obras *mexicanas* de Steinbeck no solo nos hará disfrutar de agradables momentos, sino que también proveerá elementos para reflexión y, espero, para impulsar cambios en nuestra forma de pensar y actuar" (2017, xiii).

The interconnected nature of ostensibly separate languages could be—and is perhaps overdue to be—forefronted in emerging approaches to cultural performance. Deflecting the presumed continuities and purities in English-only and Spanish-only (and other monolingual) readings, such views have an attunement that describes existence outside conventional center-margin prescriptions. This shift in focus places anxieties on purity-contamination myths and opens agencies that are rebellious to one-language prescriptive readings.[19] As Sandra Cisneros reflects: "That voice is one of a person speaking Spanish in English. By that I mean that I write with the syntax and sensibility of Spanish, even when there isn't a syllable of Spanish present. It's engrained in the way I look at the world, and the way I construct sentences and stories. I was not aware of this when I wrote *House*, but I'm conscious of it now" (2013).

WILLIAM CARLOS WILLIAMS'S TRANSCULTURAL CREATIVITY

Spanish as a locus of transcultural and translingual creativity is a topic with many relevancies for William Carlos Williams, a figure known almost exclusively for his use of English. While Williams is understood as a smith of American English, that language was not his primary means of communication until he was a teenager. At home his mother and father—who were raised in Puerto Rico and the Dominican Republic, respectively—spoke Spanish with each other and to young William Carlos, who would learn English at school and from his paternal grandmother. This circumstance had various effects on his writing—in theme, subject, grammar, syntax, and structure—and many of the transcultural depths of Williams's language have links to Spanish-language sensibilities. In many respects, the Latinx and Spanish-language dimensions of Williams's formative years are not—and indeed, cannot be—separated from the ostensibly Americanized, monolingual man he often projected in public. Williams's English should be understood as transcultural and to an extent translingual, and thus a device that performs identities and sentiments that transcend the "unhyphenated-American" label; the monolingual tool Williams used for writing—the English language—should be revisited and contextualized with the other tongues in his repertoire, in order to offer a more attuned understanding of the complexities of his mind.

Williams had to balance the cultural inheritance from his parents with a violent public climate toward Spanish-speakers in his place of residence—and New Jersey, for Puerto Ricans who lived there, was and to a degree remains a colonized space not unlike the archipelago, where Puerto Rican language and cultural performances were not only unwelcome, but signifiers of the racist and classist violence of the US colonial program.[20] Williams constructed a literary and public identity that was cleansed of Caribbean culture, foregrounding a monocultural "Americanization" that was specific to the violence surrounding him. But, as Williams clarifies in *The American Grain*, his vision is not a monocultural one but toward the hybridity in which he lived: "And to give to him [a Native American] who HAS, who will join, who will make, who will fertilize, who will be like you yourself: to create, to hybridize, to crosspollenize [sic],—not to sterilize, to draw back, to fear, to dry up, to rot. It is the sun" (1925, 121). Lisa Sánchez González's sharp analyses notes that Williams "clearly inscribes the authenticity of mestizo consciousness as *the* American consciousness" (2001, 52; emphasis added). It appears Williams's context prohibited performance of this mestizaje, that is, speaking Spanish to the tyrant: "Hence the amnesia" from critics, writes Sánchez González, "concerning Williams's Puerto Rican heritage" (2001, 62). However, as soon as we unlink "Puerto Rican" performance from the Spanish language, a transcultural dimension to texts in English appears, and this new critical space allows one to perceive other channels of meaning. Things Puerto Rican are memories concealed, emotions performed under threat—but they can be articulated in another language, including that of the tyrant (English).[21]

MULTIPLE-LANGUAGE EMPHASES ON "SPANISH"-LANGUAGE PERFORMANCES:

If a mixture of tongues complement and interrelate in all contexts, even when only one language is present, the cross-lingual dimension of life is of particular importance for migrant figures: multi-language cognition (that is, thinking in English, French and/or *frespañol*, and other tongues) would shape each person's and knowledge and use of Spanish. As linguistic conditions inform the ways ideas are organized into text, the Spanish texts in question may be interpreted as multilingual. The performance of several identities through Spanish-language writing, performing, listening, and so on, are accessible once the language-of-origin prescriptions are contextualized with the cognitive dynamic of multilingual life.[22]

To develop this concept, Spanish can be a locus of so-called "English" performance (or that of other tongues), as well as vice versa—Spanish can have "English," "unhyphenated-American" and other sensibilities, norms, and identities. Identity concerns are a key entry point for fleshing out further depths of this phenomenon: in multicompetence approaches, the plural sociolinguistic map of performances and their identities, in addition to verbal routines, is balanced into a unified, amalgamated, stable concept.[23] Thus, interpretations of some migrant and many multilingual performances in Spanish should take into contemplation the concealed significances, cognate emotional responses, and underpinned cultural values of linguistic systems that may not be present in the phrases being analyzed[24]: multi-language cognition would shape each person's knowledge and use of Spanish, a notion that moves toward a translingual understanding of creativity as a human behavior.

HEMINGWAY, THE FIRST CUBAN TO RECEIVE THE NOBEL PRIZE FOR LITERATURE

> I can speak and read French but cannot write it; nor Italian, nor German. But can write Spanish. English sometimes too, maybe.
> **Ernest Hemingway, 1950 (Hemingway 1981, 696)**

> Spanish [is] the only language I really know . . . [if I had been born elsewhere] I would have written in Spanish and been a fine writer I hope.

> As it is I must write in English, a bastard tongue but fairly maneuverable. Spanish is a language Tu.
>
> **Ernest Hemingway, 1947 (Hemingway 1981, 828)**

Ernest Hemingway spoke Spanish more often than English after age twenty-nine, including during his residence in Key West and at his family residence in San Francisco de la Paula, Cuba: "Here in the house," he said of life at the Finca Vigía, "we talk Spanish always."[25] When he received the Nobel Prize for Literature in 1954, he refused interviews with the US media but welcomed the Cuban press into his home. His only reception address was in Spanish—and he described himself as the first "cubano . . . a recibir este premio." He also made clear that he did not want people to call him a "yanqui," that he was a citizen of Cojímar, and that the people of Cuba represented "mi pueblo."[26] (Like Steinbeck, Hemingway had a life-long unrealized dream to live in Mexico.)[27] His Cuban experience summons intriguing questions about multilingualism: how do linguistic habits—like thinking in genders—shape how we experience the world and write about it in English? To what degree do semantic tendencies from one register drift into our thinking in another? How would such phenomena be chronicled in writing in "one" language? In addition to at home and with family and friends, Hemingway used Spanish in his public life, including when addressing large groups for civic events. One of these speeches reflects on his own idiosyncratic Spanish: "Ilustres politicos, militares, senoras, senores y amigos. Hablo muy mal el castellano porque lo aprendi en tales lugares como Madrid, Pamplona, Andalucia, Regla, y La Muelle de Caballeria, cada uno con su accento distinto" (qtd. in Herlihy-Mera 2017a, 21, Hemingway's eccentricities included throughout). While public communications and correspondence with his staff are exclusively in Spanish, what is perhaps more characteristic of Hemingway's quotidian writing in Cuba is the frequency of cross-lingual devices. Nearly all his letters to Adriana Ivancich[28] are enlivened by multilingual puns and code-switching—and he would usually close these letters with several paragraphs written in monolingual Spanish. Here he describes his lament for missing his son's wedding: "Es que hay que morir y casarse al mismo tiempo para ser bastante en Baltimore? No me voy. Ni en broma. En la boda de Bumby estuvo representado para el Embajador nuestra en Paris. Cosa normal. Pero esta? Me faltan embajadores. Siempre puede mandar el Cubano, claro. (o oscuro)" (qtd. in Herlihy-Mera 2017a, 22). In addition to indicating that the Cuban ambassador can represent him, a cultural performance in its own, he also uses the term "claro" (literally clear or light, meaning "of course" in idiomatic Spanish) with "oscuro" (meaning, literally "dark") translanguaging the pun. "Work hard on Spanish," Hemingway writes to Ivancich in another letter, "because I think the things we need to say to each other we will be able to say quite well in Spanish"—and another correspondence between them discusses the multilingual nature of their communication: "Now I write you in Spanish (Castellano we call it) so you, nor nobody will understand it: Esta cárcel, estos hierros en que el alma está metida" (qtd. in Herlihy-Mera 2017a, 22). There is also evidence that Hemingway used Spanish to organize his mind. Raúl Corrales recalls: "Lo consideraban un americano loco, y yo también lo creía porque hablaba solo. Lo oí algunas veces y me llamó la atención que monologara en español y no en inglés" (qtd. in del Carmen Ramón 2011, 1). Spanish and Spanglish were the principal languages of Ernest and his fourth wife Mary Welsh, and their home, by the late 1940s. Use of those languages began to transcend their presence in Cuba, and the couple would speak them together elsewhere. In Africa, as Hemingway recalls, "Spanish was regarded as Mary's and my tribal language" (1999, 128). Hemingway noted that Mayito said Hemingway's Swahili was shaped by Spanish, and had "a strong Camagüey accent" (1999, 128). Hemingway also spoke to the animals in Spanish, "talked to [the lion] very softly in Spanish . . . . all the time I was stroking him and talking to him in Spanish" (1999, 63) and to his apparent lover, Debba: "At first I only spoke to her [Debba] in Spanish. . . . I never spoke a word of English to her and we retained some Swahili words but the rest was a new language made up of Spanish and Kamba" (1999, 35). Hemingway also speaks in Spanish with people in Africa who don't understand it (1999, 238, 259). There is some evidence that Hemingway dreamed in Spanish, often considered a trait of linguistic dominance: "You were talking in Spanish [while sleeping]," his wife Mary comments: "It was about there being no remedy" (1999, 71). His love-talk with Debba is in Spanish as well, "'You have very beautiful hands,' I told her in Spanish" (1999, 64). And he says that he "thinks" of her with a Spanish possessive adjective and a formal, though jestful, form of address, "In Spanish I thought of her as Nuestra Señora de los Apple knockers" (1999, 229). Hemingway endeavored to teach Debba some of his language and, significantly, as was the case with Adriana, the tongue he imparts to her is Spanish: "'No hay remedio,' I said. It was one of the first things I had taught her to say in Spanish and she said it now very carefully. It was the saddest thing I knew in Spanish and I thought it was probably best for her to learn it early" (1999, 63–4).

Hemingway's perception of the shaping effects of the Spanish language, social transplantation, and migration in his life appears in a 1947 letter to Faulkner: "Difference with us guys is I always lived out of country (as mercenary or patriot) since kid. My own country gone.... Found good country outside, learned language as well as I know English" (qtd. in Monteiro 2000, 100). Returning from Spain at the Havana airport on November 4, 1959, he said to the Cuban press: "I am very glad to be here again because I consider myself Cuban.... I sympathize with the government and all *our* difficulties" (qtd. in Fuentes 1984, 238; Hemingway's emphasis). Hemingway knelt and kissed the Cuban flag and said, "I kissed it with all my heart, not as an actor." The FBI's investigative file on Hemingway called this "subversive" activity (qtd. in Herlihy-Mera 2017a, 22–26).

The theory that Hemingway was an English-dominant, unhyphenated American who should not exist in Spanish-language cultural pedagogy or research does not correspond to a great deal of the material discussed here. Yet he is, to my knowledge, wholly absent from syllabi in Spanish courses and his declarations of Cuban identity are rarely cited—and when they do appear, they tend to be treated cursorily. The concepts embedded in his reflections about Spanish, identity, migration, and language mixtures call out for a more diverse critical perspective, one that is more sensitive to how Hemingway self-identified as a Spanish-speaking Cuban.[29] As Ricardo Salvatore observes, attention to such circumstances has "produced remarkable studies connecting issues and fields that remained until recently unrelated (such as 'American Literature' and 'Latin American Literature'), and has opened new lines of research that will certainly enhance our understanding of the flows of culture in the Americas" (2015, 363).[30]

THE CROSS-LINGUAL INTERSE(X)TIONALITY OF "LATINX"

The interlingual coalescence of Spanish and English includes a common lexicon in "English," across an array of popular and academic texts: "Latinx" in both languages illustrates some important facets of this phenomenon. Whether it be labeled a proto- or neologism, the cross-lingual noun/adjective "Latinx" aims to transcend the male privilege in *Latino* and to unlink *Latin@* from the channeled significations of *a* (feminine) and *o* (masculine) in Spanish. The gesture toward linguistic intersectionality stems from a suffix endowed with a literal intersection—*x*. The root of *neologism* (*neo* = new; *logos* = logic/reason/thinking) is accurate: A new word is a new logic—and a new logic often requires a new word. As original lexes appear, they are put into hierarchies aside already-codified equivalents, tested and probed in various contexts, and re-examined over time and across media.

"Latinx" is often—though not exclusively—used in English. The word invites us to rethink some of the philosophic, communicative, and linguistic maps that are conventionally understood as contained within each (supposedly separate) language system. In English, the cognate sensibilities embedded in Latinx refer to Spanish grammar and insinuate that the ostensibly discrete nature of Spanish and English is in fact more of a mix. Latinx crosses the frontiers between languages in ways that are not always accessible in conventional translation. What's particularly interesting about Latinx is that the cross-lingual has become interlingual: The word inaugurates nuance in both registers of the Spanish-English amalgam. In English, it invites us to rethink the ways words maintain some of the gradations and underpinned meanings from the original tongue; in Spanish, it summons reflection on the utility and ethics of gendering nouns, articles, and adjectives—particularly those that refer to people. Use of a linguistic structure from Spanish in English, and the use of a new suffix in Spanish, make Latinx remarkable in both languages, as we are no longer discussing Spanish or English but where they meet—and how we respond to circumstances in which existent language structures fail to articulate value in appropriate ways.

Some argue against the notion that Spanish grammar should be transformed in these ways. "Like it or not," write Gilbert Guerra and Gilbert Orbea of Swarthmore College, "Spanish is a gendered language. If you take the gender out of every word, you are no longer speaking Spanish . . . the result could be words like 'hermanx' [for siblings] and 'niñx' [children]" (2015, 1). But there are precedents for such sea changes—in fact, contemporary Spanishes are the result of one of them: When classical Latin was interpreted by the diverse communities with which it came into contact, vulgar variants added definite articles and reduced or eliminated noun-declensions and cases, abandoning genitive and dative and modifying ablative and accusative. These reformations shaped how fundamental linguistic units like nouns and adjectives could be used. It is not unlike the ways *x* has grown into the linguistic vacuum created by a culture that values inclusivity over the ideologies embedded in *a* and *o*.

Situated in new circumstances, languages change radically. The shift toward x in reference to people has already occurred in many communities. Both traditional and inclusive grammar appear in the humanities department at the University of Puerto Rico; for many faculty, hermanx and niñx and their equivalents have been the standard on syllabi, email, and formal and informal departmental memos, among other documents, since the first decade of the 2000s. It is clear that the inclusive approach to nouns and adjectives is becoming more common, and while it may at some point become the prevailing tendency, presently there is no prescriptive control toward either syntax.

This situation has resulted in structures that appear unpronounceable in Spanish, which has been met with confusion and disregard from some. However, as Roy Pérez of Willamette University observes, "We learn to pronounce new things all the time" (qtd. in Funes 2017, 1). "Spanish is evolving to be more inclusive," writes Yessina Funes, and it's "more than a middle finger to the patriarchy" (2017, 1). It is a recognition of the exclusionary nature of our institutions, of the deficiencies in existent linguistic structures, and of language as an agent of social change. Latinx has also been singled out as a Eurocentric reiteration of ideologies that obfuscate indigenous, African, and other non-European heritages. Kurly Tlapoyawa has inquired, "Why [do] the promoters of the Latinx term feel the need to cling to a Eurocentric/anti-indigenous identity in the first place" (2018, 1). Lissette Rolón Collazo, a professor of comparative literature at the University of Puerto Rico, has pointed out, "We do not have to agree on the strategy. But suffice it to recognize that the *o* does not name all of us" (2014, 1).

While the words in monolingual writing are often appropriated by states, nations, and academies, they do not always repeat the myths those institutions presume—within them exist multiple agencies and identities that do not correspond to traditional balkanized models. These circumstances represent many opportunities for expanding the notions surrounding "Spanish" and the ways it can be taught and institutionalized: the internal maps of multilingual people have qualities and depths that are not readily accessible in traditional one-language methodologies. If "Spanish"[31] has the latitude to transcend words prescribed as "Spanish" in dictionaries, the vision of a coherent model of intellectual activity organized around Spanish-centric (and Spanish-only) myths, disintegrates to a degree before an immense mosaic of localized, personalized, and idiosyncratic linguistic and cultural experiences and the cultural materials related thereto. Multilingual "Spanish" is a site of anxiety from which to anchor decolonial pedagogies and initiate intellectual projects that are attuned to trans- and multilingualism as an ordinary human condition: by extension, faculty who specialize not in transnational or transatlantic emphases, but in fields that locate migrant and multilingual cultural performances, would move toward some of the institutional conditions that recognize some of the post-Hispanic centers that decolonization requires. The pedagogies, degrees, publications, activism, and other activities of scholars specialized in trans- and multilingual Spanish would, unlike Spanish-only exigencies, engage a democratized participation that offers agency to performances, communities, and individuals explicitly marginalized and silenced in the contemporary academy.

4

SPAIN

THE ARABIZED PROVINCE OF LATIN AMERICA, OR, WHICH QUIJOTE DO WE NEED?

> El español es el de América, el de los 19 países que en él insultamos o rezamos. No el de España que desde hace mucho dejó de ser la metrópoli y hoy es una provincia anómala del idioma, cosa que no saben en España, empezando por la Real Academia, que en estos días está cumpliendo 300 años . . . del español que se habla aquí, en esta tierras, no sabe un carajo.
>
> . . . [The RAE dictionary is] acientífico, monárquico, y clerical, que del español que se habla aquí, en esta tierras, no sabe un carajo, y en el que llama 'americanismo' a las palabras y giros propios del español americano. . . . Se equivocan, señorías. . . . De lo que tienen que hablar ustedes es de 'españolismos,' porque ustedes son un solo país frente a los diecinueve y no suman sino cuarenta y tanto millones frente a más de [400] millón.
> **Fernando Vallejo, qtd. in Alfredo Morales,**
> **"El autor colombiano Fernando Vallejo" (2013, 1)**

> *Spain is a province of Latin America.* By some kind of Bolivarian fiat, the discipline should also liberate Spain from its 21st century, Iberian, retro-imperialist fantasy and reinsert it in the republican history that created what is known, after Francisco Bilbao, as Latin America. . . .
> In this context, Spain would become the least studied.
> **Joseba Gabilondo, "Spanish Nationalist Excess" (2014, 31, 32)**

> Idea-dying . . . has not been sufficiently studied nor understood.
>
> Ana Marjanovic-Shanea, Sohyun Meachamb, Hye Jung Choic,
> Samanta López, and Eugene Matusov, "Idea-Dying in
> Critical Ontological Pedagogical Dialogue" (2017, 68)

The argument I would like to develop in this chapter engages how conventional Hispanic/Iberian studies paradigms, informed by what Joseba Gabilondo has called "retro-imperialist fantasy," should "die" and concurrently construct non-exceptionalist narratives. Toward that end, I argue that 1) Spain should be considered a province of Latin America, and 2) Arabic and Islamic cultures should become central to Peninsular curricula, balancing the traditional received Latinate, Christian, Castilian-centric ontologies. Any widescale reform of traditional Peninsular studies, especially when contextualized within Latin American emphases, would transition the cultures, languages, and communities of Spain from exceptional to ordinary. Within such a mold, as Gabilondo argues, "Spain [like the United States] is a province of Latin America"— and Iberia should be "the least studied of all Latin American" topics (Gabilondo 2014, 31; brackets mine).[1] Thus, if that study should continue within an areas studies design, parsed down to a significantly smaller portion of hires, courses, degrees, publications, study-away programs, conferences, and other intellectual activity, how might this Latin American studies subtopic be de-exceptionalized? What myths dominate the grand narratives that envelop "Spain?" What colonialist stories do contemporary Iberian/Hispanic pedagogies mobilize and reproduce? Aside the recognized subnational groupings, how do Castilian-, Latin-, Christian- and other traditional centers enforce marginalization? If we retreat from the traditional master signifiers and their claims of causality (historical and contemporary Spanish national affiliation; Christianity and Latin languages), what characteristics remain and what new depths emerge?[2]

This very task that has recently emerged as an important emphasis in Peninsular studies: "Challenging traditional Hispanism," notes David Wacks, "is to decenter Castilian and develop approaches that integrate texts, voices, and materials from the other linguistic traditions of the Peninsula" (2018, 1). Engaging Wacks's inquiry, building on Vallejo's views and Gabilondo's notion of Spain as "a province of Latin America," this chapter argues that, in comparison to other Latin American regions,

Spain's uniqueness derives in part from the historical, cultural, and linguistic interrelation with Arabic and Islamic cultures. As the notion of Spanish as a unified language does not preexist Arabic contact, and the traditional conceptual mapping of Spain expressly elides those emphases, the historical, linguistic, and cultural bases of "Spanish culture(s)" may be understood as a marginalization program of those dimensions of the cultural base.[3] Decolonized views, then, engage the traditional margins (and the wholly elided components) as central nodes toward a flattening of the imperial ontology. While this treatment centers largely on the systemic marginalization of Islamic/Arabic traditions native to Iberia, similar arguments are worthwhile to posit in relation to Judaism/Judaic, Celtic, and Greco-Roman cultures and languages since Christianization,[4] as well as Basque, Catalan, Galician, Canarian, migrant, and multilingual performances, among other foci that nuance the Castilian/Christian/Latin traditions. Abandoning thesis-antithesis myths that distort Christian tradition as "native" and Islamic culture as "foreign," a focus on Arabic and Islamic influences offers not only a plentitude of material to mine but also many new approaches to discuss the traditional figures, movements, and material culture generally celebrated in Hispanism pedagogies.[5]

INTENTIONAL RELATION AND MEMORIES OF "SPAIN," A PRESCRIBED UNITY THROUGH TIME AND SPACE

Area-studies paradigms generally bind a priori knowledge—in this case, prescriptions of Spanishness, Spanish culture, and what "Spain" is—"is" in the *ser* sense rather than *estar*. Conventional area studies epistemes maintain the cultures produced by residents of the spaces in question are "Spanish," and this Spanishness, often institutionalized through Castilian-Latin-Christian axes, is self-evident and indisputable. The myth of unity across time and space is among the operative fables: "Hispanic unity," as Joan Ramon Resina notes, "in Spain as in Latin America, was accomplished for the purpose of political administration and obedience to Castilian rule through methods of domination that eventually led to independence and the birth (rather than fragmentation) of a constellation of republics" (2013, 17).[6] The myth of Spanish/Hispanic unity is also a structural component of the ways the cultures in question have been institutionalized in educational spheres, subtly engaging what Gabilondo terms the "anti-multicultural structure of the state" (2014, 48) as a predominant archetype in historical, aesthetic, and pedagogical categorizations.

"Time and again," notes Resina, "the demographic weight of Castilian is held out as an unassailable argument for cultural hegemony" (2009, 207). In the same way that "American studies" oppresses all other experiences of reality into hyphenetic subordination to specific unhyphenated "American" Eurocentric myths—e.g., Christianity, English language, and the range of racialized and classist notions generally embedded in "American"—the term "Spain" unpacks a similar cascading map of a priori assertions relating to Castilian Spanish, Catholicism, Latin, Greco-Roman myth, and so forth, a program that relegates other experiences in the same spaces to subaltern statuses: "Spain" as Gabilondo explains, "continues to be an ahistorical construct that is not altered, challenged, and limited by those very same subaltern groups. Spain is a transhistorical container where hegemonic and subaltern groups exist without politically constituting the very same container, the Spanish state" (2014, 44). The notion of "Spain" monoculture-izes (or attempts to homogenize) various transnational, spiritual, pluricultural and linguistic groups in spaces claimed by the crown: traditional Spanish/Iberian/Hispanist pedagogy presume *that* center, the myths against which all other experiences in the spaces and times in question must be judged.[7] While the failures of this logic make area studies methods to a degree an unreasonable (and sometimes irresponsible), and despite criticism from many scholars,[8] the structural fantasy of the unity yet upholds much of the available questions within the discipline.

PEASANTS INTO SPANIARDS, FRENCHIFICATION AND SPANISHIFICATION

It is worthwhile to consider Eugen Weber's *Peasants into Frenchmen: The Modernization of Rural France, 1870–1914* in relation to similar "Spanish" treatises and myths. Weber's argument evidences that many residents of spaces claimed by the French government did not understand the notion of "France" in 1870 or 1914—and many performed acts of bodily violence (self-mutilation) in protest to forced Frenchification. Many demographies (Weber focuses largely on illiterate, non-French-speaking peasants) had life experiences, worlds, and realities that extended to the limits of the village: such identities were and are ungrammatical within a priori, external, and imperial French prescriptions of being. Weber describes the essential role that translators from local languages into French maintained into the mid twentieth century. But even if language is set aside as an identity metric, Weber's work deftly illustrates how the national phenomenon in Europe was, until very recently, exclusively the domain of the elite (specifically the literate) and thus to a degree inaccessible to the supermajority of communities in question—that is, to those who received "national" labels. While "France" may have existed in the minds of French-speaking, literate communities near Paris, and perhaps in urban centers in other regions, the notion that those in the countryside had corresponding or even comparable sentiments is largely fanciful.[9]

The peasants had meaningful worlds and identities, but these were (and largely are now) unrecognized and unimportant to the French conquerors. A nineteenth century traveler described: "Every valley is a little world that differs from the neighbouring world as Mercury does from Uranus. Every village is a clan, a sort of state with its own patriotism" (qtd. in Zeldin 1977, 663). Not unlike the treaties that uphold Hispanic studies, the standard French political, social, cultural and academic narratives prescribe the notion of unity with France across both space and time, so as to appropriate the activity of the communities under a French umbrella, regardless of other emotions and performances. "To stress the obvious," notes Walker Connor, "a French identity had still not penetrated the rural masses hundreds—in some cases several hundreds—of years later than scholars had presumed" (1990, 92).

As French-centric myths are promoted across all social and cultural arenas, "the acts, thoughts, and words of the illiterate," notes Weber, "remain largely unrecorded" (1976, xi). When martial conscriptors descended into the provinces in 1870 and again in 1914, those in non-French-speaking communities were thousands of times more likely to commit self-mutilation (often cutting off trigger fingers) to avoid military service for a nation that, despite being externally applied to them, many could not perceive. The illiterate, as Weber observes, "were not in fact inarticulate": self-mutilation was an elegant form of resistance to forced Frenchification; for many, the loss of a finger allowed them to escape death in a trench on behalf of a foreign government. There was "no uniform concept of [French] patriotism at the Revolution or at any other time in our period, and that patriotic feelings . . . far from instinctive, had to be learned" (Weber 1976, xii, 114).[10]

The French experience is not unique. While south of the Pyrenees was perhaps more rural than nineteenth and twentieth century France, Spanish cultural and social paradigms engage a similar tendency, prescribing "Hispanic" or "Spanish" unity forward and backwards in time, across all claimed spaces: like French histories, the received Spanish intellectual models are unpacked as a natural phenomenon, unassailable and irrefutable. Save some important exceptions, many presumptive knowledges about Spain and France among other territorial-based grouping mechanisms, are to a degree farcical, as the people involved "regularly identified themselves in terms of some other identity or identities" (Connor 1990, 92) and had no access to the skill (literacy) that could potentially integrate them into the imperial cultural system. Given that Hispanic studies (especially literary ones) are largely restricted to a performance—reading—specific to the elite and bourgeois, the contemporary myths upon which Hispanic/Spanish notions rest are significantly more recent than the traditional pedagogical models presume or allow.[11] Nevertheless, such structures "have often been passed off for fact" (Connor 1990, 93) and they yet colonize the available latitude of inquiry. Rodrigo Díaz de Vivar is often grouped across time and space with figures like Isabella I, Goya, Picasso, and Francisca Aguirre, and structural exigencies command that we develop no other grammar: "Hispanic" or "Spaniards" or "Spain" and the rest of the terms are presumed as logical, accurate, and precise for use concerning all epochs and in all spaces.

TRADITIONAL HISPANIC STUDIES PRESUMPTIONS

While area studies approaches in Hispanic studies "continue to mobilize nationalist anxieties" (Gabilondo 2014, 30), some scholars argue on behalf of a federalized approach that aims to de-hierarchize "Spanish" communities through multiculturation: these often have tones of a multinational Spain, and sometimes expressly so.[12] But there are some ostensibly irreconcilable theoretical miscues with replacing pure "Spain" myths with ontological moves into just as pure non-Castilian national interests, be they founded in language, history, presumed civic ties, or another cultural dimension. These same uncertainties burden the multi/

cross/trans/national inquiries, and in some ways, as Gabilondo notes, the application of area/trans/national studies to an Iberian frame "cannot be reconciled with reality" as "every 'Iberian nation' is quilted by the Spanish master signifier" (2014, 37).[13] As Claudio Guillén has noted, "as an object for literary history, [Spanish] national literature is, in most cases, from a historic-literary perspective, not only an insufficient institution . . . but also a spurious and fraudulent one" (qtd. in Seixo 2016, 651), and as Gabilondo shrewdly affirms, "with a subtle alchemy of a little Bhabha and a pinch of Anderson, they have managed to skirt the problem" (2014, 24).[14]

In the same way that medieval and feudal reasoning faded slowly,[15] during the prolonged abandonment of nation and trans/nation-based certainties, whatever logics succeed such myths in relation to the peoples and cultures of Iberia will bear the burdens of Hispanism—and this will be the case for centuries. Amid the protracted and piecemeal process during which Hispanism coexists with the modes which succeed it, there are several paradigmatic shifts that appear obtainable through available means; that is, within the area studies prescriptions and limits that characterize how the academy has organized these fields. Thus, an operative inquiry here is: within the exigencies and failures of an area studies mold, what new perspectives can complement existing certainties about Spain and its cultures?

In a federalized, multinational replacement apparatus for this subdiscipline of Latin American studies, many presently marginalized spheres link across disciplinary competencies in both time and space: in this vast category we find work by women, any non-heterosexual/cisgender performance, migrant competencies, age-based views, trans- and multilingual communication, among many others. Irrespective of how the new (national or area) groupings are articulated, subdivided, and historicized, there are Islamic and Muslim influences across nearly every language, culture, gender, and nation (as well as multinations and multi-cultures) performance of the peninsula—and inclusively outside the Iberian Peninsula in Europe, Africa, America, and Asia. Thus, so as to differentiate this topic, an option would be to describe Spain as the most Arabized province of Latin America—and thus shift intellectual focus to how Arabic languages and Islamic cultures, while embedded structural components of Spanish traditions, have been (and are) actively concealed, omitted, and obscured to the degree that "Moor" and "Spaniard" are often unpacked as linguistic—and thus communitive and cultural—binaries, rather than as synonymous or linguistically substitutive of one-another. Moving the critical register toward views in which "Moor" and "Spaniard" are not only related, inflected and mutually harmonized, and indicate a degree of unity instead of opposition, a new Iberian studies observes Islamic and Arabic as part of the same intellectual infrastructure as the traditional emphases.

SPAIN, THE ARABIZED PROVINCE OF LATIN AMERICA

> The meaning of an image is never inherent, but it is jointly generated by the producer and viewer. Hence images have only a meaning potential with a preferred reading.
>
> **Orsolya Putz (email to the author, May 29, 2019)**

While Spain and the rest of Latin America have cultural systems, languages, aesthetics, nomenclatures, and social structures inflected by Islam and Arabic Cultures, the linguistic structures, cultural traditions, social histories, religious tendencies, and political sensibilities of the Arab/Islamic world are virtually absent from Peninsular curricula, even in early medieval material. In Iberia specifically, the forming influences from Islam and Arabic, across the geographic region (space) and over millennia (time) have been institutionalized through an apparatus of intellectual distanciation that is characterized by near (if not overt) denial, disavowal, and rejection that imagines this set of subjectivities not as infrastructural but at most as an "occupation" or "convivence" that are superficial rather than integral parts of the edifice. The traditional paradigm cleanses many topics from possible studies, which has cascading effects on institutional frameworks and biases; one of the key exclusions, as Gabilondo deftly describes:

> *The Arabic "nation."* No Iberian studies proposal has located the origins of "Spanish" and Iberian literature and culture in the Peninsular Arabic tradition of Al-Andalus, also practiced by Jews and later expanded to Hebraic literature by writers such as Judah Halevi, as well as Moriscos, Mozarabes, etc. in what has been named without much success as "Arabicate culture.... An Iberian literary history that would begin with Arabic as "truly" Iberian language and literature would similarly create another trauma (the

orientalization of Spain) against which the master signifier of Hispanism, now refashioned as Iberian studies, reacts as symbolic reorganization and fantasy. Indeed, Iberian studies, as it is discussed today, is not too far from Menéndez Pelayo's thesis at the turn of the 19th century. (2014, 41)[16]

In "How Christian was Iberia in the Middle Ages?," David Wacks argues that this circumstance is largely because the "narrative is based largely on Christian sources" (2016, 1). In relation to this bias, María Rosa Menocal observes the following:

> The untidy truth is that medieval Spain was home to a greater variety of interrelated religions and cultures, as well as more languages and literatures, than seem plausible or convenient to attribute, as origins, to the literature of a single modern national literature. If unified nations and single national languages are the benchmarks for the divisions of literatures established in the modern period, then the medieval universe which precedes it cannot be fit into those same parameters and divisions, without distorting the past to make it seem as if its only lasting value was in laying the groundwork for a distant and ultimately unimaginable future. (2004, 61)

The migration of Muslims to the Iberian Peninsula that began in 92/711 (Islamic and Christian calendars will be used throughout) brought languages, traditions, aesthetics, and ways of life that blended into diverse cultures that flourished under Muslim political rule for nearly eight centuries (92–897, 711–1492). Major advances in science, medicine, irrigation, architecture, astronomy, culture, and other fields made the cities of Al-Andalus a key center—and for much of the fifth/tenth and sixth/eleventh century, Córdoba was the most populated urban center in the world. In contemporary Arabic, as David Wacks notes, "[Al-Andalus] means wealth, opulence, and artistic refinement" (2013). Over half the population in Al-Andalus/Andalucía had voluntarily converted to Islam by 390/1000, and by the sixth/twelfth century, "there were almost no Christian communities left" (Fierro 2005, 207). Arabic language flourished and yet flourishes in Al-Andalus/Andalucía among those who remained Christian. Initially there was discrimination vis-à-vis "old"/ "new" (مولد, *muwallads*) Muslims, though these distinctions disappeared by the fifth/eleventh century. Even today, in the fifteenth/twenty-first century, "many Spanish Muslims do not consider themselves converts, rather . . . they are *re*verting" (Roberson 2007, 249).

Despite the intercultural nature of medieval and contemporary Iberian society, the terms "Moor(ish)" and "Spanish" regularly appear as separate, distinct, and unconnected cultural and social entities—a theoretical tendency that also appears in the critical scholarship about the cultures in question. This circumstance produces academic language like the following: "Images of the Moor find their way into representations of the Spanish people, Spanish history, and Spanish culture. Indeed, I argue that the figure of the Moor becomes a double in these texts for the space of Spain itself" (Ramos 2011, 41). Reports like this hinge upon a binary linguistic separation between "Spain," "Spanish people" and "Spanish history, Spanish culture" with "the figure of the Moor"; they strive to disassociate blended, interrelated, and shared and unified cultural histories into discrete communities.[17] The externalization of non-Catholic groups results in a counterfactual binarization, mapping the master signifier: "It was a place where bishops spoke Arabic, imams spoke Ladino and Jewish viziers advised caliphs and gave dinner parties for Muslim poets in their presidential gardens" (Almond 2011, 28).

Many historical documents contradict the notion that Moor-Christian polarity was a motivation for violence, conquest, or cultural expression. Jaime I of Aragón voiced his conquest as one in which: "both Christians and Saracens, present and future, are bound to [continue congregating here] for baking their bread" (qtd. in Lowney 2006, 203); nor was the invasion of Grenada (or the Christian conquest of Iberia more generally) merely a religious intervention. The Tratado de Granada (881/1491) stipulates there would be no conversions; Islamic law would remain in effect; coerced relocation or cultural modification were expressly prohibited; and Arabic would be the official language on public documents. The intercultural resonance is also clear in religious structures (from Islamic and Christian traditions): the Court of Lions at the Alhambra has amalgamative symbols[18] and many Medieval Christian temples, even those in the far north of the peninsula, are adorned by what are often termed Islamic and Mudéjar aesthetics. The Convento de las Huelgas in Burgos houses the tomb of Doña Berenguela, Catholic Queen of Castile whose funerary headrest was inscribed in Arabic with shahâda (First Pillar of Islam, "There is no God but Allah") and decorated with a figure in a turban and four Rub el Hizbs. The communitive nature of Iberian culture has been, as Chris Lowney argues, "virtually unavoidable" (2006, 203). The Islamic military interventions in the north were similar: when Al-Mansur invaded Compostela in 387/997, he kept vigil at the tomb of Santiago "to protect the site of James the Greater's remains from being sacked. And many other Muslims journeyed to the Christian site" (Moore 2015, 135).

While traditional historical and religious narratives construct binary positions (Islam-Christian), these are not generally representative of the peoples of Iberia or their cultures: "What today, through historical analyses, we consider Islamic Spanish, we put into a political-religious quality of Muslim; *this would not occur in the same way at the time of the events*. It is likely that many characteristics, forms, symbols, and artistic and cultural fashions that we [today] define as 'Islamic,' at that time were considered simply 'Hispanic'" (Momplet Míguez 2008, 126; my emphasis). "Muslim and Christian traditions," as Moore deftly observes, "more than parallel one another: they are overlapping" (2015, 135). It is important to clarify that, if the patrons, architects, and artists had Jewish, Christian, Moorish sentiment; a blended, circumstantial, or transitional relation to one, several, all, or another system; or if they were indifferent to these logics entirely; or if they engaged with them as mercenary goods to secure commissions; becomes unimportant as soon as the critique unpacks the notion of "Islamic/Moorish" as dissimilar from "Christian/Spanish" onto the artefacts. While there is a poverty of evidence toward Moor-Spaniard distinctions, those ideological positions (and their binaries) are important to contextualize here, as they arise as *central* points of rhetorical emphasis in nearly all cultural and social histories in question.[19]

CONVERSION TO ISLAM AND BACK AGAIN

Very soon after the Christian conquest of Grenada, the Catholic church and state broke the treaty and initiated religious violence (compulsory conversion to Christianity). The importance of involuntary Islam-Catholicism conversions in Iberia—and their profundity and outcomes as cultural performances—varied significantly depending on the context, government, and broader community activity. As Leonard Patrick Harvey notes, "What happened to Spain's Muslims after they had all been forcibly converted is, surprisingly: nothing very much. No energetic campaign of mass evangelization, no wave of repression or persecution followed" (1993, 222). The communities were left as semiautonomous entities in which: "Spanish crypto-Muslims did a number of things to continue practicing Islam and hold themselves together as communities. One of these was the practice of *taqiyya*, a religious dispensation by which Muslims under compulsion or threat of injury were relieved of their religious requirements, including the observance of Ramadan, daily prayers, and dietary restrictions. This flexibility built into Islamic religious practice allowed crypto-Muslims to adapt their faith and religious practice to their difficult situation and thus continue on as Muslims in a real sense" (Barletta 2005, xxvii–xxix). Similarly, Ahmad ibn Abi Jum'ah's "Oran fatwa" examined Islamic practices under the Inquisition and decreed that Muslims may practice Christianity as well as consume alcohol and pork, and realize other prohibitions, if they were under compulsion or persecution. Abi Jum'ah's fatwa was disseminated widely among Muslim and Morisco communities in various Christian kingdoms and was translated to Spanish in 1563 and 1609 (Stewart 2006, 265–301). The crypto-Muslim practices involved concealed rituals, including language, burial, and betrothal, and as López-Baralt notes, "Crypto-Muslims refused to forget Arabic. . . . The secret Muslim community managed to teach its members not only how to marry according to Islamic law but also how to die within the faith" (1997, 28, 32). The state-backed ethnic cleansing campaigns document that crypto-Islamic rites continued at least until the eighteenth century (if they ever ceased). In "Los Moriscos que se quedaron: La permanencia de la población de origen islámico en la España Moderna," Enrique Soria Mesa's examination of the Kingdom of Granada shows that thousands of descendants of Muslims remained after 1609, and many circumvented the royal decrees by concealing their origins. In the seventeenth and eighteenth centuries, some in this community accumulated great wealth and controlled the local silk business, while more than one hundred held public office. The crypto-Islamic nucleus that remained was prosecuted by the Inquisition in 1727. López-Baralt has studied extensively the ways that these practices informed life throughout regions claimed by the Spanish government, noting that "reading Spanish Islamic literature is a sobering experience indeed" (1997, 36). In the face of the forced Christianization of the Inquisition, these rituals, as López-Baralt notes, demonstrate a "collective effort to persevere against all odds the community's Islamic identity" (1997, 23). Additionally, some ostensibly Christian prayers have Islamic resonances, such as "there is no God but

God and Jesus is the spirit of God" (qtd. in López-Baralt 1997, 33), and there is, to be sure, a "nostalgia for their lost Iberian motherland" and a tradition telling that "the King of the Christians will be captive, and be sent to the city of Valencia. There he will become a Muslim" (López-Baralt 1997, 25).

REBELLIONS OF THE ALPUJARRAS AND THE INSTITUTIONALIZATION OF ISLAMOPHOBIC LEGISLATION AND CULTURE

The rebellions of the Alpujarras underscore the limited success of the Inquisition and the importance of Islamic cultural and Arabic linguistic performances after the change in government. These revolts—from 1499 with occasional interruptions until 1571—were in response to Christian violations of the Treaty of Grenada, which forbade forced religious conversions and stipulated that Arabic remain in use. The Inquisition prohibited Morisco culture (bathing, language, clothing, food, etc.) as well as Islamic practices, policing them throughout the peninsula. The cultural cleansing program was codified by the Pragmática of 1567, after which possession of texts in Arabic was a criminal act and stipulated that contracts in that language be annulled, Christianization of dress and betrothal rites became compulsory, "Moorish" names were banned, ceremonial tattooing was prohibited, Friday celebrations were forbidden, and Arabic-style baths were destroyed. Francisco Núñez Muley expressed opposition in the following terms: "Paramos cada día peor y más maltratados en todo y por todas vías y modos, asní por las justicias seglares y sus oficiales como por las eclesiásticas; y esto es notorio y no tiene necesidad de se hacer información dello. ¿Cómo se de quitar a las gentes su lengua natural, con que nacieron y se criaron? Los egipcios, syrianos, malteses y otras gentes cristianas en arábigo hablan, leen y escriben, y son cristianos como nosotros" (qtd. in Caro 2000, 160). In the wake of the resistance, the Spanish government forced around 80,000 deportations, which included seizure of properties that were later allocated by the government to Christian colonizers (commonly termed "settlers"). These events hastened the expulsion of the Moriscos in 1609 and 1614.

In addition to physical and religious violence, the Christianization program was also cultural and ideological.[20] Some of the principal protagonists of the western cultural and literary canon—Roland, Cid, Othello, and Quijote, for instance—are celebrated through selective readings that privilege an Islamophobic stance, one that is often contrived and occasionally counterfactual to historical treatments. While Roland and Charlemagne were in battle against Basques in Orreaga-Roncesvalles, their adversaries were codified as Moors in "Song of Roland."[21] Similarly, Rodrigo Díaz de Vivar is often celebrated as the anti-Islamic hero par excellence, but he grew up in a transcultural community, spoke Arabic and Latin vulgates, had many Muslim friends, and spent nearly a decade serving on the courts of al-Mutamán and al-Mustaín II. While he "reconquered" Valencia for Alfonso, many Muslims had important military and administrative roles in his government.[22] He often fought with Islamic governments and their armies against Christian governments and their armies, and his nickname—*Cid*—is an Arabic honorific. Albengalbón, perhaps Cid's closest friend in the *cantar*, greets him in Arabic fashion, kissing the shoulder.

IS DON QUIJOTE A LITERARY ALLUSION TO MUHAMMED?

Was Cervantes a Christian, Jew, Muslim, or several (or none) of these? "Whether Cervantes was a converso or not," note David Castillo and William Egginton, remains "crucial to disentangling the meaning of his texts, to finally getting to the original, unquestionable, and intentional truth of Don Quixote" (2006, 50). Much like Rodrígo Díaz de Vivar, Miguel de Cervantes spoke and likely read and wrote Arabic and had extensive experience with and reverence for Islamic cultures. Arabic and related diglossias were common among Christians and Muslims—and converts to both traditions—in Iberia during his lifetime,[23] and apart from Cervantes's friendships with Moriscos and mozárabes in his homeland, he spent just under six years in Algeria before writing *Don Quijote*.[24] Cervantes's stint in north Africa was definitive for his literary career—he had published almost nothing until that point. After Barbary pirates abducted his ship near Roses in 1575, he was held in bondage by Ottomans in Algiers until 1580. As a man of means, Cervantes was held for ransom, not manual labor: his social status allowed him to move freely about the city.[25] While terms like "bondage" and "slavery" appear often in biographical depictions of these years, and thus insinuate a harsh and brutal treatment, voluntary conversion to Islam was common among Christian captives in Algiers. While Cervantes ostensibly did not convert, if he were a crypto

Muslim in Spain, in Algiers he could perform rites that were concealed in his native land. While conversion from one religion to another—and sometimes back again—is a process characterized by fluidity, terms like "Muslim" and "Jew" and "Christian" suggest immutable categories. The words themselves are sometimes deficient: they belie how transitions among faiths occur (especially when conversion is forced). *Don Quijote* aims at the spaces in between. During those years Cervantes lived daily life in Arabic and other tongues, experiencing and perhaps observing Ramadan, as well as Salat and four of the Five Pillars. As María Antonia Garcés notes, there may have been a "love affair between Cervantes and a Moorish woman" (2005, 50). Alberto Sánchez maintains, "la asimilación de la cultura musulmana por Cervantes no procede de los cinco años de esclavitud en Argel, puesto que ya estaba impregnado de ella a través de la propia cultura materna y española, completamente híbrida y mestiza" (1997, 23). Nevertheless, the directional axis of Cervantes scholarship often hinges on the idea, as expressed by Luis Fernando Bernabé Pons, that "Cervantes es un cristiano que busca convencer a los demás," and in addition this supposed evangelism, "no estoy de acuerdo . . . de que Cervantes tolere Islam, o que respete el Islam. Cervantes es un cristiano. Quería que los Moriscos se conviertan convencidos" (2015).

Cervantes appears to have included some important dimensions of Muhammed's biography as a subtext in *Don Quijote*: Don Quijote and Muhammed have the same birthmark, manner of death, last words, and vision of their professional callings—and both, like Cervantes and Díaz de Vivar, speak Arabic. The Muslim prophet was known to his followers as "Dhū al-Shāmah" or "The one with the birthmark." This mole—called "The Mark of Prophethood"—was between his shoulders. In chapter 30, Don Quixote says, "Sancho my son . . . help me to strip." Dorothea asks, "What does your worship want to strip for?" "To see if I have that mole," answered Don Quixote. "There is no occasion to strip," Sancho interrupts. "I know your worship has just such a mole on the middle of your backbone, which is the mark of a strong man." Quijote and Muhammed's deaths occurred after fevers and nine days of delirium; both used their last words to sort out possessions. Both had watershed moments at age forty-nine and said they would have been shepherds if not called unto their respective vocations. The narrator wants the reader to know Quijote speaks Arabic:

Albogues son—respondió don Quijote—unas chapas a modo de candeleros de azófar, que, dando una con otra por lo vacío y hueco, hace un son, si no muy agradable ni armónico, no descontenta, y viene bien con la rusticidad de la gaita y del tamborín; y este nombre albogues es Morisco, como lo son todos aquellos que en nuestra lengua castellana comienzan en al, conviene a saber: almohaza, almorzar, alhombra, alguacil, alhucema, almacén, alcancía, y otros semejantes, que deben ser pocos más; y solos tres tiene nuestra lengua que son Moriscos y acaban en i, y son: borceguí, zaquizamí y maravedí. Alhelí y alfaquí, tanto por el al primero como por el i en que acaban, son conocidos por arábigos. Esto te he dicho, de paso. (2004, capítulo LXVII)

Cervantes reports that his novel was translated from Arabic and authored by "Cide Hamete Benengeli" or "Lord of Commendable Eggplants"— eggplant was introduced to Spain by Muslims and has a spiritual role in Islam: it is traditionally consumed during Eid al-Fitr, the feast marking the end of Ramadan. Quijote also mentions "incidentally" his Saturday (part of Islamic sabbath[26]) meals are "duelos y quebrantos los sábados" or "trials and sorrows on Saturdays." The dish is comprised of eggs and bacon. Pork had become something of a national dish in Spain during the Inquisition, a gastronomic method to feign and/or perform Christianity. The cleansing of Moriscos from Spain (1609–1614) coincided with the publication of *Don Quijote* (1605 and 1615), and Cervantes—or Hamete Benengeli—addresses this directly: Ricote, a Morisco expelled from Iberia, returns in disguise and says: "Doquiera que estamos lloramos por España, que, en fin, nacimos en ella y es nuestra patria natural" (2004, chapter 54).[27]

Mukadder Yaycioğlu skillfully argues that, in *Don Quijote*, translation (Arabic to Castilian Spanish) and transcription (from Arabic characters to the Latin alphabet) merge thematic components that span time, experience, and community:

Si tratamos de entender en qué consiste el juego, nos damos cuenta de que no llegamos a entenderlo a fondo hasta terminar la lectura y hacer otra doble: una retrospectiva y otra futurista; volver del **final** (que equivale a **ahora/el presente**) al **principio** (que equivale a **antes/el pasado**) y viceversa para prever **el futuro**. Es el *eterno retorno* que nos salva de la amenaza del olvido de la historia. Con esta estructura tanto lineal como circular en la que se funden las culturas occidental y oriental y por medio del texto aljamiado y su transcripción al romance, Cervantes crea un juego/engaño intercultural y confronta el sistema de escritura de las lenguas semíticas; el árabe y hebreo (que se efectúa de derecha a izquierda y de atrás hacia adelante) con el latino que se realiza en el sentido contrario, para demostrar que la diferencia entre los dos sistemas no pasa de ser una realidad formal y no cambia el concepto de principio y final. (2010, 97–98; boldface in original)

The irony and satire of Cervantes's novel ask questions that are otherwise unutterable—questions about religion and state policy, about language and belonging, and about writing and culture and their role in history. While his critique emphasizes the distance between truth and fiction, between perception and reality, the context from which and in which he wrote was not bound by Latin, Spanish, Catholicism, and the other traditional lenses used to describe "Spain."

ISLAMOPHOBIC AXIS OF THE CAMINO DE SANTIAGO

Each literary treatment thus far noted here references St. James's posthumous presence in Iberia, a story that first appeared eight hundred years after the Christian apostle's death in part as a method to promote the nascent and somewhat counterintuitive notion that Spain and Western Europe may be understood as Christian spaces. Circa 40 on the Gregorian calendar, James was said to be on a mission trip to the Ebro region, near present-day سرقسطة-Zaragoza. He later returned to Judea and was beheaded by Herod in 44. The first version of the story ends there, in Judea. After Islamic peoples migrated into much of Iberia (including سرقسطة-Zaragoza) and southern Gaul/France in 89/711, a second phase of the James story was conceived: circa 191/813 a new narrative component tells us that upon execution, James's body was brought by angels (or perhaps other Christians) to Galicia and interred seven hundred years before. The rediscovery of the remains—the basis of the pilgrimage—occurs during the reign of Alfonso II (169–220/791–842). The James myth is nuanced to another degree not long after the rediscovery: the apostle appears on horseback in Clavijo in 222/844, fighting against Muslims. The most common icon of Santiago in Spain is on horseback (a white horse), and James is termed "The Moor Killer."[28]

"The Camino also served a political purpose," notes Rick Steves. "It's no coincidence that the discovery of St. James's remains occurred when Muslim Moors controlled most of Spain. The whole phenomenon of the Camino helped fuel the European passion to retake Spain" (2010). While few scholars examine the Islamophobic axis of the pilgrimage, Steves—a travel writer—emphasizes that this current is central in the rite: "Propagandistic statues of James are all over [Santiago de Compostela]—riding in from heaven to help the Spaniards defeat the Muslim Moors. . . . St. James is depicted taking such joy in butchering Muslims" (2019, 1). His account goes on: "Historians figure the 'discovery' of the remains of St. James in Spain was a medieval hoax. It was designed to rally Europe against the Muslim Moors, who had invaded Spain and were threatening to continue into Europe. With St. James—a.k.a. 'the Moor Slayer'—buried in Iberia, all of Europe would rise up to push the Muslims back" (2019, 1). There are important geopolitical concerns in the sudden apparition of Santiago in Galicia specifically. Placing the tomb five hundred miles west of سرقسطة-Zaragoza was opportune as Galicia was among the only vestiges under Christian political control on the peninsula after 89/711,[29] making it an opportune site for the relics. A central point in locating the tomb in this Christian-controlled polity was "the cult offered . . . the germ of a political ideology" and "integrated Santiago into a larger narrative" (Deswarte 2015, 481, 493). In that narrative, "The pilgrimage and the holy war," notes George Zarnecki, had become "in many minds the same thing" (1966, 67). Thus, Peregrino and Matamoros iconographies may be understood as "complementary, not antithetical" (Raulston 2008, 349), a situation that has been termed an "irreconcilable dichotomy" (Moore 2008, 313). In this sense, the institutionalized pilgrimage narrative interrelates the St. James imaginaries in both "pilgrimage and reconquest" manifestations as "iterations of the same narrative" (Moore and Spaccarelli 2008, 13).

Locating Santiago's remains in Galicia was also convenient as there was a Celtic pilgrimage to the "Coast of the Dead" and the "End of the Earth" at Finisterre, which was already sacred to many peoples throughout Iberia, Gaul/France, and the rest of the Celtic world.[30] Celtic religious traditions were strong long into the so-dubbed "Christian" period—and the Christian faith itself in these Celtic regions, including much of Iberia, France, and the northern isles, is layered with pagan resonances. Despite the claims of Christian overlords, many in Galicia—and around Spain and France in general—were ambivalent to Christianity during the medieval period; while priests had to expressly forbid Celtic fertility rites on the pilgrimage trails, those activities continued centuries into Christian domination: "During the 18th Century priests had to campaign to stop eager-to-be parents from copulating on what were considered fertility rocks" (Herbert 2014, 1).[31]

Richard Fletcher has argued that religious conversion is not a sudden or abrupt shift but a gradual one that occurs over generations and takes centuries. He notes that country people, like those in the northern regions of Iberia, are "notoriously conservative" with traditions and mores that "were not going to yield easily, [and] perhaps were not going to yield at all, to ecclesiastical injunction" (1998, 54). David Wacks has observed that, in the context of pre-Christian rituals performed in the region in 1907, "priests found it more convenient or expedient to allow the people to persist" and argues that the church encouraged these practices, "partnered" with such communities, allowing non-Christian practices "in order to maintain hegemony" (2016, 1). Wacks continues, "In the case of Spain there has been very little academic work synthesizing the evidence from art history, folklore, and literature. . . . This [likely] has to do with Spain's relatively recent disestablishment of the Church" (2016, 1).

Notwithstanding the limited acceptance of the new dogma, the posthumous component of the Santiago story was institutionalized in the third/ninth century as a method to justify (and sanctify) war—it is precisely this *pre*scription that sanctions the prefix "re" before "conquest." The Santiago pilgrimage involved distant peoples in this cause,[32] in a narrative that scaffolds an ideological program to culturally engineer some traditions as "natural" and "native" in Iberia. The Santiago myth thus participates in the Catholic/native, non-Catholic/foreign binary that for centuries has sanctioned violence against Muslims, Jews, Protestants, pagans and others, and links to the cultural and ethnic cleansing programs, under the auspices of Catholic and Castilian colonial mores.[33]

The Camino de Santiago is not the sole Iberian pilgrimage: the arm of Muhammed and an original Koran were long-held in the Mosque of Córdoba, and many made the pilgrimage to worship before them, but there is no contemporary public recognition or funding for these Spanish rites with Islamic ties.[34] The ideological dimensions of the Christian occupation of Iberia endeavors to elide Islamic ceremonies in order to maintain the myth that one system (Catholic) is "natural" while another (Islamic) is "foreign."[35] These stories do not engage Christianity vis-à-vis Iberia (and the West more generally) as malleable, situated, and ultimately fleeting worldviews, but as permanent or unchangeable conditions that exist forward and backward in time. Physical and cultural violence enforces this position. In this sense, the spiritual rites of Christian pilgrimage cannot be extricated from the matrices of power that Santiago codifies: the shift from military to cultural violence emblazons the development of power over time, and demonstrates how the appropriation of space through cultural frames is ultimately shielded into nonviolent passivity, such as that of a pilgrim's piety. However, the presence of the pilgrim in the space itself—be she, they, or he Angela Merkel, Charlemagne, Letizia Ortiz Rocasolano, or Rodrigo Díaz de Vivar—is also a symbolic articulation of rights: to breathe, pray, experience sunsets, and so on, in those spaces, while others doing the same are prohibited, under penalty of law.

The passivity of the pilgrim is perhaps the final adjudication of the conquest—it is a manifestation of power in the seemingly trivial, commonplace, and as a literary performance in the case of Cervantes, Picasso, *anónimo* (author of *Cid*), Hemingway, Cormac McCarthy, Cortázar, and many others who engage the Camino as a literary motif. These are the imperial cartographies of pilgrimage that we are instructed to overlook and ignore: in the ways Hispanic traditions are institutionalized, non-Christian experiences of Iberia are to be relegated (often labeled "alien," "foreign," or "Moor") against supposedly appropriate spiritualties and aesthetic sensations. Such myths have been buttressed through novels, stories, art, and supported by public funding, and they have also been codified into law: aside from the prohibition of Islamic vestments and burial rites around Spain, many Muslims exercising the same acts as Camino pilgrims—praying at sacred sites—have been incarcerated by Spanish authorities for doing so (Keeley 2010, 1).

The construction of "we" and mythic unity through cultural performances like pilgrimage and Christian-centric multidisciplinary retellings of the Christian conquest of Iberia privileges certain demographics: Ernest Hemingway's Robert Cohn (a Jew) and Cervantes's Ricote (and the ostensible author of *Don Quijote,* Cide Hamete Benengeli) are excluded from the pronoun and its possessive adjectives by such mappings of the term. The exigencies embedded in those pronouns are perhaps more important to reconsider today, as the intercultural nature of the communities in Spain are moving beyond Christian nationalisms, toward a period in which "we" is mapped with distinct coordinates.

SPANISH AS A VARIANT OF ARABIC

> From the perspective of the human agents that engaged it, temporal frameworks, such as specific times in the Islamic calendar or hours of the day and the devotional practices that correspond to them, can take center stage. This feature is of course not limited to aljamiado-Morisco literature . . . it is such a salient feature of the handwritten texts of the Moriscos of Castile and Aragon.
> **Vincent Barletta,** *Covert Gestures* **(2005, 156)**

While the quotidian use of Andalusian Aljamiado or the linguistic structures of Andalusian Arabic rarely appear in US curricula, Arabic has had a seminal importance on the development of the Spanish language. While studies vary to a degree, approximately 25 percent to 50 percent of Spanish derives from Arabic[36] and 50 percent to 60 from Latin, but Spanish is rarely described as a dialect or variant of Arabic. To my knowledge, there are no pedagogical or curricular programs in the United States that recommend study of Arabic or Islam as bases to learning about the "Spanish" language or "Hispanic" culture. Nevertheless, the linguistic influences "cover almost the entire lexicon," note Kees Versteegh, and are particularly dominant in terms relating to culture, agriculture, names, commerce, construction, gastronomy, and leisure (2001, 228). Nearly all words with "al" as well as many common surnames in Spain (Almeda, Alcalá, Medina, among others) and the names of more than a thousand locations (including Madrid, Sevilla, Murcia, Valencia, Andalucía, Jaén, and Ronda) from all over the region stem from Arabic traditions. The Castilian borrowings in Andalusí Arabic also reflect "a considerable degree of bilingualism" (Versteegh 2001, 227), and some of the most traditional expressions in Spanish, like *ojalá* and *olé*, are taken from Arabic—and some linguists maintain *usted* derives from *ustadh* (Chejne 1969, 16).

Andalusí Arabic also has influences in the other direction, into the Islamic world. A notable case is the tradition of *muwashshahat* (vocalized poetry) that is generally written and performed in standard/classical Arabic though nearly all end with two to four lines written in *aljamiado*: these last lines, as Habeeb Salloum notes, "summarised the entire meaning of the poem. This last verse was known as a *kharja* and from it was derived the whole inspiration of the poem" (2015, 1). The *zajal* was a popular form of *muwashshahat*, performed in vulgar (rather than classical) Arabic. Among Muslim and Christian communities, these songs from Spain "spread throughout the Muslim world with remarkable rapidity" (Salloum 2015, 1). Spain has an interesting role in the contemporary the Islamic world, as well: "Cordoba gets quite a few Arab tourists," and their focus tends to be the Mezquita as well as the food and architecture, which are perceived by some as tinged with exiled Islamic resonances (Amar 2011, 1).

FOOD AND DRINK

The Arabic influence on Iberian culture is ubiquitous in food and drink, and the ceremonies surround them, including the use of utensils, serving dinner as a third meal, and a variety of ingredients and forms of preparation. The same vocabulary is shared in both traditions—including rice, saffron, watermelon, coffee, and lemons, among many others (incidentally, the Latin term for olive oil—*oleum*—was superseded by *aceite* from Arabic). Muslims also introduced sugar, which largely replaced honey as a sweetener, and the tradition of regular fruit consumption, including oranges and apricots. Methods to dry raisins, dates, and other fruits, as well as their consumption, were also integrated as cultural rites. Arab expertise in irrigation engineering caused the population to soar after 92/711, and was key to many of these dietary shifts. The Muslim culinary traditions included use of clay pots and wood-burning ovens, kebabs, churrasco, as well as the practice of frying in olive oil and using vinegar as a preservative. The *jarabe* pestle from the Middle East was used to grind almonds and peanuts into creams used in *ajo blanco*, a precursor to gazpacho. These revolutionized food consumption and were not limited to Islamic peoples, as Juan Castilla Brazales notes, "[Many Christmas meals] served in the south of Spain are Arabic" dishes (2017, 1). While many of these performances may be implicitly linked to Islam, as Olivia Remie Constable notes, "clothing practices were merely elements of local culture and style; they were not based on faith traditions" (2018, 3). She continues, examining further layers of inquiries: if we review the "issue at hand from a question of religious identity (Christian vs. Muslim) to one of linguistic and regional identity (first Granada and Arabic vc. Castile and Castilian) . . . the Moriscos were also willing to die and suffer to preserve their regional identity, language, and customs, even while being Christians" (2018, 14).[37]

MORISCO AMERICANS—INCAN MUSLIMS IN THE SPANISH CONQUEST

> Columbus's ship of conquest was piloted by a Moor. . . . Between 15 and 30 percent of the enslaved West Africans were Muslims.
>
> Denijal Jegić, *Trans/Intifada* (2019, 128)

Another topic that is nearly absent from (Catholic/Latinate/Castilian) "Spanish" pedagogies and intellectual frames involves the role of Morisco and Islamic cultures in the colonization not only of the Iberian Peninsula and Canary Islands but also the Americas, Africa, and the Pacific. The Arabic and Muslim influences reaching into "Spanish" peninsular cultures were present in the lives of the colonizing crews, migrants, and sojourners, many of whom were Moriscos and crypto-Muslims. How would Arabic and Islamic practices influence the colonial initiatives? While Islam was practiced in Spain in hiding until at least the eighteenth century, Moriscos may have practiced the faith in the Americas significantly later. Cardinal Jiménez de Cisneros complained that Islam was being openly practiced—and some of the Muslim cultural resonances in food and dress were common well into the republican period, such as the Tapada Limeña (similar to the Cobijada de Vejer, in Andalucía) in Perú (for more on these topics, see Hernán Taboada 2004, 115; Harvey 2014, 325).

Many slaves the Spanish forced from West Africa to the Caribbean and elsewhere were Muslims, but the relations between Moriscos and Muslims they held in bondage is a topic that has received very little attention. Sir Francis Drake liberated several hundred Muslims in bondage from the Spanish colonies in the Caribbean, and ultimately returned about half of them to Islamic cities around the Ottoman Mediterranean—the other half, it has been surmised, were sent to Roanoke (Abd-Allah 2010, 2). The emerging and evolving role of Islam in the Spanish colonies was addressed by the royal decree of 1543, "In a new land like this, one where faith is only recently being sowed, it is necessary not to allow to spread there the sect of Muhammad" (qtd. in Diouf 2013, 40). As Sylviane Diouf notes, concerning Spanish Islamophobia in America: "Another indication of the fear that Islam and the rebellious Muslims inspired in the Spaniards . . . can be found in the [game called] Moros y Christianos [sic]. This was a special type of anti-Muslim play that colonists imported from Spain and Portugal. The settlers made the slaves in the Americas play out the struggle between the Moors and Christians in Spain" (2013, 149). The overwhelming presence of Islamic practices—both crypto and among the enslaved—in the Americas caused the Spanish to have "a genuine fear that Muslims would proselytize among the Indians." In Cuzco in 1560 Luis Solano (son of a Spaniard and female slave) was burned and Lope de la Pena (from Guadalajara) received a life sentence for participating in conversions. The slave rebellions among Muslim slaves in the Caribbean and elsewhere, reports Diouf, were "without a doubt indignant about being made the slaves of Christians" (2013, 147, 149).

CONTEMPORARY SPAIN AND THE REPETITION OF CHRISTIAN-CENTRIC ESSENCES

While the Muslim population of Spain increased by more than 60 percent from 2010 to 2020, the traditional narrative of Spain as Christian remains preeminent: "In Spain, in the schools," Yasin Maymir observes, "they would never teach you about the [country's] Islamic history" (qtd. in Macguire and Stewart 2017, 1). While conventional Spanish pedagogies in the United States follow this alignment, Muslim Spaniards are generally studied as migrants and newcomers, rather than participating in the continuance of a Spanish tradition. The institutionalized national heroes, Cid and Santiago Matamoros, who attained fame by killing Muslims, represent many avenues of critique of institutional Islamophobia and the extra-territorialization of Muslims and Islamic cultures, as do the comments from figures like José María Aznar: "¿Cuál es la razón por la que Occidente siempre debe pedir perdón y ellos nunca? ¡Ellos ocuparon España durante ocho siglos! . . . Debo decir que yo soy un partidario de Isabel y Fernando" (qtd. in Pardon 2006, 1).[38] As extremism infiltrates democratic bodies around the world, including the Spanish government, these tendencies have a shaping effect on the codification of historical materials throughout Iberia: the Mosque of Córdoba was converted to a cathedral subsequent to the Christian conquest in 633/1236, though for centuries the building itself has been known colloquially as the "La mezquita de Córdoba." The nomenclature "mosque" was removed from its listing on Google Maps in early 1435/2014, a digitized linguistic appropriation that continues the systematic cultural cleansing of Islamic symbols in Iberia that has occurred since 897/1492. While the bishop of Andalucía claimed that he was unaware of the cartographic change, the official brochure for the mosque/cathedral removed text characterizing the temple as "the foremost monument of the Islamic West" and "the Hispano-Muslim style at its greatest splendor"—and replaced it with a call "to be respectful to the identity of this building as a Christian temple."[39]

The Spanish government recently offered citizenship to descendants of those expelled, but only those with specific (Jewish) religious ties: "The Spanish state should grant the same rights to all those who were expelled" including Moriscos, notes Bayi Loubaris; "otherwise their decision is selective, if not racist" (qtd. in JTA 2014, 1). The weight of these expulsions is important to consider now, as University of Puerto Rico professor Abdelrahman Elsaid eloquently comments:

> The Moriscos were aligned with the Iberian peninsula just as Egyptians are to the strip of land called Egypt, as Arabs are to Arabia, as Persians are to Persia, and as the English are to England.
>
> Nostalgia was a natural feeling for those who were exiled.
>
> Today Muslims feel pain for those [Spaniards] who were treated unjustly, and the feeling is similar to the pain that exists for the Ukrainians with the Russians, Native Americans with the US colonialists, the Irish with the English, and the imperial provinces with the Romans. It is a pain for the displaced.
>
> The nostalgia that exists today for Spain is for the civilization, for what Andalusia represented as a human achievement. Andalusia is/was looked at as one of the enlightenment centers in the world, but again, this came with the flavor of Spanish/Andalusian identity that made those indigenous people different and unique in having their own sensibilities which they shared not only with Europe, but with other Muslim nations as well. The sensibility also came to America, within the men and women who ran the ships. And also within those who came in chains. (Email to the author, 11 March 2022)

METHODS, PEDAGOGIES, AND INQUIRIES

In addition to focus on Islamic and Arabic sensibilities in Spanish cultures, a methodological shift toward a non-Castilian/Catholic/colonial dominant intellectual paradigm allows further pedagogical inquiries to rise in importance: What does it mean to be Jewish, Muslim, atheist, pagan, *and* Catholic in a mono-religious/cultural polity? How do forced spiritual conversions shape emotions, community, language, identity and culture? How do Jewish, Islamic and pagan scaffolding inform and influence contemporary and historical Spanish spiritualities, myths, identities, languages, and material cultures? In what ways do imposed collective identities (i.e., "Spanish Catholic") fail to rearrange core beliefs, inspire extremism, or mobilize anarchy? How are the spaces between forced identities and emotional sensibilities codified in food consumption, dress, language, bathing, and other performances in colonized communities? What is the lifespan of a religion's "facts" after conversion, forced or otherwise? How many generations do the prohibited religious and cultural tenets exist in concealment—do they continue in perpetuity? How do the cultures of atheism vary across Islamic, Jewish, pagan, converted, and Catholic Spanish communities? In what ways do forced and voluntary religious conversions make Spain unique in Latin America—and how do they relate to contemporary cultures, languages, identities, communities, aesthetics, and other social performances? In a broader sense, to what degree do externally prescribed definitions—Catholic, Islamic, pagan, and so on—inform emotion and the cultural performances that stem therefrom? The maintenance of Castilian/Christian/Roman/Latin axes curbs the evolution of such inquiries, and thus, the developed epistemes are, often explicitly, designed to relegate questions to the margins of significance: more important is that the pedagogical epistemes be developed in concert with traditional certainties at all levels, including PhD, thus facilitating potential employment in the academy, publication, and grants and other funding opportunities, among many other opportunities.

"Arabicate culture," notes María Rosa Menocal, "in that place we now call Spain" involved translation of Bibles into Arabic in a place where there are "all members of a community of Arabic language and culture first[,] in al-Andalus[,] and then in what will become Spain" (2006, 14, 13). The historical and contemporary institutionalizations of "Spain" are too burdened by Christian/Latin-centric inertia, by the conventional (disciplinary and popular presumptive) exclusions,[40] but there are some available channels to consider:

1) Cultivate nostalgia for things Arabic/Islamic in Spanish histories and cultures
2) Require knowledge of Arabic as a part of Spanish language studies
3) Involve studies of the Koran and Islamic histories, customs, and traditions
4) Unlink unity from Castilian prescriptions
5) Develop non-Castilian national and subnational cultural and linguistic epistemes in relation to Arabic/Islamic traditions
6) De-interpellate Spanish from received Latin, Christian, Roman presumptions

CLAIMS OF CAUSALITY

While the monologic of Spain-centric cultural pedagogy may be under slow decay, the deconstruction of the cultural understandings of the present and past[41] is a piecemeal process that occurs slowly and differently depending on context. Hispanic studies as a paradigm pursues a melancholy spiral: it retains an intentional relation to Christian, Latin, and Castilian masters of signification that weaponizes pedagogies as methods of exclusion. As passive and innocuous as received claims of causality may seem, they have immense power. As Michael Jarrett notes, it is "woefully oversimple but tremendously reassuring—to assume that we choose the objects of our affection" (1996, 1)—and it may be the case that, as Ania Loomba argues, "Eurocentric roots of comparative methodologies are so deep that it is impossible to denaturalize the habits of mind that have emerged from them" (2009, 501). That affection has been engineered, plotted, curated, and strategized in concert with Eurocentric presumptions of a field that they serve to maintain. But criticism of that model, part of which hinges on Spain's non-exceptional and provincial status in a Latin American frame, can gesture toward forms of relation that bind to a series of interconnected margins, to plurality, and even to malleability, in ways that have the potential to moderate the exclusions enforced by Hispanism.

ON THE PUERTORICANIZATION OF US HIGHER EDUCATION

OR, THE AWKWARD CONSTRAINTS OF USING ONE LANGUAGE

> Se dice que Estados Unidos es un cementerio de lenguas.
> **Jorge Durand, "Cemeterio de lenguas" (2015, 1)**

> Have you ever hurt about school?
> I have, because I learned a lot of words from school,
> And they are not my words.
> **Apache student, Arizona, qtd. in Courtney Cazden and David Dickinson, "Language in Education" (1981)**

> Our teachers come to class,
> And they talk and they talk,
> Till their faces are like peaches.
> We don't;
> we just sit like cornstalks.
> **Navajo student, New Mexico, qtd. in Cazden and Dickinson, "Language in Education" (1981)**

> Students of all ages do learn words in school. But all too often . . . their own ways of speaking are denigrated.
> **Courtney Cazden and David Dickinson, "Language in Education" (1981, 459)**

Borderlands are not particular to the Southwest.
Gloria Anzaldúa, *Borderlands / La Frontera* **(1987, 2)**

I talk in the language that the class needs from me.
Anonymous UPR student

Language shifts in class? Cuando sucede me mantiene más atento.
Anonymous UPR student

There are some awkward constraints to using only one language. I understand we must do it sometimes. It limits how and what I feel, and how I express myself. It's like swimming with just your legs. I would rather not do it—but I can.
María Biaggi , UPR student

For me taking criticism from someone who only speaks one language would force me to challenge them to learn about their world. But people from that mindset usually can't see beyond themselves, so it's not worth even the effort to say it to them in their own language.
Cristina Martín, UPR student

Changing languages changes meanings even on the same book or poem. No sé que más decir.
Anonymous UPR student

Students for whom [two languages] was not something exotic or even particularly noteworthy, but a fact of life, its absurdities and fucked-up politics and violence and juxtapositions not so much a story to tell as a backdrop against which the satisfactions and preoccupations of daily life were set.
Daniel Tyx, "The Year I Didn't" (2013, 63)

A linguistic persona of this kind is fundamentally different from one that is molded in a circumstance where monolingualism is the default assumption. . . . This pattern of language use appears odd only to those who assume that monolingualism is the normal human condition. To people who live with linguistic plurality it doesn't seem at all complicated or problematic: indeed, it seems perfectly normal.
Amitav Ghosh, "Speaking of Babel" (2020, 287–88)

Nearly all US educational organizations embrace English as the sole language for gradation certification, any and all credentialization, teaching (save "foreign" languages), funding and admissions paperwork, academic awards, institutional messages, and so on. While the academy could be a space where the binary between Spanish and English is rethought (if not demolished), which is appropriate, which is proper, which is correct, which is—in some cases—legal to use in public life are subtly reinforced in universities and through all levels of the education system. At universities, rethinking these policies could address both a cultural injustice and an enrollment cliff: almost all demographics are in a precipitous matriculation decline (one that predates COVID-19), yet across the United States and across disciplines, Latinx enrollments have exploded, and the trend is likely to continue for decades.

For all the virtues of the US university system, institutional monolingualism as a "best practice" has many nefarious effects—for English-dominant students and those who regularly use multiple languages. While the way students and faculty use Spanish and English (and their mixes) at the Universidad de Puerto Rico tests the semantic rules in both languages, the intellectual competencies developed on our campuses pose serious challenges to the monolingual university as an institution, especially in Spanish-dominant areas. Multilingual maps in an educational setting allow (and in effect nourish) not only the coalesce of varied realms of thought, social, and intellectual traditions, they also expand the implied dimensions of citizenship in ways that needle the subtle controls on whom may participate in civic affairs. A shift toward a model like ours would almost certainly increase Latinx enrolment, retention, and graduation rates—and it would have significant benefits for monolingual students from all backgrounds: many studies show multilingual learning has profound cognitive and social benefits.

SPANISH AND ENGLISH AND SPANGLISH AT THE UNIVERSITY OF PUERTO RICO

Spanish is the dominant language on our campus, though English has co-official status. Each are used for specific purposes. As Kevin Carroll points out, "English has held a privileged role in higher education where institutional policies have allowed professors to teach in English or Spanish." He goes on to note that "the majority of [Puerto Rican] institutions have de facto open-language policies, which allow instructors to use textbooks largely published in English and present their lectures and assessments in Spanish or a mixture of Spanish and English" (2015, 260). Besides the classroom, language blending occurs in institutional communications, assessment and accreditation paperwork, faculty meetings and social gatherings, as well as across media including websites, e-mail and Zoom conversations, and the gamut of everyday interactions.

If languages speak us, the ability to switch between them layers what can be done by a university—it introduces experiences, perceptions, and complexities that exceed the range of English-centrism. Especially in literary and cultural studies, cross-lingual conversation allows students to engage more directly with how narrative structure and word choice, expression of feeling and desire, and emotions arise in a language/cultural tradition vis-à-vis another. When a learning environment draws from the students' language repertoires in this way, it also engages people to recognize themselves and their communities in new ways and to create and co-construct culture and memory across a broader set of experiences.

There are also cognitive and social benefits that reach across multiple domains of academic life. Anatoliy Kharkhurin comments that multilingual institutions afford "an advantage in intelligence," since students outperform in divergent thinking; language fluency, flexibility, elaboration, and originality; also on insight problems and imagination tasks. These "superior abilities" are "qualitatively distinct" from monolingual comparison groups (2016, 357, 355). Scholars who prepare in such settings are "less likely to jump to conclusions prematurely" and demonstrate greater creativity, spatial awareness, and depth of attention (Dewaele 2016, 413). Vaid and Meuter have called monolingual environments "conditions of deprivation" (2016, 92). Languages are words and syntax—and they are also social experiences. As Vamsi Koneru, assistant professor of psychiatry at the University of Connecticut School of Medicine, observes: "People score differently on cognition tests; tell stories differently; name their communities differently, and self-identify differently depending upon where they are, with whom they are speaking, and in what language" (2013). The linguistic truncation characteristic of English-centric practices has many detrimental effects that have been blurred into the normalcy of US academic life.

Many correctly perceive the presence of English in Puerto Rico as a colonial exigence, an external linguistic control designed and published in a granite office building in Washington over a century ago, but still implemented this very day in places like Mayagüez and Vieques. But the colonial mission failed: English has been appropriated in Puerto Rico into a linguistic ecosystem robust and expansive enough to rewrite its limits, localizing *inglés* in accordance with how it is useful in Aguadilla or San Germán in ways that play with the external controls, overwriting the directives from Georgetown or Logan Circle. Beyond an archaic colonial program, translingualism allows the institutional dynamics at the UPR to transcend a closed-in homogeneity subtly enforced by monolingual policies (be they English-only or Spanish-only). Martha G. Abbott, executive director of the American Council on the Teaching of Foreign Languages, envisions "a 'new normal' of multiliteracy and multiculturalism" that would cultivate "linguistic and cultural development for all its citizens." Implementation of Green Linguistics, or institutional policies that develop with local circumstances, would mean multiple languages could be an inevitable part of (scholarly) life in the US. Such a move would resist the standard US programs, which not only "efface Latinx experiences, reduce and problematize bilingualism, [but also] demonize U.S. varieties of Spanish and Spanglish" (Carter 2018, 251). It would appear Abbott envisions applying a model like that of the University of Puerto Rico to the rest of the United States.

English-only university life is sometimes imposed by law—but often it is subtly enforced in higher education by funding opportunities, institutional assessments and accreditation metrics, governmental oversight, and fiscal documentation, among other forms of accountability, that are only available in one language. English-only "best practices" in degree conferral, curriculum design, cultural events, scholarly appointments, institutional-level communication, and the cascade of other university activities, have important symbolic weight, especially in Spanish-dominant communities: they represent not only the power to define a linguistic and cultural reality, but also to make others accept it. In this way, the US system of higher education unequivocally foreignizes languages other than English even when they are local to campus and truncates the range of questions scholars may pose. English-only universities in Spanish-dominant areas are particularly misguided—aside from ignoring the significance of Spanish to a community, they explicitly disallow multilingual and translingual knowledge cultivation, which are competencies with many cognitive benefits. While the prohibition of fluidity, interchangeability, and variability of language among students, faculty, and local communities, has obvious unfavorable effects in cultural fields, it shapes all disciplines: many studies show that in multilingual environments people have sharper attention skills, demonstrate enhanced self-control, make more logical decisions, are more creative, have greater facility with abstract knowledge, navigate "foreign" ideas with increased receptiveness, and are more adept at disregarding irrelevant material (Dewaele 2016).

The way we communicate is not incidental to what we (can) know, but in monolingual utopias, that fact is misunderstood: and so goes the apology, *Knowledge is neutral and a-linguistic. Texts can be translated. As the de facto national language, English is indispensable in higher education. Students should learn, practice, and use it in all facets of academic life. It is the language of science, of the humanities, of business; it is the system of the future, of the present. Nothing else can come close. The English language must be the center of what our universities do.* While higher education is vital to professional formation, skills-training, and specialized experience, it is also central to the cultivation of critical social responsibility: who valid people are, the languages they (may legally) use, the nature of the relationships they develop, and the composition of community interrelate closely to a university's mission. Inasmuch as citizenship is a status, it is also a process—part of which is linguistic. *What language speaks us?* is related to another inquiry: "What languages speak our university?"

The links between language and identity cannot be overstated: "Identity is circumstantial, conditional, contingent upon surroundings," notes Vamsi Koneru. "We see the impacts of this psychologically, neurologically, psychosomatically, and physiologically" (2013, 1). Cross-fertilization studies demonstrate that mixing languages—having more than one language accessible and available—appears to prime the brain in ways that are unfeasible in monolingual settings. As Ying-yi Hong et al. note, linguistic-based cognitive benefits function "as an interpretive frame only to the extent that" each language is "cognitively accessible" (qtd. in Herlihy-Mera 2018a, 173). English-only institutional policies limit this frame, and thus, they explicitly restrict and colonize: 1) students' brains and 2) the forms of citizenship imagined, enunciated, practiced and recognized.

UNIVERSITY OF PUERTO RICO, ¿UTOPÍA TRANSLINGÜE?

Part of what makes the UPR notable is that our institutional environment identifies use of multiple languages not as incendiary but ordinary. Engaging, thinking, experiencing, and performing several languages and traditions each day allows our students to complement their technical preparation with a unique set of cultural capacities—skills, philosophies, and experiences unavailable at almost every other US institution of higher learning. Recognition of these as qualities or intellectual virtues cannot, or at least does not, occur in part due to the nature of competitions that rank scholars: be they in admissions, funding, publications, grants, hiring, prizes, scholarly appointments, and so on, UPR students and faculty fail across all rankings in no small part due to the ways competitions subtly but specifically prohibit recognition of multiple-language—and any other-than-English-language—communication as valid. In these competitions, and in the US in general, multilingual agency is not a metric of excellence but an eccentricity. Despite a distorted location in the rankings, UPR students have the scholarly infrastructure available to develop unique sensibilities across all disciplines—if the lower, mid-, and top ranked universities across the United States were more like our campus culturally and linguistically, this would be of great benefit to the students, faculty, and to the communities served. The English-centric demands of US higher education inhibit the study and practice of many multilingual and translingual sensibilities and competencies that are natural on each campus. The implicit "best practices" channel all activity into not only English-only administrative and extracurricular activities, including all institution-level communications, but also across course and degree offerings: activities, seminars, and degrees in subjects like local and national histories, mathematics and natural sciences, social and human sciences, the arts and world/modern languages, among others, are subjected to an English-only prescription. This institutional "best practice" even inserts English as, in effect, a center of "Spanish"-language and cultural university programs and activities—a circumstance that imbues all relations to the monolingual base as well as its implicit philosophies, attitudes, and views.[1]

What languages speak a decolonized university? What benefits do flexible, transitory, conditional, situational, and multiple centers of linguistic performance bring to a pedagogical environment? How does translingual learning benefit students and their communities? Engaging axes of institutional multilingualism as a forum for decolonial pedagogy gestures toward arenas of scholarship, resistance, engagement, research, and community activities that are largely inaccessible in English-only environments.[2] Upon an institutional philosophy that appreciates multilingual cognition, translingual meaning-making, and the outcomes of language shifts in a classroom setting, if the educational template developed at the Universidad de Puerto Rico were engaged across the United States to counteract the colonial experience presently celebrated as a "best practice," would open students to experiences, agency and intellectual benefits that are limited to "oddities" within the colonized university.

Especially in Spanish-dominant areas, monolingualism is a primary tool in the exercise of empire, and one closely linked to public universities. As Eva Cherniavsky observes, the "university is an imperial worldmaker, balance of critique and apology" (2017, 52). And the monolingual maps encourage, if not demand the implementation of imperial value systems that John Muthyala describes as: "Determining life and death but by controlling all realms of life itself; that is, empire exercises its power through administering social life by bringing all aspects of life under the domain of observation, classification, and digitization, and by intertwining the various strands of the social, political, cultural, and economic in complex and pervasive ways. Its power extends throughout the realms of social existence, and because of its reach, empire presides over the management of entire groups, classes, races, masses of peoples, and their living environments" (2012, 45). In limiting recognized and participatory communication to a monolingual base, as Lourdes Díaz Soto and Haroon Kareem note, "The colonizer imposes his culture upon subjugated groups and seeks out their cooperation by pacifying their minds. This pacification limits the creativity of vision of the subjugated and destroys their ability to act in their own interest" (2006, 21). This "linguistic terrorism" amounts to "the continual expression of white supremacy and its continual advocacy to Americanize all others." These linguistic controls "perpetuate social control" (23, 25) and "linguicism has taken over from racism as a more subtle way of hierarchizing social groups" (Phillipson 1992, 241); during the Trump administration, this shifted yet again back to overt racism combined with linguicism as explicit governmental policy.

While the US imperial rules allow an institutional-level awareness of other languages, the "best practice" relates other systems as subordinates to English: the colonized institutionalizations of non-English ways of being, as interrogated through monolingual organizations, generally follow three phases: 1) celebration 2) appropriation 3) destruction. The destruction phase occurs through saturation of English in all institutional media (books, videos, tweets, speeches, etc.), prohibition of languages other than English on "official" communiques, and tokenization of non-English media (which is sometimes translated to English or italicized), among other mechanisms. Among the primary and inevitable consequences of English-only education, as Díaz Soto and Kareem note, "Teachers and instructors systematically negate the cultural experiences of subjugated [multilingual and non-English-speaking] children and refuse to allow them to exercise their own reality as a foundation of literacy" (2006, 29).[3]

The maintenance and creation of unequal relationships between communities is enforced through the monolingual university—and this circumstance is part of what makes Universidad de Puerto Rico's language policies unique and worthy of specific attention: notwithstanding crushing economic violence, natural disasters, and perpetual colonial exigencies from *la junta* (appointed by the US government) and its educational accrediting bodies,[4] my university has many linguistic and cultural depths that make it exceptional in comparison to top-ranked universities across all disciplines. But the intellectual environment in humanities is particularly lively: as Spanish and English coexist, conversations in all fields weave in and out of several languages, philosophies, worldviews, and intellectual registers; even undergraduates have proficiency in three or more traditional languages (Spanish, English, and a "foreign" tongue), including the several variants of Spanish and English used on the island, as well as a diverse map of Spanglishes, all of which are used interchangeably, not only in research initiatives and tertulias but also in classrooms, at public events, and the gambit of institutional activities.[5]

The intellectual dimensions that these circumstances provide are difficult to measure precisely on paper—or to comprehend from the outside. Perhaps for that reason UPR scores so inappropriately low in all standard measures, rankings, categorizations, and other forms of institutional scaling—including external humanities grant funding competitions from Mellon, NEH, NEA, and ACLS, among others. But each person's experience on campus is augmented by the social and cultural latitude that this environment offers: the preparation our graduates realize transcends knowledges available at top-ranked universities in all regions, but recognition of these as qualities or competencies cannot (or, at any rate, does not) occur due to the nature of the competitions: be they for grants, admissions, hiring, scholarly prizes, and so on—even competitions on Puerto Rican or Caribbean Studies, trans/multilingual culture, etc.—those affiliated with top-ranked monolingual universities win them.

While colonial inflections can be unavoidable when using English in Puerto Rico, institutional recognition of multiple languages on campus allows what is fugitive communication in the United States (that is, Spanish and Spanglish) a location for institutional agency in ways that elide the social truancy concomitant in monolingual institutions, undoing some of the built-in assumptions that frame all activity, including teaching, degree-granting, as well as daily life, through the English-only restrictions that are characteristic of nearly all US universities. Puerto Rico and its universities are colonized spaces but they are also exemplary of the ways translingual agencies may nourish sensibilities and create social maps with performances, forms of inquiry, and depths of analysis that are impossible under monolingual domination: in short, the Universidad de Puerto Rico is what other universities cannot be without wholesale structural shifts—it is futuristic, democratic, plural, and erudite in ways Abbot wishes the United States could be.

SPANISH-ENGLISH INSTITUTIONAL ENTANGLEMENT WITH PRE-COLUMBIAN LANGUAGES

The emphasis on English as sole mediator of linguistic existence in US universities has serious effects on the study of inter-, multi-, and crosslingual exchanges amid Spanish and Native languages, particularly in the US Southwest. While Puerto Rico's decolonial engagement is mainly Spanish-English based, such a model could be applied across whatever linguistic map exists in the communities of each institution. This practice may have specific emancipatory outcomes in spaces where pre-Columbian cultures and languages exist, that are presently claimed by the US government. In these regions, along with many other tongues, Yaqui, Keresan, Taos, Tewa, Zuñi, and Hopi, and several variants of Spanish developed in entanglement with one another, an exchange that involves loanwords, grammatical cues, and pronunciation tones, among other lexical forms, across each system; while in a colloquial and quotidian sense, the role of Spanish in these contexts may at first appear an ordinary one, some of the more fascinating anti- and decolonial linguistic processes in the Americas from recent centuries involve these gradations.[6]

While many Yaqui in Arizona, Texas, and Sonora are trilingual (Yaqui-Spanish-English), their colonization by Spanish Jesuits since the 1600s was, at least initially, realized in Yaqui—a circumstance that informs their specific multilingualism today. As Jerry Craddock notes, the Spanish priests used "the Indian language" to conquer reflexively, a mode that involved "persuasion rather than force to influence the religion, social organization, and material culture of the Yaqui" (1981, 203). When the Mexican government colonized Yaqui areas in the 1880s many Yaqui migrated to Arizona, then as now claimed by the US government. The Yaqui brought their specific translingual engagement with Spanish to that area: "Unlike other groups in contact with Spanish," writes Craddock, "Yaqui do not use loan translations and rarely combine Spanish and Yaqui roots. Instead, Spanish terms are borrowed" (1981, 203). The Yaqui borrowings from Spanish have Yaqui phonetical patterns and Spanish pronunciation. Meanwhile, Yaquis' use of Spanish, English, and Yaqui remain comparatively isolated from one another; each arise in context of specific functions.

Other Indigenous nations and communities have had significantly different interactions with Spanish and English. In Tewa, Keresan, and Taos, for example, Spanish appears with much less regularity. After centuries of subjugation and brutality, the Pueblo Revolt of 1680 estranged these groups from Spanish colonization in ways that are manifest in contemporary linguistic performances. Like the Pueblo peoples, Hopi and Zuñi resistance to European presence is also specific and idiosyncratic, and has similar outcomes in their languages, which have even fewer Spanish loanwords. While the Hopi and Zuñi struggle with Spanish colonization does not have an explosive moment like the Pueblo Revolt, their language maps express their resistance: "The majority prefer English" over Spanish as a third language (Craddock 1981, 204).

The US monolingual institutional exigence at universities in those regions makes such facets of linguistic history and cultural localization unrecognizable, subordinate to the wipe-away dominance of English that informs all facets of communication—official and sanctioned, internal and external. The reduction of institutional communication marginalizes pre-Columbian sensibilities in programmatic ways that are intentionally destructive: their purpose is not to lend existence to anything other than European realities, but to create systems that make them illogical. The multilingualization of universities that serve these communities would, in addition to the horizons opened by abandoning English as linguistic center of all reality, emphasize these histories in decolonial pedagogies and gesture toward the release of non-Euro-articulated ways of being.

MEANING-MAKING AS A MULTILINGUAL PROCESS: EPISTEMOLOGIES OF PLURILINGUAL PEOPLES

> We needed a language with which we could communicate with ourselves, a secret language. For some of us, language is a homeland closer than the Southwest—for many Chicanos today live in the Midwest and the East. And because we are a complex, heterogeneous people, we speak many languages. Some of the languages we speak are:
> 1. Standard English
> 2. Working class and slang English
> 3. Standard Spanish
> 4. Standard Mexican Spanish
> 5. North Mexican Spanish dialect
> 6. Chicano Spanish (Texas, New Mexico, Arizona, and California have regional variations)
> 7. Tex-Mex
> 8. Pachuco (called caló)
>
> Gloria Anzaldúa, *Borderlands / La Frontera* (1987, 55)

How does language influence what we remember and what we forget? In a monolingual setting, what stories can survive? What stories vanish? How does monolingual policy shape the understanding of multilingual stories? How do such policies cause silence? What historical narratives can survive a monolingual onslaught, sanctioned and celebrated in universities? Is translation sufficient? What are the limits of Spanish narratives and histories when recounted in English? Cross-, inter- and multilingual pedagogies engage meaning-making as a multi-nodal process with generative links and parallels to student knowledges and student experiences. Retreating from the certainties of the monolingual university allows our educative processes to understand and recognize that societies create meaning in ways that transcend uni-nodal knowledge.[7] Multilingual pedagogies effect an emancipative legitimization of the ways students and their communities use voices, construct agencies, and make meaning through use of several languages and the spaces between them, to the degree that the myth of "in-between" or amidst mythically pure languages dissolves into criticisms of the structures diving and prescribing these divisions.

In this way, the theoretical and the epistemic bases of pedagogy in Puerto Rico have lived dimensions that contribute to meaning-making in ways unachievable in monolingual intellectual contexts: such meaning processes are critically engaged, locally attuned, and in perpetual reconstruction. They arise not in relation to the colonial matrix of power but as meta-colonial processes, external to the conditional and circumstantial exigencies of the US political body's prescriptions for, about, and pertaining to the community.[8] Recognizing that traditional linguistic systems cannot contain these extra-linguistic identities emancipates them and decolonizes their performance; their existence is not contingent to colonial mores but metacognitive to them, situated within other axes of performance. As Aneta Pavlenko notes in *Negotiations of Identity in Multilingual Contexts*, "Identities are best understood when approached in their entirety" (2001, 16) and as the interactional accomplishment of meaning-making in such an environment engages multiple axes holistically. Cross- and extra-linguistic interventions are situated within gender, race, class, ethnicity, generational, geopolitical, and institutional affiliation, toward nuanced views on the ways "each aspect of identity redefines and modifies all others" (Pavlenko 2001, 16). These trans-, cross-, and extra-lingual conditions, with cascading constellations of meaning-dimensions, may appear "fragmented, decentered, and shifting," they create and recreate coherence, using language as a resource to shift, jam, and play with decolonial tropes that avoid imperial grammars of categorization in ways that "produce new identities, and assign alternative meanings to the links between language and identity varieties" (Pavlenko 2001, 18, 27).

A focus on multilingual meaning as a creation process allows entry to an epistemological turn that de-ontologizes communities and individuals from the already-power of nations, transnations, their codified and "official" languages, and other iterations of knowledge that maintain the myth that supposedly homogenous groups—or hybrid ones, articulated within the terms of the coloniality—can be the only meaningful bearers of memory. A multilingual university, then, de-balkanizes these emphases and extracts them from charged terms like "transnational" and "hybrid" and the discrete colonialities that they reinforce, engaging with them in a lived and embodied sense: that is, an institutional recognition of commonplace and ordinary ways of being, instead of decentered and marginalized in relation to a "pure" center.

THE CULTURAL NEUROLOGY OF TRANSLINGUAL SENSIBILITIES

> We are your linguistic nightmare, your linguistic aberration, your linguistic mestizaje, the subject of your burla. Because we speak with tongues of fire we are culturally crucified.
> **Gloria Anzaldúa, *Borderlands / La Frontera* (1987, 58)**

> "So, do you feel more South African or Portuguese?" I always feel "put on the spot," as I don't feel more or less of one or the other and I always feel like a traitor if I chose one over another. I'm not even both.
> **D. N. Ibrahim, "Being Bilingual . . . Multilingual Identities" (2013, 1)**

While ethno-relative linguistic sensibilities may be recognized with greater facility in multilingual environments, Gloria Anzaldúa's intrepid thinking unlinked Ernesto Quiñonez's barrio aesthetics from the exigencies of traditional grammars in ways that correspond to recent studies in neurolinguistics and pluricultural psychology. The use of multiple languages "interact[s] with cognitive functions, such as perception and memory" and has a close "relationship between language and conceptualisation of objects, actions, and relations that we express in language" (Filipović and Pütz 2014, 6, 7). While sole-language textual codifications (for instance, "literature in English" vis-à-vis "literature in Spanish") are dealt with almost universally as separate and isolated from one another, many linguists have noted, "There is no reason why a person who speaks both English and Spanish should behave in the same way as a monolingual speaker of either language," (Paul Meara qtd. in Kecskes and Papp 2000, ix). It has been shown that the "transfer of sociocultural norms and patterns of interaction" occurs when changing code (Kecskes and Papp 2000, x).Thus, in the case of multilingual performances restrained to one language or another, "communication transcends individual languages" and "transcends words," reflecting not separate linguistic silos but a unified linguistic base across the languages in a person's repertoire (Canagarajah 2013, 6). The multilingual university normalizes this multiplicity, facilitating new public and democratized forms of communication, the study of them, and the memory-making processes that engage those conditions.

MULTILINGUAL TEACHING OF MONOLINGUAL SUBJECT MATTER

The texture of a thought or feeling is queried, interrogated, and refined when a language change occurs—be it in a classroom, senate meeting, or gas station. While it may appear counterintuitive, multilingual teaching of monolingual subject matter opens channels of inquiry and interpretation that are only theoretical when our language availability is strained down to one system. In addition to de-foreignizing and decontaminating multilingual culture,[9] such methods provide many innovative ways to interpret monolingual texts. Many courses at the Universidad de Puerto Rico, even those taught explicitly in English or Spanish, involve interactions with language that are interlingual, translingual, and extra-lingual: faculty often use the multiple-competencies of our students and community in ways that evoke skills toward collective, generative, and nuanced knowledge-creation that transcend monolingual strictures.

Cora Monroe is a professor of comparative literature and French; she engages students by using specific accents, languages, and their mixtures to allude afield from the subjects at hand in ways that allow her classroom to flesh out underpinned meanings and significances embedded in each linguistic variation. Watching Cora Monroe lecture is like being in the presence of an electric storm: a thunderstorm storm often begins innocuously, far off on a horizon—occasionally flashes of light appear and disappear; far-off thuds report. You aren't sure if the storm is approaching you or moving away. A veil of mist falls. Dull thuds transition to booms that shake the room. At some imperceptible moment your attention has shifted from whatever is happening in your daily life to the tempest upon you. Thunderclaps sound, car alarms wail: lightning strikes tear at spacetime and timespace. And then the rain begins; everything around you has changed.

Like electric storm environment changes, Monroe's lectures move from language to language and accent to accent as they move through philosophies, worlds, and themes of study. She navigates several Englishes—central-Massachusetts taciturnity, North Carolinian African-American, flat CNN midwestern—and these transition into Frenches (with nuance that escapes me) and into Spanishes (and Spanglishes) of Aguadilla, Mayagüez, and Kissimmee, occasional cut-vowel jíbaro, and even more occasional nasal-heavy peninsular Castilian. Each intonation and dialectal shift lends distinction to a specific topic or subtopic, engaging subtle undertones in ways that illustrate concealed themes within the lesson—as well as to mark transitions from subject to subject. Watching and listening and participating in this form of pedagogy commands fluid boundaries not only between languages but subject-disciplines and communities, and while it may forefront a connectedness between ostensibly unrelated entities—Mayagüez and Martinique, Massachusetts and Haití, North Carolina and Castile—the languages of her pedagogy reflect the mobility, complexity and plurality of our classrooms. English-only and Spanish-only restrictions cloud what Cora Monroe and those like her do. "This is a circumstance that cannot be properly represented with solid blocs of color," argues Amitav Ghosh. "It calls instead for images borrowed from fluid dynamics—in other words it demands metaphors of liquidity, of flow rather than stasis. . . . Languages bleed into and mingle with each other in such intricate ways that everyone becomes individuated by their own, idiosyncratic conjunctions of language" (2020, 287).

While revelations available in multilingual pedagogy may be complicated within "best" practice exigencies of the monolingual university, Sara Castro-Klarén recommends that universities consider "offering courses in English as well as bilingual courses" in Spanish-language-cultural themes, a concept that would give counterbalance to "language stalls, which are assumed as incapable of communicating across the barrier that separates them" (2016, 10).[10] While creating, teaching, and learning across languages is treated as an aberrance by the monolingual university, using more than one language increases intellectual capacities beyond language, including enhanced abilities in goal-oriented activities, ambiguity tolerance, problem solving, concentration and attention levels, and task switching. The higher executive control has been described as a "neural signature" (Kovelman et al. 2008) that is manifest in less intellectual decline through ageing, and a "more perceptive understanding of the world" (Goodrich 2018, 1).

TRANSLINGUAL STUDENT LIFE

These mostly anonymous student comments, taken from surveys from 2018 to 2021, look in on how multilingual university life shapes and informs learning and development. Some responses are ironic and amusing, playing with the survey itself (which was—in the interests of this book, with a touch of irony—monolingual in English); the poignancy and fluency bring together many qualities of a translingual environment as both a knowledge-creation device and an identity-performance space. (Spelling and syntactic idiosyncrasies included.)

Do you ever mix languages in the same conversation?
A: Nunca mezclo ambos idiomas en una conversación.
A: Well, sí. Spanglish is a mix of spanish and english, which helps us understand english words, but in our way.
A: I do mix languages. The advantages of doing so are that I can express things faster. If I try to stick to one language, sometimes I tend to slow down because I am thinking of the correct term in the opposite language. Casual or friendly conversations tend to trigger these language shifts more than formal settings.
A: I do mix languages in the same conversation and I feel like I can get a better message across usually.
A: Yes, I mix languages! The advantage is that people actually get the concept of what I am saying if I forget how to say it in one language. It can happen at any time.

Is it ever difficult to limit yourself to one language? Have you experienced anxiety about a monolingual setting?
A: No pero a la vez sí.
A: Sometimes it is very difficult for me to speak only one language because my mind thinks in both languages.
A: There are some awkward constraints to using only one language. I understand we must do it sometimes. It limits how and what I feel, and how I express myself. It's like swimming with just your legs. I would rather not do it—but I can. (María Biaggi)

Are there emotions or thoughts that are accessible in one but not another?
A: There are some feelings and emotions available in Spanish, but

not in English. For example, anger and frustration arise in Spanish. Every time I have these emotions I tend to express them in Spanish only.

A: Spanish insults insult me more than the exact same thing in English.

A: Yes, it is very hard to express different types of love or affection in English. And Spanish lacks the cold, business logic that accompanies speaking in English.

A: In Spanish they are mostly anger, "love," and disappointment emotions/feelings. "Trolling" or the feeling you get from "trolling" is in English.

A: Spanish is more complicated and it includes genders and some verbs like "te amo" and "te quiero" that in English will just be "I love you" for both of them. So in that example English is less emotional, because there's only one option.

A: All of my romantic love life was in Spanish. I like Spanish because it is much more poetic. It is also really fun to play around with the wording in Spanish. English is more technical for me.

Have you ever been embarrassed because of your language use?
A: Only the Spanglish. But not in Puerto Rico.
A: Yes, in Spanish and English. It happened in the US a few times. And in Spain. I try not to listen to comments about accents and other things like that because most of the ones directed were made by people who are practically monolingual. For me taking criticism from someone who only speaks one language would force me to challenge them to learn about their world. But people from that mindset usually can't see beyond themselves, so it's not worth even the effort to say it to them in their own language. (Cristina Martín)

What advice or instructions would you give to faculty about language?
A: Sing it, live it, and have fun with it.
A: More languages make classes better, more interesting and engaging. Even when you can't understand them all. Each one has meanings and colors. Changing languages changes meanings even on the same book or poem. No sé que más decir.

A: I think more than one language can be "first" and classes in two languages is natural.

A: Changing languages in our discussions connects me more to the [monolingual] reading.

A: I talk in the language that the class needs from me. They should do the same.

A: Changes of language in instruction, cuando sucede me mantiene más atento.

These remarks are from Wireliz Soto-González, a graduate of Universidad de Puerto Rico, on the transition to another multilingual university, for graduate studies at Universitat de Barcelona:

> It was surprising that Spaniards use many words from English that we don't use in Puerto Rico. Like "bol" instead of "envase," referring to a bowl, and "footing" in Spain means "jogging" rather than what it means in English. They also modify the spelling of some English words to make them more pronounceable in Spanish, like "cúter" for "cutter."
>
> There's no doubt that Spanglish is a way of life. I came to reason with myself, and became very cautious about my expression depending on with whom I spoke. At the beginning I tried speaking only full-on Spanish; it didn't work. The occasional "so . . . " and "anyway . . ." and "OK . . ." were constantly present. When I forced it, I couldn't even translate them to Spanish. But in the end my Spanglish was more useful than anything: All of my peers said they envied it. Even with my faulty Spanglish-to-Spanish translations, my Castilian with these nuances seemed more complex, more eloquent, and sometimes more expressive than that of my Spanish peers and professors.
>
> How I could change from one language to another in the same sentence without any problem—my peers loved it, and actually asked for help with their English. On the other hand, professors didn't like it, and instead asked that every international student take a Catalan-language course (because we were in Catalonia, not Spain) and improve our Castilian.
>
> I realized in Spain that my English was excellent, and that sometimes it was easier to communicate in that language instead of Spanish. (qtd. in Herlihy-Mera 2018b, 1)

INSTITUTIONALIZATION OF LINGUISTIC HUMAN RIGHTS

A multilingual university licenses students to speak across their languages without humiliation or irony. Thus, the Universidad de Puerto Rico—in comparison to mainland institutions—is innovative, egalitarian, plural, decolonial, and emancipative in ways that monolingual institutions expressly prohibit and penalize. Our students' translingual agency empowers them to critique and design the interrelations between citizenship, culture, and language in our most important social institutions, and for that, it is the opinion of this author, that UPR graduates should be hired, admitted, elected, and chosen more often for positions of influence. The US university community should consider what we do as exemplary instead of an oddity.

To dwell on the obvious, a decolonized society requires multilingual public institutions. "In order for our educational programs to move beyond colonialism," note Díaz Soto and Kareem, "our learners need to be able to read the word and the world bilingually, biculturally, and multiculturally" (2006, 32). In the United States, laws command that elected officials be fluent in English; political naturalization even in Puerto Rico involves an English exam; even the smallest municipality cannot name Spanish as "co-official" language without a national outcry. Plurilingual ideas may appear utopian from within the monolingual violence of the status quo. But the notion that monolingual existence should continue in perpetuity is a dangerous delusion. While myopic ignorance is celebrated in many facets of US national culture (including presidential elections, like 2016) it is important ideas like "our universidades should be multilingües" be voiced if nothing more than so that they be said. Como bien dice Ernesto Cuba: Si no las nombramos, no existen.[11]

While a sudden or gradual shift to a multilingual university may be framed as detrimental to monolingual students in English (or other tongues) the overwhelming benefits—competencies that relate to mental capacities and physical health—are as sufficient reason to consider such a move. Significant economic, social, and cultural advantages would accompany the shift, as would the mental agility that has been shown to merge into non-language-related fields and activities. The advantages of extending multilingual ontologies of a community into its educational institutions may seem self-evident, but such a move in the United States would require both decolonial thinking and action. In relation to

Spanish, engaging multilingual knowledges in United States universities would normalize and academicize the performance of local Spanishes and Spanglishes, and as they shift from foreign to domestic, to normal, and to ordinary, some of the Euro-, Peninsular-, and English-centric constraints of the traditional learning settings would inevitably lose some of their toxic self-evidence. A fundamental notion of English-centric universities is that cultural knowledges performed in Spanish are objects that exist independently of our knowledge of them—and that English is the most-appropriate institutional vehicle to develop that knowledge. These conditions and social relations structure the conventional forms of knowledge-production and programmatically influence their outcomes, content, and event horizons in ways that keep local Spanishes and Spanglishes marginalized and "foreign" per institutional definitions.

The fundamentalist position that maintains an English-only institutional framework is a best practice at almost all universities and professional organizations belays the ways language and knowledge are interrelated: the way we communicate is not incidental to knowledges developed and what forms of community and belonging may be cultivated. The ways studies in Spanish-language cultural themes are entangled with English-centric institutions obfuscates, makes Eurocentric, and foreignizes the interactions, and while mindfulness of this constraint makes the failure of monolingualism apparent, the colonial grip that fundamentalist English-only forms of thinking has on institutions is perhaps axiomatic. Undoing this control requires a constellation of critical reflection and collective voices that reach into legal statutes, cultural norming, social traditions, and political exigencies. Opening multilingualism as practice, method, pedagogical emphases, and legitimizing apparatus could be understood as a multifold shift in institutional values; as a process, "plurilinguicization" of the university would involve:

1) Multiple languages could be understood as an inevitable part of scholarly life. This move would undo a tacit assumption: languages other than English that students have in their repertoire are useful only to the degree that they permit students to acquire English, the sole center of literacy in spaces claimed by the United States, thereby undoing the received monoliteracy exigence.
2) A linguistic policy based on lived realities of students, faculty, and the communities: Developing sensibilities through the commu-

nities' languages gestures toward a decolonization of institutional values in ways that engage students in generative knowledge-creation that is localized

3) Unlinking meaning-making from the mythologies of monolingualism: The ideological contamination of a monolingual university causes "the awkward constraints of using one language" (María Biaggi), while English-only mandates ensure a situation in which institutions cannot realize their missions for all students. The (dis)service to the multilingual community that a single language model enacts would be replaced by meaning-making processes that transform the role of local communities into voiced, sovereign spaces, descriptive of their populace instead of carriers of colonized cultural and linguistic violence.

In "The US: A Cemetery of Languages," Jorge Durand notes that in many places, not merely regions like Miami and Los Ángeles, "la lengua franca es el español."[12] If domestic status were recognized in Spanish and English (or other tongues), the work of the university would gesture toward institutions that domesticate, localize, and internalize communities now implicitly, explicitly, or de facto "foreign" to constituent components of the social group. These forms of institutionalization have enormous power: "With that recognition," writes Gloria Anzaldúa, "we became a distinct people. Something momentous happened to the Chicano soul—we became aware of our reality and acquired a name and a language (Chicano Spanish) that reflected that reality. Now that we had a name, some of the fragmented pieces began to fall together—who we were, what we were, how we had evolved. We began to get glimpses of what we might eventually become" (1987, 63).

CONCLUSION

OVERCOMING THE TRADITION OF SILENCE

I will overcome the tradition of silence.
Gloria Anzaldúa, *Borderlands / La Frontera* (1987, 59)

Cada palabra que redactas en español está mal escrita y merece
ser subrayada con el color de la sangre.
Héctor Huyke, on Microsoft Word, in conversation (2020)

We had no language to resist our own erasure.
Henry Giroux, qtd. in Brad Evans, "Histories of Violence" (2019, 1)

While for centuries Spanish has been weaponized in political and cultural affairs, since 2016 this phenomenon has accelerated, and some of the most toxic and sinister segments of contemporary US society—the racist, misogynist, ethnocentric, classist elements (including Donald Trump and many of his supporters)—directly benefit from how Spanish is foreignized in US universities.[1] More than a curricular focus or faculty specialization trend, the Euro-fetishization is a system of "identity politics" that extends far beyond campuses. Overloading the intellectual labor toward Spain,[2] focusing on material distant in time and space from our classrooms, encourages marginalization of students' cultures, languages, and experiences—a dismissal that forcefully and violently situates local traditions and Spanishes not only as "foreign" but also as inferior, substandard, irrelevant, and unworthy of scholarly attention. The monolingual university constructs and defends this architecture.

Teasing out the political and social mechanisms embedded in the "foreign" Euro-"masterscript," local Spanishes cannot be "correct," accurate, aesthetic (only folkloric or heritage), or desirable: always secondary to English *and* inferior to Peninsular tracts, US Spanish is institutionalized in a way that forces Latinx students to pass into "correct" linguistic patterns that further invalidate their cultures and experiences. Organized around certainties that "reproduce Western-centric dominant and imperial values," notes Donaldo Macedo, these pedagogies disrespect the linguistic and cultural "knowledge that students bring to the classroom," urging a student to "eradicate her Spanish dialect so that she can learn standard Spanish, preferably Castilian" (2019, 10–11). Local cultures are disparaged to the point that students rarely interact with their community to "practice, say, the Spanish they are currently learning. The expectation is that they will go to Spain to be fully immersed in the 'model Spanish' reflected in the curriculum, visit the Prado Museum in Madrid, and admire the Roman monuments left behind in Spain" (Macedo 2019, 10). The very notion of bilingualism, notes Macedo, is scaled and racialized in ways that "typecast[s] Latinx ethnically so as to devalue their human worth. Their bilingualism, unlike the bilingualism achieved [through 'foreign-language' class and study abroad,] represents vestiges of colonialism in which the minoritized speakers experience subordination in speaking both their mother tongues . . . often under coercive conditions" (2019, 8).[3]

Academicized and institutionalized into "official" and "best" practices, this systematic eradication of local cultures is largely premised upon transnational myths: such tradition may be extinguished because the only valid and recognizable vessel of significance—the (trans)national container—is self-evident and unassailable. If the nation's symbols, protagonists, memberships, narratives, and language(s) are established beyond dispute, universities only disseminate the already-known message: English is domestic; Spanish is foreign. Since Homi Bhabha's interventions decades ago, hybrid approaches have been institutionalized with English as the unquestionable center and imperial tongue of the United States, the site from which all hyphenation is to occur: to think, write, speak, or interact in Spanish is to engage in a hybrid, signifying inferiority; membership in such a group requires subaltern status forward and backward in time, in eternal subordination to an "American" qualifier. In this way, transnational and transatlantic knowledges redouble a priori imperial coordinates—the binary essences of pure and discrete cultural groups are centers of the system: these are the failed codes of Americanism and Hispanism.

Disputing and disrupting this absolute form of knowledge resists "the very definition of the United States," notes Mark Bauerlein. "Are we a 'Western' nation? Is there any *unum* in the *pluribus*?" (2020, 1). The cultural and linguistic implementation of *unum* upon others is a source of immense power, and like other fundamentalist apology, Bauerlein foregrounds trans/national and "Western" experiences as the only recognizable locus of experience, mapping "we" through colonial theses that repeat archaic and toxic myths of conquest:

1) imperial directives (an English-language, Christian, neoliberal, and industrialized life in which Spanish is foreign) are the "root" experience for all who reside in spaces conquered and claimed by the United States;
2) the language, writing, art, creativity, and aesthetics of all residents have been profoundly (or relationally) influenced by these colonial directives; and
3) the existence of US empire (including colonized university curricula that repeat these linguistic and cultural prescriptions) is beneficial to the lives of all exposed to it.

While Bauerlein presumes a center that is Eurocentric and English-speaking, in his imagination Euro-, Christian-, English-centric cultural supremacy is self-evident in places like Puerto Rico, Texas, and Iowa. Iowan congressman Steve King reflects on the intersection of higher education and the application of this power: "Why did I sit in classes teaching me about the merits of our history and our civilization?" He continues, "White nationalist, white supremacist, Western civilization—how did that language become offensive?" (House Resolution 789 2020, 1)?[4] Bauerlein and King's narratives are trapped in a toxic transnational history that makes possible (and perhaps inevitable) systematized murder and deportation, grisly police-death, and what Eduardo Galeano termed "murder by poverty" (1971, 5). In all spaces claimed by the United States, these are the costs of colonial social power. The language, communities, and foreign/domestic myths in relation to Spanish and Spanish-language cultures recodify those centers through monolingual universities.[5]

Bauerlein and King, among many others, cannot address the reality that trans/national containers are nonexceptional experiences—nor that they habitually fail as descriptors.[6] The overarching insistence that social and academic systems rely on them, use their codes and received knowledge as universal—and unexamined, singular—truth, is a method to conserve the status quo and its Eurocentrism by force, a track that guides the very nature of what occurs in US universities, from accreditation to administration to classroom learning. Bauerlein insists he is not against content changes, but he maintains faculty must "set them within a similar structure" and goes on: "One lineage excludes others, but that exclusion is necessary to a successful course. . . . This is a cognitive matter, and perhaps an aesthetic one, too" (2020, 1).[7] The colonialist and racist farce that European material culture is imbued with superior cognition or aesthetics is a legitimizing apparatus that is strategic, deceptive, prejudicial, jingoist, fascist, and—lamentably—ordinary: restricting degree programs, course themes, tenure lines, faculty specializations, and departmental/professional-association nomenclatures to specific patterns of time, places, geographies, trans/nations, Atlantic crossings, and language developments are designed to impose order and exert colonial power. They press the status quo's failures onto Latinx immediate realities, emotions, cultures, languages, and ways of being. "In this context," argues Paulo Freire, "the invaders penetrate the cultural context of another group . . . they impose their own view of the world upon those they invade and inhabit the creativity of the invaded by curbing their expression" (1970, 152). Racism and linguicide are not distant consequences of this pedagogic canon, and one central myth is reiterated across disciplines and institutions: trans/national approaches (with all their failures and exclusions) are an appropriate—and sometimes the *only acceptable*—method to discuss material culture, community dynamics, and individual agency. This buries the Spanish language deep within an a priori milieu that makes hyphenations and subordination and other aphorisms for "foreign"[8] in relation to English the only possible institutional characterization.

While this legitimization apparatus has been academicized and institutionalized for centuries, recent views dispute its certainties: "If we are trapped in the [national] state model," queries Manuela Lavinas Picq, "if we can only think of ourselves as 'American,' 'French,' 'Ecuadorian,' 'Guatemalan,' 'Brazilian,' how do we move out? How do we see the [trans/nation] as one option?" (2018, 1). She envisions this shift as a creative, generative process, one that is urgent and overdue: "If they don't exist they are to be invented" (2018, 1).[9] Institutional mores defined through nonnational metrics have been organized around language, age, culture, digitality, city-states, and (as argued in this book) local communities and their sensibilities. While such additional scaffoldings are antidotes to some of the exclusions that characterize Spanish-language cultural studies in the United States, until the national and transnational exceptionalisms cease to dominate the structures of life and death, imperial directives (concerning foreign/domestic, Spanish/English, valid/invalid human beings—and their communities) will continue to define and legitimize academic treatises that trace the existing outlines through English-centric institutions of higher education.[10]

These epistemes legislate imminent danger: while more than 230 people of Mexican descent were murdered from 1848 to 1928 in Texas by extrajudicial mobs or lynching—some by Texas Rangers (Gamboa 2017, 1)—a resurgence of Juan Crow laws in Alabama, Arizona, New Mexico, Georgia, and elsewhere continues. The surge in Latinx-targeted legislative discrimination is fueled in part by what John Tanton describes as his desire to have "a European-American majority, and a clear one at that" (qtd. in Buser 2011, 1). Thomas Saenz observes that 2017 Texas Senate Bill 4 "has racism written all over it," while John Morán González comments, "This is a step backwards in terms of having Mexican-Americans thought of as really US citizens, as opposed to foreigners rather than interlopers" (qtd. in Gamboa 2017, 1).[11] This is increasingly a "Juan Crow world," notes Richard Cohen, where "human rights are trampled, communities terrorized and families torn apart all in the name of getting tough on 'illegals.' Anyone who looks or sounds 'foreign' [i.e., speaking Spanish] is a suspect" (2008, 1). And when the US military enters homes in Georgia by force, finding "the wrong kind of 'Mexicans'; they were US citizens," there is no penalty, recourse, or apology for these lawful forms of terrorism (Lovato 2008, 1).[12]

The social engineering of Spanish as foreign is central to this legislative and "civil" brutality. Foreignization is enforced through violence and death but buttressed by English-monolingual social institutions, imperial narratives in history, politics and culture, and colonized Eurocentric Spanish-cultural studies at doctoral, master, baccalaureate, secondary, and primary levels. The system of miseducation enacts hierarchical planes of existence and channels the notion of literacy itself through English and away from Spanish, wholly defaulting on the latter.[13] Aligning with these colonial literacy programs, in all disciplines (and at nearly every institution) Spanish-speaking faculty must "demonstrate high and near native proficiency in English, whereas their native proficiency and literacy in Spanish [is] generally ignored" and "routinely dismissed" (Macedo 2019, 1). The imposition of English as the "standard colonial language" is a method to destroy any Spanish-speaking "way of being" through the university and its activities, a program that "is not viewed as racism" or linguicide "but as progress" (Macedo 2019, 14).

These tendencies are toxic in all regions but are acutely violent in Spanish-dominant areas. "Socially created by the dominant ruling class," observes Macedo, they "create an ideological distinction so as to devalue, dismiss, and dehumanize. Once the distinction is achieved, its sole purpose is to devalue the corresponding cultures . . . races, ethnicities, and class" (2019, 11). Eurocentric, monolingual (English-only, Spanish-foreign) universities endorse circumstances in which Spanish-speaking students and faculty must explore local cultures and ways of being as inferior, meaningless, peripheral, exotic, and external to everything that is institutionally routine and common. The ideas in this book ask scholars who work in traditional modes of inquiry, pedagogy, and knowledge creation to test the limits of their worlds, to challenge English and Eurocentrism as unassailable tenets, to dismantle the monolingual university and its exclusions, and to move away from the known domains of knowledge and colonized certainties that characterize contemporary Spanish-language cultural studies. My university is an example of how to do this: if US higher education were Puertoricanized, if literacy were realized per decolonial epistemes—i.e., largely *in Spanish* where English is *de facto* secondary, requiring literacy *in Spanish* for degree conferral—and if linguistic and cultural expertise were cultivated at the intersection of Spanish and English, this would allow a de-exoticizing, domesticating quality in the lives of students for whom two languages is "not something exotic or even particularly noteworthy; but a fact of life, its absurdities and fucked-up politics and violence and juxtapositions not so much a story to tell as a backdrop against which the satisfactions and preoccupations of daily life were set" (Tyx 2013, 63).[14]

Ignacio Sánchez Prado believes "the academy has failed to address an open war" on these students and their communities, a situation that is pointedly ironic in a neoliberal sense: while nearly all demographics are in a precipitous enrollment decline, "we are in the midst of a boom of Latinx students" (2020, 1). Nevertheless, the material is "taught as a *social problem* but seldom as the source of some of humanity's most important cultural works," a reality that "replicates the stereotypes affecting Latinxs and Latin Americans in U.S. society at large."[15] Sánchez Prado has astute comments about the role of academic categories in this social matter: "Spanish is lumped together with other 'foreign' languages—even though it is definitely not a foreign language" (2020, 1). Further obstacles are constructed by university officials and "are the consequence of the outright discrimination," observes Sánchez Prado. "An administrator once told a friend of mine that the only reason he supported the Spanish department was because students needed to be able to communicate with the help" (2020, 1). Sánchez Prado also critiques the ways national publications and professional associations participate in the system of inequity, saying it is "hard to elicit solidarity from people in fields like Spanish when the problems of English monopolize fundamental conversations critical to many other fields, particularly in venues like this one [the *Chronicle of Higher Education*], read carefully by administrators with the power to decide our extinction"; moreover, the centrality of English is reflected in the "MLA's usual practice of scheduling English and foreign-language panels in separate hotels altogether" (2020, 1).[16]

Research in these fields is underfunded due to their externalized and peripheral roles, a circumstance that Sánchez Prado relates to Alfred Coester's 1916 book, *Literary History of Spanish America*, which "serves as a testament to . . . how little things have changed in the century or so since its publication"; and Coester's "question ('*are Latin American writings literature?*') comes to my mind every time the press laments the demise of literary studies and the humanities" (2020, 1; my emphasis). If 1916 vanguard ideas like American Adam, Frontier Myths, and the Transnational Theses maintain their central ontological and epistemological supremacy in perpetuity, English and studies thereof will remain the threshold of existence, social participation, and intellectual legitimacy, as the sole "authentic" and "American" communicative axis. That set of narratives has required—and has enjoyed—Eurocentric monolingual universities as sites of ideological implementation.[17]

THE POWER OF DECOLONIAL MEMORY-MAKING

Sin imágenes, no hay memoria

Malinche, qtd. in Laura Esquivel, *Malinche* (2006, 27)

While "states," "districts," "territories," and other polities claimed by the US government are seldom discussed as colonized spaces, the institutional foreignization of Spanish in US universities has echoes of the 2005 French law on colonialism, which requires textbooks to "acknowledge and recognize in particular the positive role of the French presence . . . especially in North Africa" (see article 4 in "Loi portant reconnaissance de la Nation et contribution nationale en faveur des Français rapatriés"). As Bélen Fernández notes: "Americans, too, quickly mastered . . . methods of exoticization, dehumanization, and disempowerment, as well as other handy tricks for facilitating imperial conquest; after all, in strategically valuable areas, . . . one can't be burdened with natives who fancy themselves in control of their own destinies" (2019, 24). Higher education is an integral part of systems of ideology, power, and legitimacy that are designed to ensure any credentialled intellectual experience is "very state-centric, very colonial, very Eurocentric" and that attempts to construct a reality in which "we only exist through the state in the world" (Lavinas Picq 2018, 1). The silence produced in these institutions is programmatic—and monolingual literacy in English[18] codifies the oppression: "Research finds that the overwhelming dominance of [monolingual] Euro-American perspectives leads many [Latinx] students to disengage from academic learning" (Sleeter 2011, vii), a situation that summons an important inquiry: If Latinx students and their communities, languages, and cultures were to have a domestic place at the US university, what would the studies look like? How would the curricular scripts, institutional architectures, and epistemological focal points reexamine the connection between pedagogy, cultural reality, language, community, membership, and the received exigencies of monocultural and monolingual centers? What would become of English (and heritage speakers of English), Peninsular Spanish, and Spanglish? What about the colonial metanarratives that frame the institutions and provide cultural cohesion to weave the social orchestration together? Will the hierarchies that characterize the status quo survive decolonization?

It is incumbent upon faculty to equip students with the tools to address those uncertainties, to write their own stories about their own worlds in their own words. As students move outside culturally assigned labels in ways that jam traditional metanarratives, their images, texts, digital and print literatures, languages, politics, and systems of reality enunciate emancipative opportunities that narrate interconnected presents, futures, and pasts in Spanishes that are seldom recognized by their institutions. Since English and Spanish are pre-embedded in systems of authority, simply replacing or complementing English with Spanish (or vice versa) could be read as a power struggle—and, as Víctor Figueroa has argued, "To oppose power is still to be defined by power" (2015, 77). But such a shift may be characterized as a *process* external to the binaries of struggle: such a reconceptualization "changed my life" notes Paulo Freire; "It gave me a language that enabled education to be understood as a political *process*" and one that "changed the conception of what it means to work with people who were normally considered 'voiceless,' and understand that they do have a voice and can narrate to themselves" (qtd. in França 2019, 1, my emphasis). In this way, decolonial praxes test "what Fanon and Césaire required," writes Edward Said in "Representing the Colonized," the process of "abandon[ing] the fixed ideas of settled identity and culturally authorized definition" (200, 315).[19]

If student-creation exists above, away, within, beneath, and beyond the state and its authorized (often transnational) exceptionalisms, a decolonial turn in Spanish-language cultural studies would transcend the superficial externalities of Hispanism and Americanism, leading toward an encounter that is more relatable to students' lives and attuned to local sensibilities. The narrativization of student experience would have important de-fetishizing effects, reanchoring notions of belonging in educational institutions that are defined by and for local communities through study, creation, resistance, and critique. A move to cultivate new consciousnesses and institutionalize them, through complexity and critical pedagogical modes, requires students and faculty to cross languages, codes, histories, centers, and modalities. In short, it requires exploration of historical disunities and discontinuities that have been crowded out by the exigencies of Spain-centrism.

DECOLONIAL EXCEPTIONALISMS IN LOCAL, LATINX, TRANSLINGUAL, AND COVID-19 CONTEXTS

The institutional shifts suggested in this book imagine a structural condition in which Hispanism's narrative erasures and historical gaps come into focus—not merely as appropriate intellectual concentrations but as structural inevitabilities: enrollment would mean expertise in local languages, traditions, cultures, habits, histories, Spanishes, and the trans and multilingualisms that characterize here and now, futures and pasts. Such a tact perceives Hispanism as a problem to overcome rather than project to complete. Reappropriating and criticizing the clarifying terms has the potential to denaturalize Eurocentrism into a pedagogical shape "in which many worlds fit" (Shenker 2012, 432): in this procedural and democratizing turn, the common ground of localization involves "circumspection vis-à-vis the very categories we use to define social reality" (Kramsch and Zhang 2018, 216).

An important aspect of the received exceptionalism in the US academy[20] can be documented across two centers:

1) Eurocentric epistemes; and
2) fetishization of intellectual labor realized at top-ranked research universities that have less than 50 percent Latinx enrolment.[21]

A decolonizing structural move across these disciplines would nudge both axes:

1) Latinx languages, cultures, and experiences, in their complexities and multiplicities, would displace Spain-centrism as the essential matter of one-to-one scrutiny, research, critique, and teaching.
2) Valuable ideas would become enunciable by students at universities like mine. One hopes these students would then begin to dominate tenure-line appointments, publications, grants, external funding, and the other metrics of academic life that are largely cloistered off to scholars at a small set of institutions, many of which are wealthy and private; none approach 50 percent Latinx enrollment.

Moving "exceptional" from traditional centers and institutions toward Latinx realities requires further critique, analysis, and consideration. Since COVID-19, things have shifted dramatically—looming budgetary concerns will decimate jobs, increase teaching loads, and erase whatever research support existed. But at the institutional cohort that tends to dominate academic appointments and external funding (including NEH, ACLS, Mellon, and other organizations), the effects will be minimal in comparison to universities with 50 percent or more Latinx enrollments.

In light of the emerging crisis, ACLS (American Council of Learned Societies) launched a shift in programming to support new and recent PhDs in humanities and social science fields. "The profile of our grantmaking is changing considerably," comments ACLS president Joy Connolly. "We stand to lose whole cohorts of PhDs to the pandemic's financial impact, and we hope to be able to help mitigate its effects" (Connolly, email to the author, May 7, 2020). The 2020 initiative is similar in aims and structure to the ACLS "New Faculty Fellows" program implemented in the wake of the 2008 meltdown. That iteration (2010–2013) resulted in postdoc positions for PhDs from the following universities (number of positions received, institution):

13—UC Berkeley	3—Princeton	1—Pitt
12—Harvard	3—Virginia	1—USC
10—Yale	3—Duke	1—Case Western
10—Chicago	2—Maryland	1—Carnegie Mellon
9—UCLA	2—Illinois	1—Brown
7—NYU	2—Northwestern	1—UC Irvine
7—Michigan	2—Stony Brook	1—Tulane
7—Columbia	2—Arizona	1—Rochester
7—U. Penn	2—Penn State	1—Iowa
6—Johns Hopkins	2—Colorado	1—Indiana
5—Minnesota	2—Texas	1—U. Washington
5—Wisconsin	2—UC Davis	1—Rice
5—UC Santa Barbara	2—Vanderbilt	1—MIT
5—Cornell	1—Notre Dame	0—HHE
4—Stanford	1—Georgetown	0—TBCU
3—Rutgers	1—Syracuse	0—Tribal universities

Like NEH (the National Endowment for the Humanities), Mellon, and other cohort organizations, ACLS negotiates excellence in ways that makes receiving support more likely for applicants from some institutions: "I'll share my experience with ACLS New Faculty Fellows. There are very few fellows chosen [approximately 10 percent funding rate]. The application process is non-standard, requiring more from both applicant and letter-writers. It was a long distraction in my job application process. From both my experience and my colleagues' experience, *it's much easier to get a tenure-track offer*. I also learned, anecdotally, that a fellow who also has a tenure-track offer is encouraged to turn the fellowship down" (Sydera 2011, 1; my emphasis). While COVID-19 is exacerbating the situation, pre-pandemic data from tenure-line humanities appointments evidences that "virtually no one moves up" (Dunn 2015, 1), and thus—regardless of talent and expertise—scholars with "top" PhDs receive positions throughout the academy; "middle" PhDs, from the median and down; and "bottom" PhDs are restricted to appointments within their own cohort.[22] (The "bottom" cohort is exceptional in that faculty are hired from every sector of PhD-granting institutions.) The data for humanities awards mirror the hiring situation: "We noticed that those with an elite degree (Ivy League, Stanford, University of Chicago)," observe Claire Grossman, Stephanie Young, and Juliana Spahr, "are nine times more likely to win than those without one. And more specifically, those who attended Harvard are 17 times more likely to win" (2021, 1). If academic competition has these exclusions and controls without pandemics or economic crashes, "Where did we get this idea that only the top 1% of job candidates [who received ACLS grants] need any support or any breaks?" (Sydera 2011, 1). The ACLS "New Faculty Fellows" program is, according to Sydera, "in short: nice idea, poor implementation, helps no one."

But some disagree: after studies at University of Virginia and a UCLA PhD, Austin Graham won an ACLS position in the first iteration of the program, one of several similar grants he received before landing on the tenure track. "Postdocs rescued me," he comments. "And I know that was the case for a lot of other scholars of my generation" (qtd. in Cassuto 2020, 1). Graham has since received tenure at Columbia. While he feels his numerous pre-tenure-track fellowships were "a godsend" for him and PhDs in the elite cohort, what happened to the "others"—specifically, students at universities like mine? If data show ACLS (and similar fellowship) cohort grantees *already* enjoy such privilege in tenure appointments, fetishizing their labor in postdocs only redoubles the predicament for those who lack the social and cultural capital (or the desire, economic status, or of a combination of these) to enroll in those institutions. Moreover, many studies show top students from Latinx and other demographics systematically blocked from opportunities avoid those institutions for a variety of shrewd reasons (Herlihy-Mera 2015, 90). Their talents are often developed on campuses like the UPR, Morehouse, and Diné College. But since the valuation fetishization in both hiring and fellowships has such strict limits, those scholars are almost entirely absent from academic appointments and postdocs designed to address the crisis.

The ACLS New Faculty Fellows from 2010–2013 did not vary from that model: there were no PhDs from universities with 50 percent or more Latinx enrollment or 50 percent or more Pell Grants,[23] making the "downturn" period one of comparative abundance for scholars in the privileged cohort, as their already ample options *multiplied*. In this respect, the very notion of "crisis" should come into view: in comparison to UPR, the PhDs from the above list have experienced a significantly different "crisis" in terms of scholarly resources (fellowship opportunities, funding— for pedagogy, research, outreach, or any other initiative—or employment prospects). Yet the "crisis management" initiatives from the humanities grant-funding bodies support almost exclusively scholars who already enjoy the immense privileges of their station, and thus repeat the exclusions that this book critiques.

I was appointed to Universidad de Puerto Rico in 2009 and experienced what this downturn did to our students, to our campus, and to our community. While 2008 erased the careers of many PhDs in UPR's cohort (and in comparison, a small number from Graham's cohort),[24] COVID-19 has wrought circumstances largely unprecedented—and they will be most damaging to students at universities like mine. Since ACLS and similar associations traditionally organize merit using analogous metrics, virtually identical scales of exclusion characterize data across nearly all academic activity (admissions, fellowships, hiring, external funding, publication opportunities, and so on): ironically, universities with more than 50 percent Latinx enrollment are absent from the merit charts even in the tenure-line appointments, grants, and publications *that explicitly concern Latinx topics*. This has a direct impact on what occurs on my campus and at similar institutions: In fields like "crisis studies" (concerning colonialism, hurricanes, pandemics, or earthquakes) and even "Puerto Rican studies," data from external funding and hiring competitions, publications, ad hoc committee appointments, and so forth indicate that innovation, excellence, and "merit" on those topics *cannot* be enunciated by UPR students, faculty, or the community the way they can be articulated elsewhere; almost without exception, the resources on those topics go to scholars at top-ranked universities. Such preferences amount to an unsubtle attack on what it means to study and work in Puerto Rico, what it means to be human, what it means to endure crises, among other topics that are central to the disciplines themselves. As Musa al-Gharbi comments, "tenured and tenure-track professors exploit and perpetuate" these inequalities: "The publications and grants these faculty are able to secure, precisely as a result of this privilege, are then used to justify institutional inequality on meritocratic grounds: we deserve our advantages—'look at our rate of production as compared to everyone else!'" (2020, 1).[25] But the academy doesn't have to be like this. It is structured to be so. As Nelly Pereira comments: "Políticas y jerarquías institucionales como estas parecen fósiles vivos. Pueden vegetar mucho tiempo hasta su periodo de muda. Las incoherencias se quedan en práctica por una confianza grotesca en el relato. ACLS mantiene que la otorgación desigual de recursos es aceptable porque la jerarquía de mérito los aprueba" (Pereira 2020, email to the author, May 3, 2020).

One cannot hear UPR students because the academy has silenced them. They are foreignized, marginalized, exoticized and thus muzzled in grants, hiring, admissions, prizes, and publications. As I have argued in this book, our campus should be a model for every institution and academic organization in the United States: what has evolved here cannot occur elsewhere because of Juan Crow laws and the residual racism, classism, English-centrism, and other anti-Latinx ills that fill in the background of US life and higher education. It is difficult to dispute that students, faculty, and the communities served at Ivy + Stanford, Chicago, Michigan, Berkeley, UCLA, as well as by ACLS, NEH, and MLA (and in fact every institution and professional organization mentioned in this book) would benefit, especially but not solely in Spanish-language cultural studies, if the scholarly conditions in those institutions were more like at the UPR.[26] But the colonial power of a deep-seated exclusion—always codified in "competitions" that are ostensibly winnable by UPR scholars—pushes students like ours out of interview rooms and hastens their texts toward the editor's or prize committee's or grant reviewer's wastebasket.

COVID-19, AND A NEW FUTURE FOR HUMANITIES FUNDING?

The humanities in Puerto Rico have withstood an existential, colonial crisis that long-predates COVID-19 and Hurricane María. In the aftermath of hurricane, my humanities department endured incredible austerity cuts combined with a flotilla of grant rejections. As we consider where to apply in 2023 and beyond, it's difficult—and borders the absurd—to see so many colleges and universities that repeatedly receive funding have two resources we lack: 1) active institutional budgets for humanities projects, and 2) considerable humanities-specific private donations. Consider the past several years: Harvard, New York University, and the University of Southern California's recent humanities gifts were greater than $200 million; a single $75 million donation went to the Johns Hopkins philosophy department. At Yale, humanities-specific gifts have included $150 million to the School of Drama, an anonymous $50 million donation, and another $25 million donation.

The situation on my campus and at other universities like ours is a world apart from that sector the academy. But we apply to the same grant competitions, many of which are from public sources. Given the financial circumstances, especially at public institutions, such award practices undermine the mission of the humanities. In the era of COVID-19, grant-making organizations should be attentive to the lived realities across the academy. At my university, we have incredible teaching loads. We do not have release time or travel funds for archival research or to attend conferences. We have very little support for campus and community events. We do not have sabbaticals. All of this was the case *before* Hurricane María. Since the storm hit the island, the PROMESA austerity has cut the UPR budget by 40 percent.

Meanwhile, we are embedded in and colonially subordinated to a culture of funding that *reduces* rather than *expands* humanities scholarship: in the clearest of terms, when Harvard (or any university in its cohort) and UPR apply for a grant, and Harvard et al. are funded, one project goes forward: that of Harvard's cohort. If UPR receives an award, *two projects* will be completed: 1) UPR's, and 2) that of the Harvard et al. cohort. While one could make a case that Harvard scholars (and those in their cohort) cannot complete their work without external funding (it may be difficult to believe, but you could make the case), it is not in dispute that UPR students and faculty cannot complete or begin projects without external support: *it is a lived experience*. When any funding goes to Harvard or its cohort, the grant itself *decreases* the number of humanities projects realized. While this state of affairs is toxic, classist, discriminatory, elitist, and participates in the exceptionalist fetishization (and therefore dehumanization) of some scholarly communities, the situation is unnecessary and preventable.

In *How Professors Think*, Michèle Lamont's analyses of humanities and social science fellowship competitions make clear that "assessing need is largely framed as illegitimate—panelists do not even mention it as a consideration" (2009, 228). Written before the 2020 earthquakes and COVID-19, our 2019 National Endowment for the Humanities submission, "Engaging the Humanities in Times of Crisis,"[27] sought support amid the post-María conditions that define daily life on the island. Considering the earthquakes of 2020 and the pandemic, the aims of the proposal were prophetic. Our application requested support for release time, conferences and speakers, and materials (books, projectors, and Project Muse credentials). Many scholars have access to those resources through their universities—no external funding is required. But that's not the case at my institution. Among the rejection paperwork were comments indicating that the project was "Not Competitive" among the others:

> This project's design is not rigorous at all with regard to its critical conceptualization of "crisis" in Puerto Rico or about what the impact the practical, useful outcomes might be. Similarly, any mention of assessment lacks rigorous description and detail, as well as of actual methodological considerations. Any sort of valuable measurement in this proposal comes of primarily at an evaluation of its events. There is no discussion of how these talks/workshops, and the publication of their content, will translate into new courses, or of how these courses would be evaluated. There is just not enough serious discussion of this proposal's curricular intentions or meaningful visualization of its lasting impact. Its distinct parts are simply

not well integrated nor is their integration conceptualized as integral to the project's success.

The proposal mentions that the Center that would be created would continue to exist beyond the grant period but there is no explanation of where funding would come from for this to be able to happen, nor is there any such commitment in any institutional letter. Finally, given the importance a successful model for "teaching" about crisis and crisis management or avoidance, the dissemination plans are limited only to PR and do not take into account further dissemination beyond PR, except through a website. No conferences or other presentation formats are discussed, nor is any sharing of the materials and findings with public and other K-12 schools on the island, which are also in crisis and reeling from the very same crisis.

FEASIBILITY: In its current state, this project is not very feasible for all the already mentioned reasons and due to at least one other consideration—the primary project director's qualifications. Her CV does not reflect the kind of administrative experience or intellectual rigor she might need to successfully pull off this project.

POTENTIAL FOR SIGNIFICANT IMPACT: Given what is at its core, the project could have a very significant impact but doubtfully would due its poor conceptualization and design.

Your initial rating for this project

NC, Not Competitive

Harvard, Princeton, Stanford, Brown, and University of Pennsylvania scholars, and many others from the same cohort, have received incredible sums of money from NEH since September 20, 2017. Had scholars at those universities received the above rejection, they could file away the email and, if necessary, take steps to arrange institutional travel funds, release time or a sabbatical, or other support, in order to complete the project. When scholars in that cohort need extramural support—it is a situated need; certainly some of their proposals *require* external funding, but this is not always the case. It would appear that many scholars—not only those at Harvard, Princeton, and the like—have all the institutional scaffolding necessary to complete what we proposed to NEH regardless of external funding. For context on the institutions submitting competitive proposals, some NEH funding cycles since Hurricane María show:

Princeton University, $1.75 million;
New York University, $1.36 million;
Cornell University, $1.25 million;
University of Pennsylvania, $869,000;
University of Chicago, $804,000;
Brown University, $481,000; and
Stanford University, $310,000.

Our grant solicited $59,000. In a strange twist, grants supporting post-María projects in Puerto Rico often go to mainland colleges and universities. The Andrew W. Mellon Foundation granted $150,000 to Brown University for "Emergency Support for UPR [the University of Puerto Rico] after Hurricane Maria" and $325,000 to Michigan State University for the "Puerto Rico Disaster Archive." Northwestern University has also received more than a $1 million for Puerto Rico–centered projects since the storm (Herlihy-Mera 2021). While some of those funds reach the island, the symbolism of the situation is important.

Since 2010, my campus at Mayagüez received $22,000 in total from Mellon, while the entire University of Puerto Rico—consisting of eleven institutions—received a little more than $1 million. Meanwhile, in the same decade, Mellon awarded tens of millions to institutions including:

University of Chicago, $41 million;
Columbia University, $40 million;
Yale University, $39 million;
Princeton University, $39 million;
Stanford University, $35 million;
New York University, $32 million;
Harvard University, $28 million;
University of Pennsylvania, $23 million;
Cornell University, $23 million;
Northwestern University, $23 million;
Johns Hopkins University, $22 million.

On my campus, a 10 percent stake of any of the above totals would mean new tenure lines, robust support for our post-María and earthquake work, and incredible opportunities for our students, faculty members, and community in the face of COVID-19. It would fundamentally change our institution in ways that reflect the mission of the humanities. What circumstances cause such funding disparities? What happens during peer reviews?

Mark W. Roche, a professor the University of Notre Dame, described a stint as ACLS referee: "Besides Notre Dame," on the committee "were Berkeley, Dartmouth, Duke, and Princeton." At some stages the committee was "looking for excuses to eliminate candidates" and factors external to proposals were important: "Applicants who had a good résumé as a result of other grants and book prizes, etc., were more likely to receive support." Roche noted that "the ability to convince the audience that the applicant is the appropriate person" could be key. Echoing our NEH reviews, he observed that "candidates were sometimes described as not being up to the task." And he added that "well established scholars who write letters, endowed chair holders, leaders of professional societies, leading scholars in the field, Nobel Prize winners, carry more weight than associate professors" (qtd. in Herlihy-Mera 2021).

I don't know that scholars at the institutions serving on that committee can understand faculty life at a university like mine. They esteem social connections unavailable to me, and they respect attributes that have little to do with the proposals. The way Roche describes what they value, whose opinions are important, and how they make decisions brings to light some serious concerns about such peer reviews. Partly in relation to those evaluation practices, many faculty and students at my university are disenfranchised from these grants to the point that they do not apply. When we do apply, one must also subtract the considerable time spent drafting the proposal from the academic lives of those who do not receive funding, a part of the equation that does not exist in the institutional cohort mentioned by Roche.

We spent three months without running water and a year without regular access to electricity (there was no electricity at all for six of those months) in Mayagüez after Hurricane María. Class was in session using generators three months after the storm. Our department lost Carlos Fajardo, an artist and professor. Two non-tenure-track faculty and I published an installment of *Voces del Caribe* on "Crisis" in the aftermath without electricity and without support (institutional or external) and dedicated it to him. This was before the earthquakes in 2020 and the COVID-19 pandemic. By any metric, our department is uniquely (not to say "exceptionally") situated to take on the project we proposed to NEH. But lacking the privilege of the scholars who received funding, we couldn't and didn't continue it. As the paperwork documents, we are "not competitive."

To address the collapse in UPR funding, the external funding imbalances, the post-María/earthquakes crises, and COVID-19 in Puerto Rico, members of our humanities department reached out to ACLS, NEH, and Mellon, challenging them to make their awards more accessible to non-tenure-track faculty and scholars at High-Hispanic-Enrollment Institutions (HHEs) like ours—as well as Historically Black Colleges and Universities (HCBUs), Tribal Institutions, and universities with more than 50 percent Pell enrollment. Mariam Colón-Pizarro, Sara Gavrell-Ortiz, Héctor Huyke, and I recommended:

Applications and evaluations in Spanish. Humanities organizations should recognize that Spanish is a domestic, national language of the United States by accepting applications and conducting peer-review panels in that language.

Democratization of grant agencies. Scholars at universities like ours do not have a meaningful voice in the institutions that control external funding. This situation likely exists in part because reviewers and board members are often chosen from previous grantees. (At ACLS, eleven of the fourteen on the executive committee have ties to Harvard University.) This situation affects peer-review, the definitions of excellence and merit, the structure of competitions, and the very mission of funding organizations and agencies. Scholars affiliated with institutions that require external funding for humanities activities should be the norm—not the exception—among executives, directional committees, and peer review panels.

Single-grantee award eligibility. Several agencies have single-grantee awards that are effectively sabbatical leaves. Faculty who already have institutional sabbaticals receive nearly all these awards (Herlihy-Mera 2021). Grant organizations should reconsider the eligibility requirements to focus on scholars at public institutions that cannot afford to offer sabbaticals.

Revised institutional statements on resources. Many awards require institutional support for salary matching, post-grant release time, summer-wages and sometimes existing infrastructure. Meeting such eligibility terms on a campus like ours is an obstacle. Instead of a "Statement of Institutional Support," eligibility could require a declaration documenting that the activities proposed cannot occur without external monies.

Lottery selections. To address some problems embedded in peer reviews, a weighted lottery among feasible proposals could determine grantees. How would weighted lotteries work? In a grant competition, each "feasible" proposal would have a metaweight numerical factor based on existing resources and professional conditions. This information could be requested in the demographic section of each application:

Feasible proposal: +1
25% of students from communities systematically blocked from opportunity: +1
50% of students from communities systematically blocked from opportunity: +2
75% of students from communities systematically blocked from opportunity: +3
25% of students served eligible for Pell Grant: +1
50% of students served eligible for Pell Grant: +2
75% of students served eligible for Pell Grant: +3
Larger than median course load: +1
Larger than median class size: +1
No institutional support for archival work: +1
No institutional support for conference travel: +1
No institutional support for hosting conferences: +1
No institutional sabbaticals: +1
No institutional release time: +1
Lower than median salary (among applicants or national cohort): +1
Lowest 25% salary group (among applicants or national cohort): +1
Themes with exceptional relevance and timeliness in local communities
   (post hurricane/earthquake studies at UPR in a COVID-19 frame,
   for instance) or that discuss marginalized cultures, communities,
   languages, or traditions: +1

Weighted proposals would be put into a pool and a lottery selects grantees. Scholars with institutional support for their work would have fewer "tickets" while others would have multiple. A lottery of this type would unlink from some of the problems in traditional peer-review, making evaluation an opportunity for democratic, cross-academic conversation about (and with a broader definition of) feasibility, instead of a mechanism of exclusion that often rewards scholars and institutions that do not require external funding.

Programs for non-tenure-track faculty at institutions serving communities systematically blocked from opportunity. In the near term, humanities grant-making organizations could consider reorienting their programs toward scholars off the tenure-track at Historically Black Colleges and Universities, High Hispanic Enrollment institutions, Tribal Universities and institutions with more than 50 percent Pell enrollment. That move would support the humanities as a practice, while advocating scholars whose contributions are often overlooked.

Organizations should encourage scholars with institutional resources to focus on those funds. It should be incumbent upon scholars in affluent institutions to consider that many other scholars require extramural funds for their work. If a project can proceed per institutional instead of extramural funds (i.e., course releases, conference and workshop hosting, conference and archival travel, invited speakers, sabbatical leave, infrastructure expansion) it should be an ethical imperative that scholars in privileged circumstances *not apply*—and granting organizations could encourage this.[28]

Traditional humanities funding tends to support "people who already had a lot of advantages," comments Andrew Delbanco, president of the Teagle Foundation and professor at Columbia. He recalls what it was like to receive a grant while at Harvard:

> I was in an elite institution [Harvard] and there was a generous leave policy, there was a manageable teaching load, and so this [ACLS] fellowship came in. It basically said, "all right you know you've got even more time [and money] to do the things that you want to do." And of course, I appreciated that at the time, but now that I sit in a different place, it seems to me that philanthropy needs to think about whether it directs its resources to people who already have advantages and whether it might not be better to spend our resources on people who need them more. (qtd. in Herlihy-Mera 2021)

In a Zoom roundtable with members of my university's humanities department, ACLS president Joy Connolly remarked, "We share many values in common" and confirmed that, during her tenure, the foundation's "fellowships and grants will help support those scholars the academy of the future needs most." Not long after our conversation, ACLS took the unprecedented step to move almost their entire fellowship program toward non-tenured faculty. Given the severe economic and human costs of COVID-19, and the continuing corporatization of the academy, similar grant-making organizations should move away from traditional funding patterns. ACLS's shift toward non-tenured scholars is an important symbolic and tangible move in that direction.

These are clearly positive changes, and they must be recognized for their vision and intention; in the new structure, though, some traditional exceptionalist patterns reappeared in ACLS's crisis-engaged grantmaking. Fellows in their 2021 postdoc programs include PhDs from the University of Pennsylvania, Yale, Oxford, Berkley, Princeton, NYU, and Georgetown; there were no grantees from institutions with 50 percent Pell Grant enrollment, with a Latinx majority, or a tribal affiliation. There was a single grantee who trained at Howard (an HBCU). In their other main program, "ACLS Fellows," 50 percent of grantees are on the tenure track (all are nontenured). Among tenure-line grant recipients with income data in the public domain, all earn more than $100,000 and their average salary is $121,000. All the tenure-line grantees are affiliated with institutions that provide sabbaticals, release time, and funds for research (in addition to those salaries).[29] There was a single grantee from an HBCU, an adjunct professor at Spelman College. There were no grantees who trained at or are presently affiliated with a Tribal Institution, an institution with 50 percent Latinx enrollment, or with 50 percent of students eligible for the Pell Grant.[30]

It is important to emphasize that a transition away from these traditional funding patterns would not subsidize mediocrity: different institutional backgrounds inevitably mean multiplicity in expertise, experience, and intellectual domains. Maintaining measures that ensure top-ranked departments continually receive outsized numbers of postdoc positions, external funding, and tenure-line appointments only repeats the myth that perspectives cultivated in those communities are inherently superior to others. While academic tradition maintains that "justice" concerns are illegitimate before "merit," changing the structure of evaluation can recognize dimensions of excellence that existing valuation models fail to recognize. In order to move away from the existing hierarchies that characterize the United States at large, Joy Connolly believes, "universities are surely not the only or most important source of change"; nevertheless, she continues, "they are a place millions of people spend time learning and thinking" (2020, 1).

Eurocentric Spanish-language cultural study teaches students that the works of people distant in time and geography are more valuable than their own culture, their own language, their own histories, and their own experience. Decolonizing Spanish pedagogy cultivates students' experiences and sanctions identities students may perform, study, and seek knowledge about: decentering the US academy from monolingual English-centrism requires annulment of top-ranked fetishization and many of the received valuation models it legitimizes. It also requires more than enthusiasm and a few supporters in positions of influence, like Joy Connolly. It must be a structural and administrative strategy to bring the student and campus to a new encounter, a new experience. Gloria Anzaldúa's ideas are at the center of such a vision: she died of diabetes without health insurance or a tenure-track job. Her plight is symptomatic of an ailing and deteriorating society with an academy beset by institutions that are constructed to exclude. Moving the central focus from medieval, golden age, transatlantic, and contemporary European cisgender women and men, and away from the exclusive domain of monolingual institutions in the model of the Harvard and Yale cohort, toward epistemes that Anzaldúa cultivated and experienced, is symbolic of a revolutionary conceptual shift about what (and whose) culture has meaning. Domesticizing Spanish would give voice to intellectual aspirations that Hispanism and a tradition of Eurocentric monolingual education have silenced.

NOTES

PREFACE

1. Biden since reimplemented it.

2. In light of the confines embedded in conventional terms, my specific use of "United States" or "US" and "America/n" in the title and throughout this book indicate "spaces claimed by the US political body" or "residents of spaces claimed by the US political body," without regard to citizenship, language, race, gender, national origin, or economic status, etc. (cognate terms, like "Mexico/an" or "Spain/Spanish," engage similar characterization). While such distinctions are perhaps more important to clarify in Puerto Rico than elsewhere, retreating from the certainties and implicit boundaries of "US/American" in their traditional usage allows the discussion to engage a descriptive rather than relational tone.

3. For a discussion of the legal and ethical consequences of this prescription, see Burnett et al. 2001.

4. These form the structures in the academic appointment process, as the language of hiring announcements is regularly organized around geographic, regional, or transnational/Atlantic specializations.

5. In academic treatises, such terms are often unexamined and unpacked as though their meanings are unassailable and unquestionable. Such tendencies support the notion that if a person is "Mexican," she or he cannot be "French," and due to the weight of the external prescription, the only available—albeit sometimes incompatible—category is hybridized as Mexican-French or French-Mexican. The transnational grammar enforces these limits.

6. Enrique Dussel has developed "pueblo" as a category that encompasses various demographics who are dominated in struggle—and describes the sphere as "el actor colectivo de la transformación histórica" (qtd. in Cofré and Delgado 2018, 1).

7. If cognition and performance are understood as embodied phenomena, thus grounded in our motor and sensory systems, this represents a challenge for scholars to clarify how cultural processes and their abstract concepts (metaphor, imagery, tropes, etc.), which may not call directly on sensory or motor inputs, can be informed by experience. The experiences in focus here include institutionalized cultures, multilingualism, and local surroundings (place uniqueness)—each link to the Spanish language as cross-axis.

8. These frequently rely on geography of origin—commonly expressed in transnational terms—as stand-alone identity proxies.

9. At the intersection of scholarship, solidarity, and resistance, *Decolonizing American Spanish* endeavors to nuance and de-fetishize the "this place" / "that place," "this time" / "that time," and similar binaries, which force a verticalized contiguity and parochial sequestration into many area-studies approaches. Moving focus toward new horizons of "localization" that relate to embodied cognitive experiences as metrics of performance, I argue that these emphases could complement conventional centers of inquiry.

INTRODUCTION:
COLONIALISM IN US SPANISH DEPARTMENTS

1. All of which subtly proscribe many other forms of knowledge creation.

2. As Ann Abbott notes, "Most Spanish departments in the United States still operate as foreign language programs," and continues: "We need to focus much of our curricula on US Latinos, commit to social justice education and engage with our local Latino communities. Few departments do this, though, because few departments have truly seen this as their mission" (2017, 33). Abbott's deft remarks also critique the distance between words and actions: "A quick look at the dissertations produced in Spanish departments ('Open Access Dissertation Lists') reveals that our focus on literary analysis and linguistics has barely budged, constantly reproducing frameworks that do not actually address the societal needs the authors foreground" (2017, 33). For more on the benefits of domesticizing Spanish through US institutions of education, see Anzaldúa 1987, 63.

3. Emil Volek comments: "U.S. Latin Americanism firmly believes in the superior reality of certain formerly neglected social and cultural agencies and forms,

tends to devalue all other mechanisms, especially those of more complex cultural productions or those not fitting its many conflicting theories, and proposes itself as *the* interpretation and solution for all of the fundamental life problems in Latin America. Latin Americanism does not allow those who cultivate it to abandon it as they please. There is every reason to believe that it acts on the spirit of its performers as a kind of narcotic agent" (2006, 38). While many of the core tenets of Latin American studies democratize and localize scholarly views, the presumption of "Latin America" as a stable category of physical and cultural geographies is perhaps an inevitable quandary when engaging area study as an intellectual grammar.

4. This has been in effect since the inception of the field. While studies concerning use of *voseo*, for example, in comparison to *vosotros* or *distinción* among students have yet to emerge, the notion that Peninsular variants are used by more than 10 percent of students is perhaps an inevitable structural outcome of the hiring practices (Herlihy-Mera 2016). As Menéndez Pidal notes in 1918, an Iberian dialect (he does not specify which) "es la que responde más exactamente que ninguna otra a la ortografía secular de la lengua" (1918, 11).

5. *Decolonizing American Spanish* examines some options for new tenure-line fields such a shift would make possible.

6. While the US College Board asserts their exam materials will not be "specific to certain geographic areas (e.g., Mexico or Spain)," on the practice test, "Part A Question 1" is the following: "En Córdoba, uno de los grandes centros culturales de España, se [ ] libros del hebreo y del árabe al latín. (A) mudaban (B) trasladaban (C) impresionaban (D) traducían." In addition, the cultural focus in standardized exams like the College Board Scholastic Aptitude Test and Advanced Placement Test, secondary school textbooks, high school curricula trends, and the private-sector initiatives—like Rosetta Stone—repeat the traditional Spain-centric mode.

7. And the ways they strive to recolonize the minds of those exposed to them.

8. He continues, noting that these are linked "to the zero-sum game of state costs, a heightened individualism, and neoliberal criteria" (2016, 4; emphasis added).

9. The absence of ontological sensibilities in Spanish-language cultural studies limits the scope and objects of study. Spain-centric pedagogical exigencies marginalize local cultures and their epistemologies, but their soft limits also prohibit the exploration of other ontologies, particularly those developed in spaces claimed by the US political body and including those of indigenous peoples. By characterizing the latter as folkloric, the Eurocentric sensibility discounts the beliefs, ways of life, and myths as irrational and inferior.

10. Largely but not exclusively in relation to conventional notions of Eurocentric genders, transnationalism, hybridity, and other geography-based epistemes.

11. Robert McKee Irwin and Mónica Szurmuk maintain people and their cultures "cannot merely be thought of in national or geographic terms" (2009, 46). The tacit assumption in much geography-delimited cultural study functions on some iteration of the following frame: "person A who resides in [place—often a nation] is ("is" in the sense of *ser* not *estar*) [adjective]"—so, if area studies are to be engaged, the idea is to relink to geography in localized ways (instead of trans/national ways). The weight of geography of residence as a cultural performance metric, a central presumption in the area studies mold, has been nuanced in many fields and inquiries, but it yet maintains a dominant role in many intellectual activities. Nearly all faculty in the data from chapter 1 describe their interests in geographic terms.

12. These views stem not from traditional rhetorical intricacies but from the studies in cultural neurology and social psychology on the situational and conditional nature of identity, community, social/cultural emotion, and the performances related thereto.

13. "Stories about what a nation has been and should try to be are not attempts at accurate representation, but rather attempts to forge a moral identity" (Rorty 1998, 13).

14. As Nelson Maldonado-Torres maintains, there is much yet to mine "beyond the modern conceptions of the nation-state" (2008, 188).

15. "We have yet to develop a new decolonial language to account for the complex processes of the modern/colonial world-system without relying on the old liberal language of the three arenas" (Grosfoguel 2011, 19).

16. One could posit that we require many new interpellative bases, including aggrupation adjectives, since, as Josephine Baker notes, "the very idea of *America* makes me shake and tremble and gives me nightmares" (qtd. in Wright 2007, 244; emphasis added).

17. As an applied presumption, the argument maintains that the self (and thus the communities with which it engages) is formed in and by language and discourse; composed through multiple subjectivities and their heterogenous codes, the self (and its multiple registers and their discourses) is socially generated; these subjectivities are unequal in influence and status; their location of power derives from Eurocentric preferences; the conflicts among and between subjects codify worlds; negotiating these multiple identities, the subject positions her/him/their-self arise through cultural and linguistic performances.

Voice is a manifestation of agency: cultural performance (linguistic is one means of many) collates these calls. These selves are negotiated in relation to our historically defined identities (race, ethnicity, transnationality), institutional roles (student, teacher, administrator), and ideological subjectivity (positioning according to discourses like citizen/immigrant; native speaker/nonnative speaker), which are social constructions that are also embodied in measurable ways.

18. Questions about difference are paramount. Eurocentric modernity colonizes variance through tolerance, diversity narratives, and conditional acceptation. The non-Euro-inflected performance is subordinate (sometimes transnationalized) and does not destabilize the presumptions of the "Eurocenter." These cultures and the groups practicing them may exist *in relation to* the Eurocentric presumption. The one-world myth legitimizes this hierarchy and enforces the subordination: when any praxis or performance challenges this model, the results are usually violent. The US one-world model forces English-centric norms into almost every single classroom, meaning that speaking Spanish in any setting beyond a "foreign" language setting is not only illogical but in some cases expressly prohibited. The suppression is so normalized and nuanced that "any affirmation on the contrary must take a radical form of defense" (Querejazu 2016, 1).

19. Language speaks us. Benjamin Whorf asserts that language "is not merely a reproducing instrument for voicing ideas but rather is itself the shaper of ideas" (1940, 214).

These points are not beyond debate: language and thought may not be so fundamentally intermeshed. As John Breuilly notes, "If language is thought and can be learnt only in a community, it follows that each community has its own mode of thought" (1982, 337). Nor is our communicative device a random collection of sounds and metaphor. The words, their connections, meanings and development, relation to one another and to those of "different" languages, and their in-group gradation relate to conditions, and thus, those communicating in "Spanish" may be understood as a community of thought processes.

20. From a Facebook post on June 25, 2016. Abbott continues, in an email to the author: "Your piece in the *Chronicle* provoked a lot of conversation on social media, and it was good to begin questioning how things are done. In addition to trying to reconfigure departments and curricula to represent Latin America more, we must do the same with Spanish in the US."

21. As the contemporary structure maintains.

22. In recent years several scholars have examined the shortcomings of Latin America as a conceptual and academic unit. In *The Idea of Latin America*, Walter Mignolo notes that "America did not name itself," and this circumstance "produced silences and absences" (2005, 152, 151).

Emil Volek writes: "This 'Latin America,' concocted by the hegemonic U.S. academy for its own consumption, is then re-exported to Latin America which, paradoxically, is struggling to liberate itself from the secular plague of magic, miracles, exceptionalisms, utopias on demand, and other spells of *macondismos*" (2006, 37). In *The Failure of Latin America*, John Beverley examines an "increasingly fashionable abandonment of Latinamericanism in the academy," emphasizing that such a conceptualization yet "retains the possibility of an *alternative* modernity, not so bound to the domination of global capitalism" (2019, xviii). In concert with this vision, the vocabulary of Latin America, as an entity with a degree of intrinsic cultural autonomy that permits many sociopolitical relevancies, could be understood as a continuing decolonial project.

23. Mayhew neglects to mention that Spain receives *multiple* specialists in each department, unlike a single other possible sole-nation specialist: this one Mexicanist, multiple Peninsularist (golden age, medieval, etc.) structure filters down into all facets of pedagogy.

24. As Nicolas Shumway observes, "Our programs seldom teach national literatures of Mexico, Argentina, Cuba, or Chile, although all these countries have highly developed traditions of writers, publications, and criticism that lend themselves to being studied in a national framework" (2005, 296).

25. "No le hagas caso," responds Francesco D'Introno to Compitello's remarks. "Está protegiendo su feudo" (email to the author, Sept. 6, 2016).

26. Critical, decolonial pedagogies endeavor to achieve two ends: 1) engage students with local knowledges and methods of creative and cultivative inquiry, and 2) offer them opportunities to practice these interpretive competencies—of argument, analysis, critique, application, and communitive dissemination—in ways that nurture and grow the questions over time, nourishing and embracing their uncertainties, empowering students toward the confidence to perform agencies and critical activities upon completion of their studies.

27. For more on this topic, see Reynaldo F. Macías, "Spanish as the Second National Language of the United States: Fact, Future, Fiction, or Hope?," in *Review of Research in Education*, vol. 38: 33–57.

28. "Such a Freedom was never meant for the 'inferior' in need of civilization and Christianization. Even the U.S. rhetorical end to our daily oath of 'liberty and justice for all' was never meant to include those from African descent, nor their neighbors south of the border" (de la Torre 2017, 1).

29. The monolingual (in English) university is a central pillar of this program: it forces pedagogy into the colonial narratives and in all disciplines foreignizes any non-English communication. In a move toward a pluriverse that localizes

the center, the colonial tenets scaffolding this program of marginalization lose traction.

30. "Culturalism," notes Marie Battiste, "is a primary force in Eurocentrism." She goes on to wage forceful critique of pedagogical models that engage "'culture' as its central foundation. Forwarded by anthropology, culture incorporates the ideologies and discursive regimes of universalism, cultural racism, and cultural incompatibility in order to construct and perpetuate a 'two race' binary. It requires that anthropological notions of culture and two-race binary be privileged as the primary analytical tool for deliberations of pedagogy in all instances" (2011, 10).

1. AFTER HISPANIC STUDIES: ON THE DEMOCRATIZATION OF SPANISH-LANGUAGE CULTURAL STUDY

1. They also limit the knowledge developed. It should be clear that these outcomes were, at least initially, intended: the purpose of Eurocentric pedagogy is to reiterate and thus normalize the coloniality myths through a social institution. For more on how Eurocentrism negatively impacts students, see chapter 2.

2. As Anne Cruz observes, "From the 1990s on, state universities downsized their Golden Age faculty from the usual two (and sometimes three) members to one" (2006, 82). While defending this Peninsular subfield, she goes on to argue that the notion that "Golden Age studies, with its imperialist overtones, is somehow the enemy nonetheless dies hard among minority students" (2006, 83).

3. For more on this topic, see Anibal Quijano's "Coloniality of Power, Eurocentrism, and Latin America" and Walter D. Mignolo's "Coloniality and Modernity/Rationality."

4. In addition to the problems inherent to Eurocentric cultural studies, inundating classrooms with Peninsular accents and vernacular has a significant weight on the Spanish linguistic norms in US higher education.

5. As Héctor Huyke has noted in English about English in Puerto Rico, "The conquered need to be proficient enough to be colonized" (conversation with the author, May 13, 2016).

6. As Serk-Bae Suh argues, "To execute power colonial power . . . the colonizer has to rely on language to convey thoughts, intentions, and orders to the colonized" (2013, 8).

7. Several cases—such as that of Bolivia, where half the population did not self-identify as bilingual in Spanish until the 1970s (Wolfson and Manes 1985, 298)—rebuke the imperialist cultural mappings surrounding the supposed "His-

panic" nature of American worlds. The movement away from Eurocentric academic models was an attempt to subvert the misapprehensions associated with perceiving Latin America as a cultural subordinate to Spain: in that scholarly tradition, Latin American Spanish-language narratives (as well as other creative and visual arts) should be interpreted as derivations of peninsular spirit or a metaphoric ongoingness outside Iberia—a diasporic "Spanish" art, as it were. That aesthetic interpretation locates supposed Peninsular influences in Latin American art above those from local traditions or associated syncretizing, often imagining the work as European culture displaced to the Americas.

8. Another major dilemma in US Spanish-languages studies is the treatment of the subject itself as a "foreign" language/culture.

9. Since the United States is part of Latin America, the Eurocentric preference is particularly severe against local cultures than other Spanish-language traditions.

10. Across all cohorts, specialists in transatlantic themes were 3 percent (20), pedagogy or linguistics 19 percent (117); and other non-area specialists 4 percent (23). Other non-area specializations included: business Spanish, gender studies, creative writing, trauma studies, hétéronomies, poetics, theory, and theater and film (if no area study was explicitly indicated).

11. In relation to the faculty demographics, Pittsburgh's doctoral program has a built-in Latin American emphasis.

12. There are many exemplary initiatives at community colleges, which could perhaps serve as models for the development of similar shifts at the doctoral level. As Pablo Baisotto and Zhongli Zhang note:

> East Los Angeles College, the San Diego City College, the San Diego Mesa College and the Ventura College provide a variety of courses on specific population groups such as the Chicano, the Latino, the Mexican and the Central Americans in the United States. In most of the courses, the culture, the history, the gender and the politics of these communities are taught.... Los Angeles Mission, Laney and Rio Hondo also have courses that pay attention to the Mexican experience in the United States. There are also discussions on the Mexican-Americans in the history of the United States, the Mexican-Americans in California, the Mexican-Americans in contemporary society, the Mexican-American woman in the society and the introduction to the psychology of Mexican-Americans. (2017, 165–66)

13. The categories exclude general language courses, business Spanish, and linguistics (in courses that lack a regional indicator).

14. M. Iarocci from Berkeley noted that, "Many of the peninsular course numbers are 'dead'; in the sense that, although on the books, they are no longer used" (email to the author, March 1, 2018).

15. Many excellent reports on this topic emphasize the importance of Spanish over other European languages in the classroom but often say little on which variant of Spanish and which Spanish-language cultures (see García 1993; Fernández 2000).

16. Román de la Campa remarks that the field is "in a constant state of flux" and that scholars should "concur in the pursuit of new packaging for disciplines and scholars" (2005, 300).

17. Brown's text details "Missing Contents" (2010, chapter 4), which includes a short section on what she terms "Geographical Gaps." This three-page segment focuses on Latin America in the canon, and, more specifically, what she calls an "open secret" (2010, 107)—that Latin American studies are unbalanced because some regions are studied more than others. The problem with this approach is that she discusses regions of Latin America *within* Latin American studies as a subfield, not the field as a whole.

18. The American Council on the Teaching of Foreign Languages publishes *Foreign Language Annals*, a journal that requires submissions be written in English.

19. Save Pittsburgh, which has one Peninsular specialist.

20. Scholars have been reinterpreting the concept of "American" for decades (see Jay 1991; Carafiol 1992; Herlihy-Mera 2018).

21. It is useful to point out that these writers do not represent the Latin American median in economic, education, political, or cultural senses.

22. It is precisely this body of laws that constructs the political concept of an "illegal" person within a socially organized space. (Unless convicted of a felony, a US citizen cannot be an "illegal" in Europe, nor can a citizen of the European Union be an "illegal" in the United States because neither are subordinated to this visa process.)

23. In order to further layer an analysis of this letter, written collectively by several Latin American authors, one might consider whether such a plea would exist if Latin American governments were to subject Spaniards to the visa process. How would the same group express their perceived loss? Would these writers use such a moment to voice their perceived relationship to Spain? What makes their supposed affiliation with Spain so strong in this moment of their persecution by it?

24. This argument has been informed by Robert Young's work on postcolonial-

ism as a continuing force. As he notes: "The only criterion that could determine whether 'postcolonial theory' has ended is whether . . . imperialism and colonialism in all their different forms have ceased to exist in the world, whether there is no longer domination by nondemocratic forces . . . or economic and resource exploitation enforced by military power, or a refusal to acknowledge the sovereignty of non-Western countries, and new literary history whether peoples or cultures still suffer from the long-lingering aftereffects of imperial, colonial, and neocolonial rule, albeit in contemporary forms such as economic globalization" (2012, 20).

25. It is worthwhile to note here a specific study of Spanish-language transatlanticism, Alejandro Mejías-López's *The Inverted Conquest: The Myth of Modernity and the Transatlantic Onset of Modernism*. Mejía-López argues that Latin American *modernistas* seized both linguistic and cultural authority from Spain toward the end of the nineteenth century. In this "inverted conquest," these writers moved "the cultural center of the Hispanic Atlantic westward to America" (2009, 4). This critic deftly observes that "For Spanish critics, Spanish American modernismo and the way it was transforming and opening literary language in Spanish were a threat to the perceived purity of 'Castilian' and to the linguistic, literary, and cultural authority of the nation" (2009, 99).

26. Numerous are the ceremonies, rituals, and other aspects of Latin American material culture that aggressively reject the myth of Hispanic cultural roots. "Quemando el Año Viejo" is a New Year's ceremony realized throughout the Andean region, Central America, and Mexico, which has been interpreted as an anti-colonial rite (see Herlihy 2009, 30). Upon winning gold medal at the Atlanta Olympics, Ecuadorian Jefferson Pérez said: "With this medal, I renounce the inferiority complex that they have put upon us for 500 years" (2004, 1A). In 2006 Bolivian president Evo Morales said that Latin America's "campaign of resistance was not in vain," and continued, "We're taking over now over the next 500 years" (qtd. in Herlihy 2011, 82).

27. That specialty could develop into closer nuance with the Arab and Islamic influences, as will be discussed in chapter 4. Moreover, as the seminal dimensions of the cultures are the product of rich interlingual periods in Iberia—Celtic and Celt-Iberian presence; Ibero settlements; the Roman conquest and the Convivencia, and so on—this would require that the departmental specialist in Peninsular themes have a broader register rather than the current norms, which generally divide Peninsular study into medieval, golden age, twentieth century, and so on.

2. VETTING THE DECOLONIAL TURN

Nelson Maldonado-Torres has also argued that "Modernity/coloniality is a form of metaphysical catastrophe that naturalizes war" (2016, 11).

1. As Kavita Bhanot argues,

> The concept of diversity only exists if there is an assumed neutral point from which "others" are "diverse." Putting aside for now the straight, male, middle-classness of that "neutral" space, its dominant aspect is whiteness. Constructed by a white establishment, the idea of "diversity" is neo-liberal speak. It is the new corporatized version of multiculturalism. It is about management, efficiency, box-ticking. As writers of colour, we parrot this idea back, reminding white institutions that they need to increase their diversity; appealing to them to let us in, to give some of us a seat at the table too. To help convince them, institutions are reminded that "diversity" is actually good for them too, that it will help them to make more money. (2015, 1)

Money is often a central factor: "Debt functions as a form of coloniality" as Rocío Zambrana notes (2021, 10), wondering "what philosophy could do if it was taken beyond its disciplinary boundaries" (2021, ix).

2. In revisiting the strictures of the colonial directives, gesturing toward pluriverse-framed and decolonial praxes, the argument here maintains that "local" shifts in pedagogies (involving language and culture) de-worlds knowledge production in ways that disengage some of the (post)colonial domination of contemporary Eurocentric norms. "The idea is that there is neither autonomous logics nor a single logic," notes Ramón Grosfoguel, "but multiple, heterogeneous, entangled, and complex processes within a single historical reality" (2011, 20). Moreover, this historical frame may be understood as a multi-situational condition in which individuals and communities interact with cultural canons in disparate ways depending on circumstances like age, language, and political status, among other factors. Recognition of multiplicity is central to decolonizing the certainties of "worlded" pedagogical Eurocentrism: challenging the universalized (i.e., colonized) "modern" prescriptions (one world, many worldviews), a main shift from diversity narratives to decoloniality is that the former presume a center, the point from which all are measured. But while decolonial moves engage multiple centers, many have questioned: 1) whether material/economic and historical exigencies can allow these to be horizontal in nature; 2) if the residual entanglements

(racist, sexist, classist, heteropatriarchal, and transnationalist programs) are too comprehensive for pluriverse-framed emancipation without revolution; and 3) if pluriversal legitimacy—re-centering value locally (with several definitions of "local")—has the breadth and dimension to supplant the grand narratives. This chapter interprets pluriversal, decolonial principles in dialog with such queries, and adds to the argument by engaging inquiries on pluriverse-geared psychology: that is, asking questions concerning how surroundings and conditions (understood broadly, including region, language, age, and other spheres as forms of "localities") inform behavior, emotion, and community—and thus the cultures performed therein. As worlded, Eurocentric pedagogies are residual symptoms of these colonial mores, reexamining localization through insights from cognate academic disciplines will shed light on the context of diversity-to-decoloniality move.

3. In local themes, "There are masterworks being written" (Saldívar-Hull 2003).

4. Colonial social programs assert and maintain sovereignty through structures of perpetual violence that are cultural (pedagogies, holidays, languages, "official" and "domestic/foreign," etc.) as well as physical (incarceration, deportation, abuse). While the physical violence of incarceration and death are always looming for those in colonized spaces, the power apparatus engages cultural canons as soft mechanisms to administer all dimensions of human existence. These standards and norms attempt to organize cultural behavior into channels of "correct/domestic" and "incorrect/foreign"—and language is an important tool of the colonial proprietorship mandate. In spaces claimed by the US political body, when a language or cultural performance is assigned to the second category (i.e., incorrect/foreign), it may exist and be practiced always in relation to the dominant, always in a subordinate position: when the dominant/margin threshold is passed—for instance, declaring Spanish as an "official" language in any space claimed by the US political body, no matter how small the community—the physical, economic, and social violence are waged directly upon those who resist the colonial directives (see discussion of El Cenizo, Texas, in Herlihy-Mera 2018a, 37–40).

5. In the same way that the "top" commercial products sell the most, the "best" political leaders win elections.

6. Labeling these as folkloric, provisional, superficial, dialectical, artisanal, or another term extends those concepts to the *worlds* those words codify.

7. This colonial pedagogical norm is due in part to universalization of history—or, as Mignolo has termed it, "the universalization of universality" (2013a, 1). Curricula and pedagogies become "products" manufactured by information bas-

es, in which the sensational Eurocentric "competes" universally with other ways of being, knowing, living, acting, in competitions that cannot be one outside the imperial qualities. Any non-Eurocentric performance, as described by Eduardo Galeano:

> Que no son, aunque sean.
> Que no hablan idiomas, sino dialectos.
> Que no profesan religiones, sino supersticiones.
> Que no hacen arte, sino artesanías.
> Que no practican cultura, sino folklore.
> Que no son seres humanos, sino recursos humanos.
> Que no tienen cara, sino brazos.
> Que no tienen nombre, sino número.
> Que no figuran en la historia universal, sino en la crónica roja de la prensa local.
>
> *Los nadies*, que cuestan menos que la bala que los mata. (2000, 59)

8. In *How to Write the History of the New World*, Jorge Cañizares-Esguerra recommends using "evidence from linguistics, natural history, ethnology, and geology" that has the scope to take precedence over colonizing chronicles (2001, 13). Local works were dismissed as authorship from "peoples with inferior mental qualities" was unreliable (2001, 119).

9. These are generally inaccessible in the modern/colonial paradigm.

10. In this sense, decolonial approaches to knowledge and institutional norms are remarkably applicable to Spanish-language cultural pedagogies: the universities in question—in nearly every region claimed by the US political body—are surrounded by unrecognized, marginalized, and silenced groups who are using the language and creating the culture and living in the worlds in question. In many cities and regions, these groups are the majority population.

In this specific context (i.e., universities in spaces claimed by the US political body), the application of decolonial options can counter the emancipations of already-power as it has been and is manifest in constructions like Spain-centric linguistic and cultural pedagogies concerning texts, graffiti, and digital media; comics, narrative, poetry, and nonfictional tracts; and film, theater, and performance art.

Emotion and desire that stem from non-Eurocentric conditions, and the decolonial endeavor aims to institutionalize these into educational praxes.

11. Decolonial philosophies offer a latitude of critique that has the potential to voice how certain events of human existence (for instance, childbirth or death)

occur without the lens of Eurocentrism. These moves concern how local cultures respond with autonomous nuance to the Eurocentrically framed events, problems, boons, migrations, traumas, as well as internal or external interventions. Such decolonized critical views will also lend insights about language as a cultural and social apparatus, its role in community affairs, and the nature of language and the cultural performance and power.

12. The looming decolonial shift will nudge the interpretive base away from Spain-centric worldviews into independent/interdependent and localized worlds, and thus decolonize the pedagogical paradigm by unlinking it from the comparative and relational "truths" of Peninsular-centric myths about cultures performed in Spanish. While Peninsular histories, cultures, and linguistic tendencies maintain a privileged and exceptional position in US classrooms, unlinked from Eurocentric exigencies, this specific pluriverse-framed praxis examines two dimensions of reality: physical spaces and language. Does extricating pedagogies in these ways *require* a rupture from relational exigencies of Spain-centric histories, logics, and imaginaries? Such a localized and disconnected view, notes Claudia von Werlhof, "is almost unimaginable anywhere, except within the indigenous worlds" (qtd. in Escobar 2018, 14). Nevertheless, victims of Eurocentrism in all communities have autonomous ways of being, living, and feeling that are unconnected to the Spain-centric presumptions—*in addition to* those specific to the indigenous worlds—and these sensibilities and their cultural material are overlooked in pedagogy. In this way, the nature of a pluriverse-informed Spanish-language cultural study is (unlike the Eurocentric, the transnational, and the transatlantic) perhaps programmatically anti-exceptional: the approach places urgency not on continual re-centering on Peninsular myth bases but on recognition of the agency, localization, and centralization of marginalized ways of being, integrating them as equivalent, peers of Peninsular parallels.

13. Whether or not pluriverses represent cultural worldviews or different worlds has been a topic of rich debate:

> There exists a world, whose main property is to be single and uniform. And there exist representations of the world, whose main property is to be plural and multifarious depending on who holds them. Ontologically speaking, this is of course a "dualist" position, related to a whole field of interlinking dualities: body and mind, practice and theory, noumenon and phenomenon, experience and reflection, signified and signifier, structure and agency and so on. But what is remarkable is that even though anthropologists have made a name for themselves by arguing against the *a priori* validity of

particular versions of such dualities, I for one know of no theoretical . . . that departs from the basic assumption that the differences in which anthropologists are interested ("alterity") are differences in the way people "see the world"—no position, that is, other than the ontological one. (Holbraad 2008, 34–35)

14. Martin Holbraad has argued that "alterity can only be understood as a divergence between contrasting representations of reality" (2008, 34–35).

The notion of environmental influences on culture has deep roots: al-Jahiz (781–869) and Ibn Khaldun (1332–1406) examined the role in climatic surroundings (desert vis-à-vis fertile valley for instance) that the environment may have on shaping influence on aesthetic pleasures and other foundational components of human experience. The color green, for example, maintains an almost sacred significance for desert peoples, due to the associations with vegetation and thus water necessary for life. These conditions are manifest in flag aesthetics in arid areas, in which green dominates; similarly, reds and yellows are more common in an inverse relationship with sunlight on flags in northern latitudes.

15. The ontological turn in cultural theory does not privilege an epistemological notion that culture is representational of *multiple realities* in *one world* but rather acknowledges the existence of *multiple worlds*.

16. He also notes that "higher levels of openness (to experience) are typically found in cosmopolitan cities that are ethnically diverse" and observes that "people in countries that have demanding climates and limited natural resources are especially likely to hold collectivistic values" (2018, 1).

17. The localized focus that pluriverse-framed cultural approaches afford, then, aligns with the psychology and neuroscience of being, culture, and behavior in ways that worlded, transnational, and national approaches cannot.

18. That is expressed in multiple mediums (verbal, visual, performative, etc.). They ask about community and cultural membership and their limits; they inquire about other kinds of worlds that have similar constitutions, histories, and memberships; they interrogate the violation of world boundaries, and examine their permeable spaces.

19. For more on external funding hierarchies, see the conclusion.

20. As a method to erase local sensibilities, the oft-silent but incredibly consequential myth asserts that Latin Americans (among others who use the Spanish language, specifically in the United States) are incapable of valid thought, *and therefore* their actions (histories, cultural production, and so on) are pedagogically irrelevant in comparison to those of Spain.

21. Some recent takes on the nature of revolutions focus on "unprecedented things" that accompany shifts in "key building blocks" of reality. What is unprecedented in this case does have precedents in different forms. The transition increases in profundity and influence "at an inflection point—a point where the curve starts to bend a lot" (Brynjolfsson and McAfee 2014, 9).

22. As Mabel Moraña has noted, such intellectual work gives "evidence of the presence of hidden and repressed subjectivities whose forms of agency, beliefs, and symbolic expressions" demonstrate "multiple and simultaneous temporalities that coexisted [and yet coexist] in contemporary history" (2016, 217).

23. It should be made clear, Saffo's deft remarks largely concern sociopolitical and economic affairs, rather than cultural emphases.

24. As Lorgia García Peña observes, these "urgent" circumstances require scholars to engage in "questioning of the multiple ways in which silences and repetitions operate in the erasure" of communities, individuals, and their agencies (qtd. in Jordens 2016, 1).

25. Horatio Alger's working-class protagonists rise to affluence and social acceptance through work, determination, willpower, and resolve. Horatio Alger was a Harvard-educated Protestant in an epoch when Harvard would not admit women, African Americans, Jews, Latinx, Asians, Boston Irish, or Catholics—and the interests of those groups were mocked in the *Lampoon* when he was on campus in the twentieth century (see Herlihy-Mera 2012).

26. Carter cites the documentary *American Tongues* in his discussion of this topic, emphasizing that the directors engage a "wholesale absence of Latinx people and languages from the film" (Carter 2018).

27. The general approach to teaching fails "to acknowledge the student's interests or possible relation to the novel" (Hernández 2015, 15).

28. What constitutes "reasonable suspicion" of immigration status? What is "illegal" presence? When asked this question, Governor Jan Brewer, who signed the bill into law, responded, "I don't know what an illegal immigrant looks like" (qtd. in Herlihy-Mera 2018a, 122).

29. In the comment section of the report on the ACLU website, a moniker "Ms. Gloria Anasyrma" adds: "They should have proved their Americanism by telling that border cop to 'F . . . off you fascist pig.'"

30. Reports from UPR graduate students who specialize in Puerto Rican studies and Caribbean studies underscore that they are (in comparison to the top-ranked cohort) perceived as inferior scholars; it is often the case that they are not interviewed for these positions.

31. Bowen 1986.

32. "How Good Students from Poor Families Get Pushed out of Elite Colleges" 2016.

33. The decisive ages, eighteen to twenty-eight or thirty, during which a scholar is subordinated to norms and directives, are informing in one's personal sensibility throughout their lifespan.

34. Such a move would have immediate effects, some of which would be linguistic. As Alicia M. Reyes-Barriéntez—who has two degrees from Baylor, a Texas university—observes, "My family spoke Spanish at home, and I was from the borderlands where Spanglish flourished alongside English. But the English spoken by professors was different and at times difficult to understand" (2019, 1).

35. As well as the broader homogenizing narratives of difference that disenfranchise many US Spanish-language communities.

36. In the context of unethical admissions policies at top universities, widespread grade inflation, the slippery politics of reference letters, and severely slanted appointment data, structural changes in hiring are long overdue ("Ivy League Admissions Are a Sham: Confessions of a Harvard Gatekeeper" 2015).

37. "General Government Spending" 2017.

38. While it may be misleading to suggest every application could be completely anonymous, the practice has become prevalent in other highly skilled professions—many symphonies hold trials with the musician out of view and companies like GapJumpers have emerged to arrange anonymous assessments that judge applicants on "performance rather than keywords on a resume." Blind reviews diversify the workforce: the presence of women jumps 50 percent when orchestras conduct blind auditions, almost 60 percent of those selected in GapJumpers' blind auditions come from underrepresented backgrounds, and companies report a 15 percent increase in community-college graduates at the in-person interview stage (Yarger et al. 2019).

Sharon Jank conducted doctoral research with GapJumpers, and noted, "Hiring managers tend to be surprised that the top performing submissions they pick to advance very often come from applicants without an elite education, training, or experience" (qtd. in Cooper 2015). Humanities search committees are not exceptional to such tendencies, and blind reviews would offer a method to address the pervasive biases that unjustly stratify who may become faculty in this climate of uncertainty.

3. MULTILINGUAL COGNITION AND ETHNO-LINGUAL RELATIVITY: EXPANDING "SPANISH" MAPS OF MEANING

1. While the realms of reading one language through another—English, for example, through Spanish—are yet emerging, recent studies in sociolinguistics suggest this directional move, as multilingualism "modulates dual mechanisms of cognitive control" (Morales et al. 2015, abstract). This treatment thus concerns a dimension largely absent from existent pedagogies and critical views, one that aims to contextualize what has been termed "the multilingual reality" of Spanish in other linguistic and cultural systems (Christiansen and Turkina 2018, x).

2. "Shame," notes Andrew Figueroa, was the dominant emotion "about my ability or inability to speak Spanish." He observes that English was the dominant language in their home in Los Angeles, "which kind of sucked," but at the same time, "struggling with language is now the new authentic Latino" (qtd. in Casa 2019, 1).

3. There are many Spanish-speaking authors who write in languages other than Spanish, and those who write in Spanish whose linguistic base is complemented by other tongues (as well as the philosophies, worldviews, sentiments, identities, community sentiments, and emotions embedded—perhaps only accessible—within them).

4. The argument here examines cultural performance (sometimes in one language) as a translingual phenomenon. More specifically, in a departure from the silo model, this chapter examines multilingual maps of "Spanish" through: (1) multilingual inflection in "Spanish"-language cultures; (2) Spanish-speakers who perform other languages (Picasso, William Carlos Williams, others); (3) the work of those who learned Spanish but worked in other languages (Hemingway, Steinbeck, McCarthy); (4) the work of those who learned several Spanishes, reaching through and across them; and (5) the work of those who cultivate Spanishes through disregard of traditional qualifiers (Spanglish).

5. And in how these are inflected into material—including into literature, music, art, dance, and other performance.

6. Boroditsky continues: "Rooted in the way different grammatical tool kits situated actions in time. English requires its speakers to grammatically mark events that are ongoing, by obligatorily applying the –ing morpheme: 'I am playing the piano and I cannot come to the phone' or 'I was playing the piano when the phone rang'" (2009, 1).

7. These shifts in mental representations also occur in text when the author is

thinking in a language other than English, as "English speakers don't include the same information in their verbs [as speakers of Spanish]" (Boroditsky 2009, 1).

8. If identities and subjectivities are constructed via words, places, others, and calling (interpellation and performativity), the implication is that regardless of the language involved, the idea of a self-same, self-identical subject is an illusion: identity/subjectivity/community and language itself are perpetually reconstructed with, as Christopher Pappas describes, a "forever-in-motion presence" (2015, 1). When interlingual dimensions of verbal (and other) communication enter our critical lens, another layer of the same contradictory expectations (conventional place- or language-of-origin suppositions, and that which presumed when "Spanish" is used) appears: does the self becomes a script that cannot be written in Spanish?

9. Futoransky's focus on "being" and "others" negotiates the feelings and complexity of her circumstance. She continues, on exile and language:

> [Exile] allows me to be autistic. What do I mean when I say that I'm autistic? The person who is voluntarily autistic, who is not really autistic, can lower the shutter on his business when the pain is unbearable. I made the word my own, in order to speak of that possibility of going into a relative retreat when the pressures around me are unbearable. Whether it's due to language, or translation, or not wanting to go where I have to go in order to do something else. Those defense mechanisms allow me a retreat that has its advantages because it allows me to grow in my own way. (qtd. in Weiss 1999a, 1)

10. The spontaneity of linguistic confluence in the mind is a recurrent theme for many in this state, including Silvia Baron Supervielle, who was raised in Argentina; nearly all of her published work is in French. She recognizes this shift causes her Spanish to develop and evolve: "I've always tried to hang onto Spanish, I write my letters in Spanish and sometimes I've been asked for a text in Spanish. The talks in Buenos Aires I did directly in Spanish, which required a lot of work." Like Biancotti, her awareness of the multi-nature of her internal cognition, that "one" language was insufficient to a degree: "It seemed to me that I would never be able to find the thread, to establish a harmony, to achieve some kind of wholeness if I kept writing in Spanish." In taking on translation (Spanish to French), she recalls, "Suddenly I found a terrain where I recognized myself and which was mine, where it was so difficult finding the word and the language that I wrote very short poems, very pared down, with barely four or five

words. Instead of translating the poems I had written, longer rhythmical poems, I thought no, I'm going to show them poems in French. That's how I started to write these poems that are of such little means, I understood that that's exactly what I am, this sort of poverty of words, this fear of the language" (qtd. in Weiss 1999b, 1). The intersection of traditionally separate languages, for Baron Supervielle, is non-geographic space with a performativity unavailable in other forms of communication: "I realized that I had found something, a place that was mine. That poverty was like a mirror that was imposed on me. What I mean is that perhaps the same thing would have happened to me in another country and with another language. It wasn't due to French, from which I also wanted to remain apart, but to that distance between the language and me, which resembled the distance I wanted to exist around me, on both sides, a distance that obliged me to pare things down" (qtd. in Weiss 1999b, 1).

11. When queried if he has a French dictionary handy when he writes, he responds: "No. I always work as a kamikaze. I'm spontaneous, I write. But then I rework. For instance, *L'Ile du lézard vert* (1992), I wrote two times entirely. *Habanera* (1994), I rewrote many times. But the real work is after the first draft. With the plays, it's the same. I write, I write, I write, and then I go back" (qtd. in Weiss 1998: 1).

12. He continues:

> I was walking in the Luxembourg Gardens and I came across Sam Beckett. We began to talk and I said, Sam, I have this problem, I'm a Cuban, I'm Spanish. "Oh, don't worry, Eduardo, don't worry. I wrote in French because I wanted to forget Joyce." The influence of Joyce. And I wanted to forget Lorca's influence on me, and Valle-Inclán. And he said to me, "Anyhow, writers are always exiles, and you write in the language that you're published. You are published in French, you are a Cuban-French writer. And I'm from Ireland. I feel even more guilty than you." So, he lifted me up. (qtd. in Weiss 1998, 1)

13. He also wrote in English, including the novel *Holy Smoke*. Similarly, Ernest Hemingway, as I will soon discuss, wrote in English to demonstrate he was Cuban.

14. Silvia Baron Supervielle, who feels "absolutely and naturally Argentine," has been recognized as in France as "a French writer who also spoke Spanish," a categorization that caused "strange sensation." When Jason Weiss asked if she sees herself as a Latin American writer, she responds:

What I know is that I do not write like the French. Many people tell me that I bring something different, a kind of fantastic realism. Although I do not see myself in most novelists and short story writers of that tendency, which I like; but perhaps without meaning to I do have something of that. Once someone told me: really, you're a foreigner on both sides. And that's how I feel. . . . Inevitably we have to ask: What notion of country and nationality do writers have? What notion of country? . . . In the middle of all that, how to define if I am Argentine? But I don't like to be told that I'm not Argentine. I am. Why? Because it is the land of my most distant memories, the most important ones . . . but at the same time I do not at all have the feeling for the *patria*, the fatherland. And if they tell me I'm French, that's not the point at all! . . . Really, in the end one is a total exile! (qtd. in Weiss 1999b, 1)

15. He also comments: "Para explicar que los peruanos aguaitamos, del peruanismo aguaitar, mientras que los españoles fisgonean, del verbo que no usamos los peruanos. Es un lío hacer periodismo así y hasta escribir un libro de recordar. En la literatura, en cambio, uno está más cómodo y la prueba es Juan Rulfo, cuyos mexicanismos a veces no los entienden ni los mexicanos y es, a pesar de ello, universal" (Bryce Echenique 1993b, 367–68).

16. A significant amount of Picasso's poetry is French.

17. Colom's library had books in Catalan, and he named the island of Montserrat for a monastery near Barcelona. He was also surrounded by Catalans throughout his life. Lluís de Santàngel, who financed him, was from Valencia (in the Països Catalans) and spoke Catalan; the first baptism in the Americas was carried out by Ramon Pané, a man "of the Catalan nation," according to Las Casas, most likely chosen by Colom, as was the first apostolic vicar of the West Indies (Bernat de Boïl) and the expedition's military chief (Bertran i de Margarit).

The Catholic monarchs received Colom in Barcelona after the first voyage, and Colom's son Diego left a silver lamp in his will to Our Lady of Montserrat "on account of the great devotion that I have always had." As Diego never lived in Catalonia, and his mother was Portuguese, a piety for Montserrat was probably inherited from his father. According to the archives of his son Fernando, the only letter Colom bequeathed to him was written in Catalan; that document and a copy (translated to German from Catalan in Strasbourg in 1497) were lost; many believe they were destroyed in part to subdue Catalonian nationalism.

Part of the mystery may have come from Colom himself. The Hebrew marginalia and references to the Jewish High Holy Days in his writings indicate that, like Lluís de Santàngel, it is possible Colom or his ancestors were converts to

Christianity. At the end of La Rambla, Barcelona's most famous street, is a two-hundred-foot-high statue of Colom. At the base are Lluís de Santàngel, the financier; Jaume Ferrer de Blanes, a cartographer; Bernat de Boïl, that first apostolic minister in the Americas; and Pere Bertran i de Margarit, the military commander. The motto of the monument is, "Honorable Colom, Catalonia honors her favorite children." Colom is pointing out to sea, with his back to Castile (Herlihy-Mera 2017d).

18. There are many "English-language" writers and popular figures whose lives were informed by distinct variants of Spanish: Ernest Hemingway (Florida, Cuba, Spain), William Carlos Williams (New Jersey, Puerto Rico, Dominican Republic), John Wayne (California, Mexico), Billy the Kidd (Arizona, Mexico), John Steinbeck (California, Mexico), and Cormac McCarthy (Texas, Mexico, New Mexico, Arizona, Ibiza).

19. The process of inter-lingual existence has been termed one in which a person is perpetually "internalizing more than one culture" and while "constructs of culture and language are [generally treated as] distinct, they are undoubtedly interwoven" (Christiansen and Turkina 2018, xv). This circumstance, note Christiansen and Turkina, "affects all areas of human endeavor" and "we must do all we can in academia" and thus "heighten the same sensitivity where it is needed" (Christiansen and Turkina 2018, xvi).

20. In this realm of cultural tension and the anxiety that stemmed from it, Williams was compelled to suppress his ability to speak Spanish—and for that, despite its omnipresence where he lived and worked, Williams's descriptions of his use of that language (including claims he could not speak it) and its role in his upbringing often belie the underlying characteristics of his sociolinguistic frame from which his creative process grew into texts in English.

21. Many writers also realize English in Spanish. A beginning pathway toward understandings, interrogations, and ultimately institutionalization of these realities begins with a scholarly environment in which languages are performable in the same ways that they are practiced outside the confines of the institution—that is: with glib interchangeability and fluidity, in place of balkanized isolation. The multilingual university provides a map that questions, contextualizes, and interprets such work and such communities with a localized facility (and relevance to multilingual students) that a monolingual intellectual environment cannot provide. For more, see Herlihy-Mera 2019b.

22. A notable scholar in this discipline is Ilan Stavans, whose book *Spanglish: The Making of a New American Language* opened new critical arenas. He describes

arriving from Mexico, expecting a "monolithic, homogenous, single-minded" environment but found "a polyphonic reality" (2003, 4).

23. In *Second Language Identities* David Block argues that separate identities based in part on language have links to social class, ethnicity, migratory-status, and other concepts (2007, introduction).

24. If a mixture of tongues complement one another and interrelate in all contexts, even when only one language is present, the cross-lingual dimension of life for migrant figures is of particular importance.

25. For more on this topic, see my article "Cuba in Hemingway" in the *Hemingway Review*.

26. His unrealized dream to live in Mexico was completed by Cormac McCarthy's protagonists.

27. After learning Spanish in Europe in the 1920s, his move to Key West (an island important in the Cuban independence movement, often described as a neighborhood of Havana), followed by his permanent move to Cuba in 1939, indicate that he was immersed in Spanish-language environs far longer than he lived in English-speaking surroundings.

28. Possibly his lover, she is often understood as a muse for *Across the River and into the Trees*.

29. There are also opportunities to locate Spanish syntax that migrated into Hemingway's English. Spanish genders nouns, articles, and adjectives, and this has been shown to influence how objects are perceived in the mind. When asked to provide a voice for a fork, Spanish-speakers tend to choose a male narrator (Aikhenvald 2016, 126) as *tenedor* is masculine. While in English time is a length ("long" or "short"), Spanish commonly uses quantity (*mucho/poco tiempo*). And subject-pronouns can be redundant in Spanish, resulting in phrases like [I/she/we] "will go home later." Hemingway was interviewed by the *New Yorker* arriving in New York from Havana in 1950: "Want to go to the Bronx Zoo, Metropolitan Museum, Museum of Modern Art, ditto of Natural History, and see a fight. Want to see the good Breughel at the Met, the one, no two, fine Goyas and Mr. El Greco's Toledo. Don't want to go to Toots Shor's. Am going to try to get into town. . . . . Time is the least thing we have of" (qtd. in Ross 1950, 1). Hemingway also designates a novel "she" (*la novela*) and addresses Lillian Ross as "my daughter," an Anglicization of *mi hija* or *mija* ("my dear"). The same tendency appears in *The Old Man and the Sea*. Hemingway endows "sea" with a cross-lingual femininity ("la mar") that provides depth for the plot and a gender-symmetry in the title. He also uses a Spanish meaning for "boy"; at one point Manolín (the "boy")

carries over one hundred pounds of fishing line *and* a gaff and harpoon to Santiago's shack. How could a boy manage that? Clarification is in the language: *chico* and *muchacho* can refer to males until marriage. (Manolín is in his twenties.) As Santiago contemplates the sky, Hemingway unpacks a translingual pun: He "saw the white cumulus built like friendly piles of ice cream" and says "Light *brisa*" (1952, 61). While *brisa* appears as "breeze" in dictionaries, in Cuba it also means hunger. *The Old Man and the Sea* is written in an English-ized Cuban Spanish, a novel that is perhaps more accurately categorized as "Cuban" rather than "American" literature, presuming the exclusions and binaries embedded in both terms.

30. The certainties upon which those binaries exist, notes Salvatore, is a result of "the centralization of knowledge that accompanied the formation of informal empire. Moreover, American Studies, the same as the new Hemispheric Studies, have demarcated a geographic boundary beyond which inquiries are less interesting" (2015, 377).

31. Nuancing a Spanish-centric critical focus offers a mine of planes of understanding that recognize how profoundly the cultural interactions in the mind harmonize into translingual writing. These philosophies, emotions, sentiments, and messages are already present in many "Spanish" texts.

4. SPAIN: THE ARABIZED PROVINCE OF LATIN AMERICA, OR, WHICH QUIJOTE DO WE NEED?

1. The institutional and pedagogical myth that Spanish cultures or histories are more important than others, more aesthetically pleasing, or in some way more relevant to study is a Eurocentric mechanism that maintains the exceptionalism that reinforces the Spain-centric status quo (a one-to-one balance in the academy) in all subdisciplines.

2. Delinked from traditional axes, how could the distinct languages, communities, nations, and diasporas in play exist in pedagogy and research? What contextual reframing would offer suitable nuance to the received Castilian-centric (linguistic, social, spiritual, and cultural) presumptions? These presumptions of cultural, historical, linguistic, and other essences achieve fictional composites of many distinct experiences, conditions, identifications, and performances. The intentionality of area studies has these controls: limits that preordain knowledge production, pedagogies, and the ways cultures and communities are institutionalized. Among these are the supposed "correctness" of Castilian Spanish and the notion of "Spain" as central historical, cultural, and linguistic axis of all world

communities that use the Spanish language, making them among the myths most ripe for deflation.

3. In her book *Metaphor and National Identity*, Putz queries, "What motivates metaphor production? What is metaphor production based on?" and specifies that "cultural knowledge has fundamental role in metaphor production and sociocultural background" (2019, 22).

4. Jentiltasuna, Irmandade Druídica Galaica, Etenismo, Odinismo, Hermandad Druida Dun Ailline, Wicca Tradición Celtíbera, and Sorginkoba Elkartea, among others.

5. As an antidote to Toledo-Burgos-Valladolid-Madrid and other (Christian, Latin, and other presumed bases in) Castilian-centric axes of inquiry.

6. Resina's deft work on this issue explores some dimensions of how the prescriptions of union (articulated in relation to Castile-prescriptions) have failed to manipulate the cultures, languages, and identities of those directed communities, in the ways intended by the administrative units. Nevertheless, that supposed colonized unity is the base of "Hispanic" and "Iberian" and "Spain" studies, which thus are charged with the failures of such a priori definitions and limits.

7. "The complex Atlantic politics of subaltern migration in areas such as Andalusia, Extremadura, the Basque Country, and Galicia prove that this is a general problem that is solved by a retroactive articulation of the Spanish state as master signifier" (Gabilondo 2014, 44).

8. Including María Rosa Menocal, Miquel Berga, Pere Gifra, Joseba Gabilondo, David Wacks, Joan Ramon Resina, Andrea Righi, and Maureen Russo Rodríguez, among many others.

9. Weber maintains that military conscription, roads, schools, and the railroad were agents of Frenchification.

10. This circumstance was part of the motivation to Frenchify the population through compulsory state education—and has tones of the role of literacy in collective fantasy, as described by Benedict Anderson in *Imagined Communities*.

11. That is to say, if those "Hispanic/Spain" absolute allegiances, group sentiments, and emotions, etc., *ever existed* as such, or *if they exist in the present day*—a tendentious if not irresponsible supposition.

12. Resina asserts that new Iberian studies could emerge as a federalist project, whereby nations may exist in a "non-hierarchical" fashion (2009, 162).

13. Gabilondo argues that "if Iberian studies are to be studied at all, they will have to be first and foremost, foundationally, transatlantic" (2014, 37), which is to say, related to a Latin American center.

14. If area studies approaches are burdened by their presumptions, promoting them as intellectual material relegates any knowledge produced therein to an equally limited circle. The Iberian reinvention of "area studies" leads the discipline to an isolationist approach that might alleviate some of the geopolitical problems of older categories such as peninsular, Spanish, or Hispanic, but does not help create a fruitful exchange and dialogue with other disciplines and areas, thus further anchoring the field in the Cold-War history that originated "area studies."

15. But still informs some institutions, perhaps especially in Spain and the United States.

16. As Luis I. Prádanos notes, "In the age of mass extinction, climate change, ecological collapse, and unacceptable inequalities, cultural criticism needs to be rethought in a posthumanist, postnational, and decolonial fashion" (2016, 51).

If the traditional *unity* (which upholds the field) existed at some fixed point or now, it is an unstable thesis to assert that it was/is unilaterally adherent to the myths of Christianity, Latin, and the oligarchical power of Christian and Latin-based myths. But the ways cultural citizenships have been institutionalized dictate that Islamic and Arabic characteristics may only be treated as "foreign" in a domestic sense, and the failures of this view maintain Christianity and Latin (sometimes vernacular versions thereof) languages and cultures as preeminent and "natural" in the spaces where social activities are performed. Attention to Arabic and Islam, a recentering of the pedagogies and field toward those margins, allows nuance both to the certainties of "foreignization" of the cultures in question and creates insights on how the myth of Spain as a Christian space is yet an active and determinative notion that is used to organize migration and language laws, as well as cultural, educational, and social expenditures that derive from public sources. When critical attention recontextualizes Islam and Arabic as infrastructural dimensions of the cultural reality, rather than "foreign" and "occupying" presences, many new realms of understanding emerge in relation to the traditional points of pedagogical and intellectual emphases, including the Alhambra, El Cid, Don Quijote, the Camino de Santiago, as well as the Spanish (Castilian) language itself, and the food, music, culture, architecture, dress, and other traditions performed in the area.

17. The term Europeans (or Europenses) was perhaps first used by Andalusian priest Isidore Pacensis, describing Christians after the battle of Poitiers in 732 (Majid 2009, 4).

18. Abu Abdullah Muhammad ibn Yusuf ibn Nasr, the original patron of the Alhambra, supported the Christian conquest of Sevilla.

19. When we examine the experiences of conventional heteropatriarchal "Spanish" cultural figures (Cid, Cervantes, and Quijote, for instance) and notable architectural footprints (Mezquita de Córdoba, Alhambra, and Sagrada Familia, for instance) many critical reports in relation thereto unpack the same terms ("Moor"/"Spanish"), discharged often without nuance, to lay out a platform to compare and describe, and the mythic binary of Moorish/Spanish functions as the axis of reflection.

20. As a metaphysical dimension of the armies of the Inquisition, this ritualized institutional Islamophobia has been practiced in Iberia (and Europe more generally) for more than a millennium.

21. As John O'Hagan notes: "Charlemagne, who was a man of thirty-six at the time of the actual Roncesvaux incident, has become in the poem an old man with a flowing white beard, credited with endless conquests; the Basques have disappeared, and the Saracens have taken their place" (qtd. in Eliot 2010, 96).

22. The ruling family of Zaragoza before the Christian conquest. Cid's Christian ruler, Alfonso VI, also served on a Muslim court.

23. Of linguistic controls levied against Moriscos in the ninth/sixteenth century, Francisco Núñez Muley (1490–1568) wrote, "How can people be deprived of their own language, with which they were born and brought up? In Egypt, Syria, Malta and elsewhere there are people like us who speak, read and write in Arabic, and they are Christians like us" (qtd. in Lévi-Provençal 2009, 509). For more on the Arabic-speaking Christians in Iberia in Cervantes's lifetime, see Dolores Luna Guinot's account of the Rebellion of the Alpujarras (1568–1571) in *From Al-Andalus to Monte Sacro* (145).

24. These circumstances inform his biting satire of figures like Cid, Charlemagne, and Amadís de Gaula, as well as the cultures that produced them. Some have argued that Cervantes's mockeries of Christian heroes demonstrate disapproval of the Islamophobia embedded in the Santiago-in-Spain myth (Graf 2007, 177).

25. He was, then in practical terms, not incarcerated in a *cárcel*.

26. While صَالَةُ ٱلْجُمُعَة Ṣalāt al-Jumu'ah occurs Friday, Saturday is ٱلسَّبْت as-Sabt or "the Rest."

27. Ricote's name likely references Val de Ricote, which is also known as "El Valle Morisco," the last region of Spain to be forcefully cleansed of Moriscos in 1614, 903 years after Muslim migrants arrived on the peninsula.

28. Historians and hagiographers, argue Françoise Meltzer and Jas Elsne, tend to focus "their attention on Santiago the Moorslayer rather than Santiago the Missionary" (2011, 187).

29. Christians invaded Zaragoza in 496/1118; it had been governed in Moorish tradition twice as long as Christian. The myth of James beholding María at Zaragoza did not reach print until half a millennia later, in the fifth/thirteenth century (Deswarte 2015, 499). In this tale, the Virgin Mary appeared on a stone pillar—the nomenclature of Ernest Hemingway's boat references that *pilar*.

30. In this geopolitical landscape, the Galician regions that were under Christian political control (though the general population could be perhaps best described as Celtic or a proto-Christian creole) proved to be an opportue site for the relics.

31. In general, the mono-causal appropriation theories about cultural imperialism are slowly being abandoned in favor of more descriptive creole, amalgamative, and hybrid approaches to the cultural interaction that occurs subsequent to military invasions.

32. Noblemen who lived far away would pay the poor to walk for them (Quesada-Embid 2008, 98).

33. When Christian armies invaded, conquered, and colonized Grenada, a city they yet occupy, Santiago's myth was an important pretext for the campaign of violence and displacement: the religious ruse linked the military and cultural campaign to the (retroactive) Christian nature of Iberia. The Santiago-in-Iberia story thus appropriated a Celtic tradition in order to justify war, and the literatures and social traditions surrounding this rite are cultural dimensions of political colonization and social domination. In this sense, Santiago is linked to violence, murder, displacement, migration, colonization, forced acculturation, and loss of personal and collective autonomy.

In this way, the pilgrimage is part of a nearly millennium-long program of cleansing Islamic, Jewish, and pagan cultures from Iberia.

34. For more on this topic, see Herlihy-Mera 2019a. These physical manifestations (bodily remains) of intangible forces sanctioned the presence of the cultural systems in those spaces.

35. The Camino de Santiago relates a charged historical metanarrative that is inherently exclusionary: latent and ostensibly innocuous literary allusions to the pilgrimage, such as those written by Cervantes but also by Picasso and Zafón among others, could be described as micro-aggressive.

36. While many studies claim the linguistic influence as between 20 percent and 30 percent, Carlos Fuentes's finds the number to be 50 percent in *Espejo Enterrado* (Fuentes 1997, part 5; Flores Montemayor 2003, 204).

37. As Abigail Agresta notes, the "categories themselves are shaped and given meaning by those in power" and thus were used to enforce difference and confor-

mity in ways that "serve those in power" (2018, 1). Remie Constable's insightful study (2018) interprets these multicultural contexts in the medieval period—but her gesture toward regional identities in Spain, and their importance in everyday existence, yet pervade cultural and social affairs. When Islamic and Muslim resonances are examined throughout cultural history around the Peninsula, it is clear that the influences across the map of federalized entities may not be of equal significance, but they have been a "unifying" dimension to "Spanish" life, and remain so. It is important to signal out that these are not specifically religious in origin but regional, traditional, and often familial. "Most people in North America and even in Europe," notes Castilla Brazales, "believe that Arab Muslims have only affected [the culture] of a small region of Spain, mostly in the south—they are wrong" (2017, 1).

38. There is a Camino del Cid, which receives significant public funding, but no institutional recognition whatsoever exists for the Islamic pilgrimages to Córdoba.

39. The relabeling illustrates how cultural engineering and meaning-making legislation often occurs in multicultural societies, especially those with imperial histories: while the prescriptions evolve in concert with the contemporary affairs, they promote the interests of those publishing the material. The seizure and attempted appropriation of iconographic material (e.g., the transition of the edifice from "mosque" to "cathedral") foregrounds the Christian ontology, but critical shifts in method can undo some of the structural configuration of the settler (in this case Christian-Spaniard) narrative in Córdoba, and in doing so, disengage specific monocultural conceptualizations of multicultural spaces, in concert with citizenship policies.

40. So perhaps like the terms "Roman," "Carthage," and "Celtic," among others, "Spain" could be allowed to deteriorate into memory.

41. That is: the social and pedagogical mechanisms that link current experiences to previous generations.

5. ON THE PUERTORICANIZATION OF US HIGHER EDUCATION: OR, THE AWKWARD CONSTRAINTS OF USING ONE LANGUAGE

1. In these contexts, English and Spanish (and other languages) are institutionalized as isolates from one another, as though they were separate, unrelated, and disconnected traditions with different histories and cultures. The tendency imagines one (English, in all cases) as domestic and others as foreign; the "best"

practice treats language mixing as ungrammatical or dialectical, or as a language "variant," rather than generatively performative methods of being.

2. In relation to cultural studies, these include: takes on the "normalcy" of multilingual identities and their performances; on use of English (or other languages) as a literary language of Spanish-speakers and vice versa; on transnational, transcultural, transregional, and translingual identities; on the ways multilingual teaching and learning expand and blend conceptual horizons in sophisticated ways.

3. Nevertheless, these forces and their process of "stripping of voice from bicultural children strips them of something more important than just their ability to have voice; it strips them of their world-view, group identification and historical experience, their commitment to their own cultural norms" (Díaz Soto and Kareem 2006, 25).

4. See Herlihy-Mera 2017b.

5. Our institution's intercultural environment allows the campus interactions—in speaking, listening, reading, and writing in class and other activities—to reflect the community in ways that monolingual exigencies of tradition best practices prohibit.

6. This dialogue is not limited to spaces claimed by the US political body. As Sandra Harding notes, "Anti-colonial arguments by Nahua intellectuals had already appeared in Spanish in the Americas by 1538 and continued to be produced by those intellectuals" (2019, 49).

7. The struggles for institutional recognition of Spanglish and other language systems that are rebellious to channel into traditional grammars and lexes are fertile.

8. By externalizing from the monolingual prescriptions, questions like "Who believes what today?" and "How does language shape thought, culture, and feeling?" are tangential to the matter at hand, incapable of the articulating inter-, cross-, and extra-meanings that stem from linguistic and thus cognitive exteriority.

9. Allowing multilingual themes to be commonplace instead of aberrant.

10. Similarly, as a student reflected on the linguistic contexts at NYU, "We study in a German department where French theory is taught in English" (qtd. in Hüppaf 2018, 1).

11. This is a play on Ernesto Cuba's eloquent aphorism: "Si no me nombras, no existo."

12. "Es posible que la excepción a la regla del 'cementerio de lenguas' sea el español" (Durand 2015, 1).

CONCLUSION.
OVERCOMING THE TRADITION OF SILENCE

Epigraph 2 (Huyke). He continues, via email: "me refiero a (1) cuándo las personas no tienen las destrezas para modificar el lenguaje de la aplicación, (2) cuando las computadoras por arte de magia vuelven al inglés como *default language,* y (3) cuando a la persona no le importa, lo que es muy común, (4) ¿qué efecto puede tener en un niño en la edad de apreciar y acoger su lengua nativa?" (email to the author March 21, 2022).

1. In step with the Spanish-foreign / English-domestic myth, Latinx cultural studies are regularly housed in English departments. Suffice it to say, these fields would be an excellent addition to Spanish departments and as independent departmental units

2. By conceptualizing Spanish and Spanish-language cultures within the one-to-one Spain-US / Latin America paradigm.

3. Any utterance outside the prescriptions of the colonial (often Peninsular) standard is "derogatorily labeled 'dialect,' 'patois,' 'pidgin,' 'creole,' and 'Spanglish,' among other labels" (Macedo 2019, 11).

4. As David Castillo and William Egginton deftly observe, these conditions inform popular media, public critique, and redouble the lesser humanity of Latinx figures vis-à-vis the imperial figures: "Pat Robertson can call for the assassination of Venezuelan president Hugo Chávez on national TV and the statement goes uncensored, while Kanye West's remarks about the president during the NBC show for the relief of the victims of Katrina (reportedly 'George Bush doesn't care about black people') are erased from the west coast airing" (2006, 48).

5. An epistemic move would retreat from the racist, Eurocentric, and English-domestic / Spanish-foreign certainties embedded in Bauerlein and King's arguments in which "United States" as a grouping mechanism subdues all outside those whom they includes in "we"—and sets the center from which all "others" are to be measured. The way communities are grouped relations is in play: these traditions make "Spanish-speaking" and "American" anti-ethical and contradictory, as one must be hyphenated, decentered, marginalized, and exist in subordinate relation to the other.

6. In a sense, they prescribe more accurately than they describe. The transnational ignorance makes that failure unrecognizable and inconceivable, and those who point it out are often considered irrational.

7. Mabel Moraña has astute reflections on the entangled nature of aesthetic and political language: "Every time that we explore the aesthetic we are approaching,

by sometimes mediated, sometimes oblique fashions, the political (the processes of cultural institutionalization, the twists and turns of official history, the problems of textual truth, the cultural politics and the material conditions from which the texts are produced and read in different contexts)" (2006, 34).

8. The ways industrialized neoliberal culture distort Latinx histories have been the focus of a great deal of critique. In "Why Hamilton Is the Most Right-Wing Musical on Broadway," Ezra Brain notes that "Miranda equates immigrants—specifically Latinx immigrants—with colonizers. This is key to how Miranda views the Founding Fathers. We are meant to see working-class people from Latin America coming to the U.S. in search of jobs in the same light as wealthy Europeans coming to the colonies to, well, colonize them." Brain's analyses examine how the demography of the actors is weaponized into capitalist myth: "[Miranda] adds insult to injury by having Black and Latinx actors portray the very people who oppressed and murdered their ancestors," and continues, "Alexander Hamilton, George Washington, Thomas Jefferson, and their compatriots are no longer bourgeois slave owners, but rather plucky freedom fighters and young men trying to make something of themselves" (2020, 1).

9. Rubén Mendoza maintains that such avenues of resistance are "social endeavors that emerge as generated effects only through collaborative work" and that creativity is key: "Development of critical-imaginative modes [are possible] through the figure of the artist-educator. It potentially can disrupt static experiences of self by facilitating student engagement with processual modes of becoming" (2017, iv, abstract). Similarly, Andrea Righi's work critically engages digital consciousness as a site of resistance (2021, chapters 1–3).

10. The violence of the foreign is "the material and symbolic horizon for the definition of [Latinx] objects and tenets" (Degiovanni 2018, 3).

11. As Michel Foucault maintains, "The role of political power is perpetually to use a silent war to reinscribe that relationship of force, and to reinscribe it in institutions, economic inequalities, language and even the bodies of individuals" (1976, 15–16).

12. These have consequences for students from my university when they are in the United States (spelling idiosyncrasies included): "I was an exchange Student last semester In rhode island and being there by myself i always felt intimidated to speak spanish even if it was with other latinos because i just felt too surounded with monolinguals in a new place all by myself it was intimidating and i felt like i could only speak english to stay out of trouble." And another: "If I think in a monolingual setting I get nervous for not being able to communicate and also for being a victim of racism."

13. The exigencies surrounding "global citizenship" participate in the silencing of US Spanish, as does the industrial education machine of study away.

14. In such communities, university faculty who prepared in far-off universities and discuss Spain before local cultures, or at best with equal importance, participate in an intellectualized and nuanced version of the same narrative: Spanish is foreign, local (US / Latin American) cultures are inferior because the people are inferior.

15. "When one considers that three of the most influential writers worldwide are Latin American—Borges, García Márquez, and Bolaño—the inability or unwillingness to support the disciplines that account for the genealogy of those writers is a glaring omission" (Sánchez Prado 2020, 1).

16. In regard to Lorgia García Peña, who was denied tenure at Harvard in 2019, Sánchez Prado notes that her situation "shows dramatically, the service that Spanish programs do in meeting Latinx students' educational and cultural needs often goes unrewarded and even punished" (2020, 1).

17. Many through the land-grant system.

18. The Universidad de Puerto Rico notably pushes back against this norm.

19. While Said situates his intervention in postcolonial terms that needle imperial grammars, critique has moved a degree away from the rigidity of those terms.

20. The exceptional norms are codified in and by professional associations, publication opportunities, scholarly awards, appointment practices, and curricular trends.

21. As Brad Epps notes, in contemporary humanities, the importance of *who may engage in intellectual activity* is of preeminent importance: "I do not take the subject(s) of the pronoun 'our' and the 'disciplines' whose state is here at issue to be self-evident. Perhaps even less self-evident is the status of work or, more specifically, academic work: not in the sense of what line of critical inquiry 'works' best, or whose 'work' is most compelling, or what 'work' needs to be done to advance the study of Hispanic issues, but in the sense of *who works, and where*, and for whom, and under what conditions" (2006, 17; my emphasis). The failures of the neoliberal university require action that allows those traditionally excluded demographics to participate: to an important degree, the demographics are those who are absent (and systemically excluded) from top-ranked universities.

22. "Prestige bias contributes to and exacerbates the structural underrepresentation of minorities," comments Helen de Cruz, and it "amplifies inequalities" in hiring (2018, 1). Similarly, as Michael Shott argues, the conventional hiring system decontextualizes candidates in toxic ways: "universalism implies that the meritorious rise or sink to their natural level regardless of circumstance" (2022, 2).

23. Of the recipients, 100 percent were from English-monolingual institutions and there were no scholars from Historically Black Colleges and Universities (HBCUs) or Tribal Colleges and Universities (TCUs).

24. While some in Graham's cohort did not receive tenure-line appointments, the figure is incredibly small in comparison to PhDs in the UPR cohort.

25. "These faculty members are disproportionately white and/or male. Adjuncts, meanwhile, are disproportionately women and minorities" (al-Gharbi 2020, 1).

26. Silence from Harvard and Yale often means more than words from UPR's cohort.

27. The proposal was written in English because NEH, like nearly every other humanities organization, does not receive applications in Spanish.

28. We recommended these changes to ACLS executives during a Zoom roundtable in May 2020. Part of the material in this section appeared in "A New Future for Humanities Funding?" *Inside Higher Ed*, May 14, 2021.

29. Employer: Williams College, NYU, Princeton, Boston University, New Jersey Institute of Technology, Columbia, Texas, Brandeis, Stanford, Tennessee, Nevada, UC Irvine, Colorado, Illinois, Valparaiso, Tulane, Iowa, Minnesota, Smith College, Utah, Harvard, University of Florida, University of California–Santa Barbara, University of California–Los Angeles.

30. At Spelman, 48 percent of students are Pell eligible.

REFERENCES

Abbott, Ann. 2016. "Many of Us Have Been Saying This for a Long Time." Facebook post. June 25, 2016.

Abbott, Ann. 2017. "Engaged Humanities and the Future of Spanish Programs." *Hispania* 100(5): 33–34.

Abbott, Martha. 2018. "Monolingualism Diminishes America's Stature on the World Stage." *Hill*, March 8, 2018, https://thehill.com/opinion/education/376707-monolingualism-diminishes-americas-stature-on-the-world-stage.

Abd-Allah, Umar Faruq. 2010. *Turks, Moors, and Moriscos in Early America: Sir Francis Drake's Liberated Galley Slaves and the Lost Colony of Roanoke*. Chicago: Nawawi Foundation.

Agresta, Abigail. 2018. "Culturally Muslim in Medieval and Early Modern Spain." *Marginalia*, August 3, 2018, https://themarginaliareview.com/being-culturally-muslim/.

Aikhenvald, Alexandra. 2016. *How Gender Shapes the World*. Oxford: Oxford University Press.

Aínsa, Fernando. 2009. "Peregrinaciones en la narrativa hispanoamericana del XIX y XX: Entre el viaje iniciático y la búsqueda de raíces." In *El viaje en la literatura hispánica: de Juan Valera a Sergio Pitol*, edited by Julio Peñate Rivero and Francisco Uzcanga, 47–65. Madrid: Verbum.

Al-Gharbi, Musa. 2020. "Universities Run on Disposable Scholars." *Chronicle of Higher Education*, May 1, 2020, https://www.chronicle.com/article/universities-run-on-disposable-scholars/.

Almond, Ian. 2011. *Two Faiths, One Banner: When Muslims Marched with Christians across Europe's Battlegrounds*. Cambridge, MA: Harvard University Press.

Álvarez, Stephanie. 2013. "Subversive English in *Raining Backwards*: A Different Kind of Spanglish" *Hispania* 96, no. 3 (September): 444–59.

Amar, Grover. 2011. "Cordoba Showcases Spain's Great Islamic Past." *National*, June 25, 2011, https://www.thenationalnews.com/lifestyle/travel/cordoba-showcases-spain-s-great-islamic-past-1.430279.

Alonso, Carlos. 2007. "Spanish: The Foreign National Language." *Profession* 1:218–28.

Alter, Adam. 2013. "Defined by Your Category." *Week*, May 10, 2013, 36–38.

Anzaldúa, Gloria. 1987. *Borderlands / La Frontera: The New Mestiza*. San Francisco: Aunt Lute Books.

Arner, Lynn. 2014. "Working Class Woman at the MLA Interview." *Rhizomes: Cultural Studies in Emerging Knowledge* 27. http://www.rhizomes.net/issue27/arner.html.

Arroyo, Danilyz. 2018. Interview with the author. Mayagüez, Puerto Rico. December 1, 2018.

Athanasopoulos, Panos. 2015. "How the Language You Speak Changes Your View of the World." *Independent*, April 29, 2015. https://www.independent.co.uk/news/science/how-the-language-you-speak-changes-your-view-of-the-world-10212854.html.

Avelar, Idelber. 2005. "Xenophobia and Diasporic Latin Americanism: Mapping Antagonisms around 'the Foreign.'" In *Ideologies of Hispanism*, edited by Mabel Moraña, 269–84. Nashville, TN: Vanderbilt University Press.

Baisotto, Pablo, and Zhongli Zhang. 2017. "The Struggle for Chicano / Latino Studies: Evolution and Development in California." *Revista Andina de Estudios Políticos* 7(2): 152–73.

Barletta, Vincent. 2005. *Covert Gestures: Crypto-Islamic Literature as Cultural Practice in Early Modern Spain*. Minneapolis: University of Minnesota Press.

Battiste, Marie. 2011. *Reclaiming Indigenous Voice and Vision*. Vancouver: University of British Columbia Press.

Bauerlein, Mark. 2020. "What Took the Place of Western Civ?" *Inside Higher Ed*, February 20, 2020. https://www.insidehighered.com/views/2020/02/19/how-revision-western-civ-curriculum-resulted-no-curriculum-all-opinion#.

Bautista, Rafael. 2017. *Del mito del desarrollo al horizonte del "vivir bien" ¿por qué fracasa el socialismo en el largo siglo XX?* La Paz: Yo soy si Tú eres ediciones.

Bernstein, Rachel. 2015. "Elitism in the Academy." *Science*, February, 12, 2015. https://www.science.org/content/article/elitism-academy.

Beverley, John. 2019. *The Failure of Latin America: Postcolonialism in Bad Times*. Pittsburgh: Pittsburgh University Press.

Bezhanova, Olga. 2014. "What Comes After the Nation-State, Part IV." *Clarissa's Blog*, September 2, 2014. https://clarissasblog.com/2014/09/02/.

Bhanot, Kavita. 2015. "Decolonise, not Diversify." *Mediadiversified*, December 30, 2015. https://mediadiversified.org/2015/12/30/is-diversity-is-only-for-white-people/.

Binder, Wolfgang. 1995. "An Interview with Roberto G. Fernández." In *American Contradictions: Interviews with Nine American Writers*, edited by Wolfgang Binder and Helmbrecht Breinig, 2–18. Middletown, CT: Wesleyan University Press.

Blanchett, W. J. 2006. "Disproportionate Representation of African American Students in Special Education: Acknowledging the Role of White Privilege and Racism." *Educational Researcher* 35(6): 24–28.

Blaser, Mario. 2014. "The Political Ontology of Doing Difference . . . and Sameness." Fieldsights: Theorizing the Contemporary series. *Cultural Anthropology Online* 13. https://culanth.org/fieldsights/the-political-ontology-of-doing-difference-and-sameness.

Block, David. 2007. *Second Language Identities*. London: Continuum.

"Bolivia's New Leader Vows Change." 2006. *BBC News*, January 22, 2006, 1.

Boroditsky, Lera. 2009. "How Does Our Language Shape the Way We Think?" *Edge*, June 11, 2009. https://www.edge.org/conversation/lera_boroditsky-how-does-our-language-shape-the-way-we-think.

Boroditsky, Lera. 2015. "'Mind & Life' Perceptions, Concepts and Self—Contemporary Scientific and Buddhist Perspectives." Sera Monastery, Bylakuppe, Karnataka, India. December 14–17, 2015.

Bousquet, Marc. 2016. "Three Posts." Facebook post. June 28, 2016.

Bowen, Zach. 1986. "'Young Blood' and Other Gothic Inspirations: The Hiring Process." *ADE Bulletin* 85. http://www.adfl.org/cgi-shl/docstudio/docs.pl?bulletin_085046.

Brain, Ezra. 2020. "Why Hamilton Is the Most Right-Wing Musical on Broadway." *Left Voice*, July 7, 2020. https://www.resetera.com/threads/left-voice-why-hamilton-is-the-most-right-wing-musical-on-broadway.244267/.

Breuilly, John. 1982. *Nationalism and the State*. Manchester, UK: University of Manchester Press.

Brown, Alan V., and Gregory L. Thompson. 2018. *The Changing Landscape of Spanish Language Curricula: Designing Higher Education Programs for Diverse Students*. Washington, DC: Georgetown University Press.

Brown, Joan L. 2010. *Confronting Our Canons: Spanish and Latin American Studies in the 21st Century*. Lewisburg, PA: Bucknell University Press.

Brown, Joan L. 2012. "What Do Graduate Students in Spanish Need to Learn, and Why?" *Hispania* 95(3) (September): xiii–xv.

Bryce Echenique, Alfredo. 1993a. *Un mundo para Julius*. Edición de Julio Ortega. Madrid: Catédra.

Bryce Echenique, Alfredo. 1993b. *Permiso para sentir: Antimemorias II*. Anagrama.

Brynjolfsson, Erik, and Andrew McAfee. 2014. *The Second Machine Age: Work, Progress, and Prosperity in a Time of Brilliant Technologies*. Brilliance Audio.

Burnett, Christina Duffy, Burke Marshall, Gilbert M. Joseph, and Emily S. Rosenberg. 2001. *Foreign in a Domestic Sense: Puerto Rico, American Expansion, and the Constitution*. Durham, NC: Duke University Press.

Buser, Susan. 2011. "'Juan Crow' Law Alive and Well in Alabama." *USA Today*, November 1, 2011. http://www.usatoday.com/news/opinion/forum/story/2011.

Canagarajah, Suresh. 2013. *Translingual Practice: Global Englishes and Cosmopolitan Relations*. New York: Routledge.

Cañizares-Esguerra, Jorge. 2001. *How to Write the History of the New World: Histories, Epistemologies, and Identities in the Eighteenth-Century Atlantic World*. Redwood City, CA: Stanford University Press.

Carafiol, Peter. 1992. "After American Literature." *American Literary History* 4.3 (Fall): 539–49.

Carcelén-Estrada, Antonia. 2016. "What Does the Sumak Kawsay Mean for Women in the Andes Today? Unsettling Patriarchal Sedimentations in Two Inca Writers." In *Decolonial Approaches to Latin American Literatures and Cultures*, edited by Juan Ramos and Tara Daly, 57–75. London: Palgrave.

Caro Baroja, Julio. 2000. *Los Moriscos del Reino de Granada: Ensayo de historia social*. Grenada: Istmo.

Carrithers, Michael. 2008. "Proposing the Motion." *Ontology Is Just Another Word for Culture*. Debate. Meeting of the Group for Debates in Anthropological Theory. Manchester, UK: Manchester University Press.

Carroll, Kevin. 2016. "Language Policies in Puerto Rican Higher Education: Conflicting Assumptions of Bilingualism." *Current Issues in Language Planning* 3–4:260–77.

Carter, Philip M. 2018. "Hispanic-Serving Institutions and Mass Media Engagement: Implications for Sociolinguistic Justice." *Journal of English Linguistics* 46(3): 246–62.

Casas, Angélica. 2019. "I'm Hispanic but Can't Speak Spanish." *BBC News*, November 18, 2019. https://www.bbc.com/news/av/world-us-canada-50395013.

Cassuto, Leonard. 2019. "8 Tips to Improve Your CV." *Chronicle of Higher Education*, July 21, 2019. https://www.chronicle.com/article/8-tips-to-improve-your-cv/.

Cassuto, Leonard. 2020. "How Can Graduate Programs and Students Prepare for an Uncertain Fall?" *Chronicle of Higher Education*, June 8, 2020. https://www.chronicle.com/article/how-can-graduate-programs-and-students-prepare-for-an-uncertain-fall.

Castilla Brazales, Juan. 2017. "Arab-Muslim Influence on the Iberian Peninsula." *Humanities BYU*, March 16, 2017. https://humanities.byu.edu/arab-muslim-influence-on-the-iberian-peninsula/.

Castillo, David, and William Egginton. 2006. "Hispanism(s) Briefly: A Reflection on the State of the Discipline." In *Debating Hispanic Studies: Reflections on Our Disciplines*, edited by Luis Martín-Estudillo, Francisco Ocampo, and Nicholas Spadaccini, 86–98. Vol. 1 of *Hispanic Issues Online*. Minneapolis: University of Minnesota.

Castro-Klarén, Sara. 2016. "Notes from the Field: Decolonizing the Curriculum / The 'Spanish' Major." In *Decolonial Approaches to Latin American Literatures and Cultures*, edited by Juan Ramos and Tara Daly, 3–18. London: Palgrave.

Cazden, Courtney, and David Dickinson. 1981. "Language in Education: Standardization Versus Cultural Pluralism." In *Language in the USA*, edited by Charles Ferguson and Shirley Brice Heath, 446–69. Cambridge: Cambridge University Press.

Cervantes, Miguel de. 2004. *Don Quijote de la Mancha*. Edición del IV Centenario. Madrid: Alfaguara.

Cervera, César. 2016. "La controvertida muerte de Billy 'el Niño,' el pistolero 'hispano' de los 21 asesinatos." *ABC Historia*, November 11, 2016. https://www.abc.es/historia/abci-controvertida-muerte-billy-nino-pistolero-hispano-21-asesinatos-201610110312_noticia.html.

Chejne, Anwar. 1969. *The Arabic Language: Its Role in History*. Minneapolis: University of Minnesota Press.

Chen, Hao, Lai Kaisheng, He Lingnan, and Yu Rongjun. 2020. "Where You Are Is Who You Are? The Geographical Account of Psychological Phenomena." *Frontiers in Psychology* 536:1–11.

Cherniavsky, Eva. 2017. *Neocitizenship: Political Culture after Democracy*. New York: New York University Press.

Ch'ien, Evelyn Nien-Ming. 2004. *Weird English*. Cambridge, MA: Harvard University Press.

Christiansen, Bryan, and Ekaterina Turkina. 2018. *Applied Psycholinguistics and Multilingual Cognition in Human Creativity.* Hershey, PA: IGI Global.

Cisneros, Sandra. 2013. "Interview with Sandra Cisneros." *Chicago Public Library Publications*, March 2013. https://www.chipublib.org/interview-with-sandra-cisneros/.

Clauset, Aaron, Samuel Arbesman, and Daniel B. Larremore. 2015. "Systematic Inequality and Hierarchy in Faculty Hiring Networks." *Science Advances*, February 12, 2015. https://doi.org/10.1126/sciadv.1400005.

Cofré, Claudia, and Arnaldo Delgado. 2018. "Enrique Dussel: 'El pueblo es el actor colectivo de la transformación histórica'" *Revista de Frente*, May 21, 2018. https://www.revistadefrente.cl/enrique-dussel-el-pueblo-es-el-actor-colectivo-de-la-transformacion-historica/.

Cohen, Richard. 2008. "Meet 'Juan Crow.'" *Huffington Post*, June 22, 2008. https://www.huffpost.com/entry/meet-juan-crow_b_107071.

Colander, Dave, and Daisy Zhou. 2015. "Where Do PhDs in English Get Jobs? An Economist's View of the English PhD Market." *Pedagogy* 15 (1): 139–56.

Connolly, Joy (@Joyhumanist). 2020. "Universities are surely not the only or most important source of change, but they are a place millions of people spend time learning and thinking." Twitter, June 19, 2020, 1:24 p.m. https://twitter.com/Joyhumanist/status/1274030328563339265.

Connor, Walker. 1990. "When Is a Nation?" *Ethnic and Racial Studies* 13(1): 92–100.

Constable, Olivia Remie. 2018. *To Live Like a Moor: Christian Perceptions of Muslim Identity in Medieval and Early Modern Spain.* Philadelphia: University of Pennsylvania Press.

Cook, Vivian. 2003. *Effects of the Second Language on the First.* Bristol: Multilingual Matters.

Cook, Vivian. 2013. "What Are the Goals of Language Teaching." *Iranian Journal of Language Teaching Research* 1(1) (January): 44–56.

Cooper, Marianne. 2015. "The False Promise of Meritocracy." *Atlantic*, December 1, 2015. https://www.theatlantic.com/business/archive/2015/12/meritocracy/418074/.

Cornelius, Wayne. 2016. "Why Immigrants Won't Self-Deport." *LA Times*, November 30, 2016. https://www.latimes.com/opinion/op-ed/la-oe-cornelius-self-deportation-20161130-story.html.

Craddock, Jerry. 1981. "New World Spanish." In *Language in the USA*, edited by Charles Ferguson and Shirley Brice Heath, 196–214. Cambridge: Cambridge University Press.

Cruz, Anne. 2006. "Golden Age Studies in the 21st Century: A View of the Culture Wars." In *Debating Hispanic Studies: Reflections on Our Disciplines*, edited by Luis Martín-Estudillo, Francisco Ocampo, and Nicholas Spadaccini, 81–86. Vol. 1 of *Hispanic Issues Online*. Minneapolis: University of Minnesota.

Cuba, Ernesto. 2017. *Si no me nombras, no existo: Guía para el uso de lenguaje inclusivo*. Lima: Mercedes Group S.A.C.

de la Campa, Román. 2005. "Hispanism and Its Lines of Flight." In *Ideologies of Hispanism*, edited by Mabel Moraña, 300–10. Nashville, TN: Vanderbilt University Press.

de la Campa, Román. 2006. "Doing and Undoing Hispanism Today." In *Debating Hispanic Studies: Reflections on Our Disciplines*, edited by Luis Martín-Estudillo, Francisco Ocampo, and Nicholas Spadaccini, 23–30. Vol. 1 of *Hispanic Issues Online*. Minneapolis: University of Minnesota.

de la Torre, Miguel. 2017. "The Pedagogical Failure of Eurocentric Methodologies." *Teaching, Religion, Politics*, May 4, 2017, https://www.wabashcenter.wabash.edu/print-blog-as-pdf/?id=209297.

Degiovanni, Fernando. 2018. *Vernacular Latin Americanisms: War, the Market, and the Making of a Discipline*. Pittsburgh: University of Pittsburgh Press.

del Carmen Ramón, María. 2011. "Hemingway y Corrales: leyenda gráfica de un día." *Cuba entre Nos ~ una ventana para re-inventar un país*, January 11, 2011. https://cubaentrenos.wordpress.com/2011/01/10/hemingway-raul-corrales-cojimar-fotografi/.

Darwin López, Liliana. 2019. "Liliana Darwin López." Faculty website, University of Oregon. https://rl.uoregon.edu/profile/ldarwin.

De Cruz, Helen. 2018. "Prestige Bias: An Obstacle to a Just Academic Philosophy." *Ergo* 5(10). https://quod.lib.umich.edu/e/ergo/12405314.0005.010/--prestige-bias-an-obstacle-to-a-just-academic-philosophy?rgn=main;view=fulltext.

De Nebrija, Antonio. 1492. *Gramática castellana*. Madrid: Juan de Zúñiga.

Dee, Thomas, and Emily Penner. 2016. "The Causal Effects of Cultural Relevance: Evidence from an Ethnic Studies Curriculum." NBER Working Paper No. 21865. National Bureau of Economic Research. http://www.nber.org/papers/w21865.

Deswarte, Thomas. 2015. "St. James in Galicia." In *Culture and Society in Medieval Galicia*, edited by James D'Emilio, 477–512. Leiden, Netherlands: Brill.

Dewaele, Jean-Marc. 2016. "Multi-Competence and Personality." In *The Cambridge Handbook of Linguistic Multi-Competence*, edited by Vivian Cook and Li Wei, 403–19. Cambridge: Cambridge University Press.

Díaz Soto, Lourdes, and Haroon Kareem. 2006. "A Post-Monolingual Education."

International Journal of Educational Policy, Research, & Practice: Reconceptualizing Childhood Studies 7:21–33.

Diouf, Sylviane. 2013. *Servants of Allah: African Muslims Enslaved in the Americas*. New York: New York University Press.

Dunn, Sydni. 2015. "Where Do English Ph.D.'s Get Jobs? It Depends on Where They Studied." *ChronicleVitae*, February 5, 2015. https://chroniclevitae.com/news/897-where-do-english-ph-d-s-get-jobs-it-depends-on-where-they-studied.

Durand, Jorge. 2015. "Cemeterio de lenguas." *La Jornada*, November 29, 2015. https://www.jornada.com.mx/2015/11/29/opinion/024a2pol.

Dussel, Enrique. 2008. *Twenty Theses on Politics*. Durham, NC: Duke University Press.

Dussel, Enrique. 2016. "Decolonialidad del poder con Enrique Dussel." *Códigos Libres*, December 9, 2016. https://www.youtube.com/watch?v=BBe1W63uLjM&.

Eliot, Charles. 2010. *Epic and Saga*. New York: Cosimo.

Epps, Brad. 2005. "Keeping Things Opaque: On the Reluctant Personalism of a Certain Mode of Critique." In *Ideologies of Hispanism*, edited by Mabel Moraña, 230–69. Nashville, TN: Vanderbilt University Press.

Epps, Brad. 2006. "Who Works Where." In *Debating Hispanic Studies: Reflections on Our Disciplines*, edited by Luis Martín-Estudillo, Francisco Ocampo, and Nicholas Spadaccini, 15–22. Vol. 1 of *Hispanic Issues Online*. Minneapolis: University of Minnesota.

Escobar, Arturo. 2018. *Designs for the Pluriverse Radical Interdependence, Autonomy, and the Making of Worlds*. Durham, NC: Duke University Press.

Esquivel, Laura. 2006. *Malinche: A Novel*. New York: Simon and Schuster.

Evans, Brad. 2019. "Histories of Violence: Life in Zones of Abandonment: A Time to Break the Spectacle of Ignorance and Violence." *LA Review of Books*, August 19, 2019. https://www.lareviewofbooks.org/article/histories-of-violence-life-in-zones-of-abandonment-a-time-to-break-the-spectacle-of-ignorance-and-violence/.

Faber, Sebastiaan. 2008. "Economies of Prestige: The Place of Iberian Studies in the American University." *Hispanic Research Journal* 9(1): 7–32.

Fain, Paul. 2016. "Poverty and Merit." *Inside Higher Ed*, January 12, 2016. https://www.insidehighered.com/news/2016/01/12/high-achieving-low-income-students-remain-rare-most-selective-colleges.

Fernández, Bélen. 2019. *Exile: Rejecting America and Finding the World*. New York: OR Books.

Fernández, James D. 2000. "Fragments of the Past, Tasks for the Future: Spanish in the United States." *PMLA* 115(7) (December): 1961–64.

Fierro, Maribel. 2005. "Mawālī and muwalladūn in alAndalus." In *Patronate and Patronage in Early and Classical Islam*, edited by Monique Bernards and John Abdallah Nawas, 195–246. Leiden, Netherlands: Brill.

Figueroa, Víctor. 2015. "In Search of the Absent Revolution: Edgardo Rodríguez Juliá's Novels of Invented History." In *Redefining Latin American Historical Fiction: The Impact of Feminism and Postcolonialism*, edited by Helene C. Weldt-Basson, 65–92. London: Palgrave.

Figueroa, Yomaira. 2020. *Decolonizing Diasporas: Radical Mappings of Afro-Atlantic Literature*. Evanston, IL: Northwestern University Press.

Filipović, Luna, and Martin Pütz. 2014. *Multilingual Cognition and Language Use: Processing and Typological Perspectives*. Amsterdam: John Benjamins Publishing Company.

Flaherty, Colleen. 2019. "Equity for Hispanic Professors." *Inside Higher Ed*, October 30, 2019. https://www.insidehighered.com/news/2019/10/30/ut-austin-faculty-group-wants-institution-fix-what-it-says-system-marginalizes#.

Fletcher, Richard. 1998. *Barbarian Conversion: From Paganism to Christianity*. New York: Holt.

Flores Montemayor, and Carlos Eduardo. 2003. *Historia, Lenguas y Leyendas Indigenas de Tamaulipas*. Ciudad Victoria: Gobierno del Estado de Tamaulipas Comisión.

Fortuna, Lisa. 2009. "Working with Latino/a and Hispanic Patients." *American Psychiatric Association*, Best Practice Highlights, 1–5.

Foucault, Michel. 1976. "Society Must Be Defended." *Lectures at the Collège de France*, edited by Mauro Bertani and Alessandro Fontana. New York: Picador.

França, João. 2019. "Henry A. Giroux: Education Should Not Be Neutral." *Truthout*, July 4, 2019. https://truthout.org/video/henry-a-giroux-education-should-not-be-neutral/.

Franceschini, Rita. 2016. "Multilingualism Research." In *The Cambridge Handbook of Linguistic Multi-Competence*, edited by Vivian Cook and Li Wei, 97–124. Cambridge: Cambridge University Press.

Freire, Paulo. 1970. *Pedagogy of the Oppressed*. Freiburg: Herder and Herder.

Fuentes, Carlos. 1997. "El Espejo Enterrado: Reflexiones sobre España y el Nuevo Mundo." Sogetel Films, Paris. Parts 1–5.

Fuentes, Norberto. 1984. *Hemingway in Cuba*. Secaucus: Lyle Stuart.

Fujino, Diane, Jonathan D. Gomez, Esther Lezra, George Lipsitz, Jordan Mitchell, and James Fonseca. 2018. "A Transformative Pedagogy for a Decolonial World." *Review of Education, Pedagogy, and Cultural Studies* 40:69–95.

Funes, Yessina. 2017. "Forget about 'Latino'—Why I'm all for 'Latinx,' and You Should Be, Too." *Salon*, October 7, 2017. https://www.salon.com/2017/10/07/forget-about-latino-why-im-all-for-latinx-and-you-should-be-too/.

Gabilondo, Joseba. 2014. "Spanish Nationalist Excess: A Decolonial and Postnational Critique of Iberian Studies." *Prosopopeya: Revista de crítica contemporánea* 8:23–60.

Galeano, Eduardo. 2000. *El libro de los abrazos*. Madrid: Siglo XXI.

Galeano, Eduardo. 1971. *Las venas abiertas de América Latina*. New York: Monthly Review Press.

Gamboa, Suzanne. 2017. "History of Racism against Mexican-Americans Clouds Texas Immigration Law" *NBC News*, June 3, 2017. https://www.nbcnews.com/news/latino/history-racism-against-mexican-americans-clouds-texas-immigration-law-n766956.

Garcés, María Antonia. 2005. *Cervantes in Algiers: A Captive's Tale*. Nashville, TN: Vanderbilt University Press.

García, Ofelía. 1993. "From Goya Portraits to Goya Beans: Elite Traditions and Popular Streams in U.S. Spanish Language Policy." *Southwest Journal of Linguistics* 12:69–86.

García Márquez, Gabriel, Fernando Botero, Alvaro Mutis, Fernando Vallejo, William Ospina, Darío Jaramillo Agudelo, and Héctor Abad Faciolince. 2001. "Protesta de intelectuales por visa a España." *El Tiempo*, March 18, 2001. https://www.eltiempo.com/archivo/documento/MAM-587296.

Gaztambide-Fernández, Rubén. 2014. "Decolonial Options and Artistic/AestheSic Entanglements: An Interview with Walter Mignolo." *Decolonization: Indigeneity, Education & Society* 3(1): 196–212.

Geertz, Clifford. 1994. "Primordial and Civic Ties." In *Nationalism*, edited by John Hutchinson and Anthony Smith, 29–34. Oxford: Oxford University Press.

"General Government Spending." 2017. OECD Data. http://dx.doi.org/10.1787/22214399.

Ghosh, Amitav. 2020. "Speaking of Babel: The Risks and Rewards of Writing about Polyglot Societies." *Comparative Literature* 72(3): 283–98.

Glatzeder, Britt. 2011. "Two Modes of Thinking: Evidence from Cross-Cultural Psychology." In *Culture and Neural Frames of Cognition and Communication*, edited by Shihui Han and Ernst Poppel, 233–48. New York: Springer.

Goatly, Andrew. 1997. *The Language of Metaphors*. New York: Routledge.

Goodrich, Kaitlin. 2018. "The Cognitive Benefits of Being Multilingual." *Brain-*

scape, October 4, 2018. https://www.brainscape.com/academy/benefits-of-being-multilingual/.

Graf, Eric Clifford. 2007. *Cervantes and Modernity*. Lewisburg, PA: Bucknell University Press.

Graff Zivin, Erin. 2009. "Luisa Futoranksy." In *The Encyclopedia of Jewish Women*. Jewish Women's Archive. https://jwa.org/encyclopedia/article/futoransky-luisa.

Grosfoguel, Ramón. 2011. "Decolonizing Post-Colonial Studies and Paradigms of Political-Economy: Transmodernity, Decolonial Thinking, and Global Coloniality." *TRANSMODERNITY: Journal of Peripheral Cultural Production of the Luso-Hispanic World* 1(1): 1–38.

Grosfoguel, Ramón, Nelson Maldonado-Torres, and José David Saldívar. 2015. *Latino/as in the World-System: Decolonization Struggles in the 21st Century*. New York: Routledge.

Grossman, Claire, Stephanie Young, and Juliana Spahr. 2021. "Who Gets to Be a Writer?" *Public Books*, April 15, 2021. https://www.publicbooks.org/who-gets-to-be-a-writer/.

Guerra, Gilbert, and Gilbert Orbea. 2015. "The Argument Against the Use of the Term 'Latinx.'" *Phoenix*, November 19, 2015. https://swarthmorephoenix.com/2015/11/19/the-argument-against-the-use-of-the-term-latinx/.

Guinot, Dolores Luna. 2014. *From Al-Andalus to Monte Sacro*. Bloomington, IN: Trafford Publishing.

Hans, Northoff. 2008. "Cultural-Sensitive Substrates of Human Cognition: A Transcultural Neuroimaging Approach." *National Review of Neuroscience* 9: 646–54.

Harding, Sandra. 2019. "State of the Field: Latin American Decolonial Philosophies of Science." *Studies in History and Philosophy of Science Part A* 78:48–63.

Harvey, L. P. 1993. "The Political, Social, and Cultural History of the Moriscos." In *The Legacy of Muslim Spain*, edited by Salma Kharda Jayyusi, 201–34. Leiden, Netherlands: Brill.

Harvey, L. P. 2014. *Islamic Spain*. Chicago: University of Chicago Press.

Hemingway, Ernest. 1952. *The Old Man and the Sea*. New York: Scribner's.

Hemingway, Ernest. 1981. *Selected Letters, 1917–1961*. Edited by Carlos Baker. New York: Scribner's.

Hemingway, Ernest. 1999. *True at First Light*. New York: Scribner's.

Henare, A., M. Holbraad, and S. Wastell, eds. 2006. *Thinking through Things: Theorising Artifacts Ethnographically*. Cambridge: Cambridge University Press.

Herbert, Kiran., Zoe. 2014. "Where Is the Seventh Celtic Nation?" *BBC*, January 20,

2014. https://www.bbc.com/travel/article/20131203-where-is-the-seventh-celtic-nation.

Herlihy, Jeffrey. 2009. "'Eyes the Same Color as the Sea': Santiago's Expatriation from Spain and Ethnic Otherness in Hemingway's *The Old Man and the Sea*." *Hemingway Review* XXVIII (Fall): 25–44.

Herlihy, Jeffrey. 2011. *In Paris or Paname: Hemingway's Expatriate Nationalism*. Amsterdam Rodopi/Brill.

Herlihy-Mera, Jeffrey. 2012. "Revisioning Migration: Stratifications of Irish Boston in *Good Will Hunting*." *ALIF: Journal of Comparative Poetics* 32:1–22.

Herlihy-Mera, Jeffrey. 2015. "Academic Imperialism; or, Replacing Nonrepresentative Elites: Democratizing English Departments at Top-Ranked US Institutions." *minnesota review* 85:80–106.

Herlihy-Mera, Jeffrey. 2016. "Colonialism in US Spanish Departments." *Chronicle of Higher Education*, June 23, 2016. https://www.chronicle.com/blogs/linguafranca/colonialism-in-u-s-spanish-departments.

Herlihy-Mera, Jeffrey. 2017a. "Cuba in Hemingway." *Hemingway Review* 36(2): 8–41.

Herlihy-Mera, Jeffrey. 2017b. "Weaponing Accreditation." *Jacobin*, May 24, 2017. https://www.jacobinmag.com/2017/05/puerto-rico-debt-crisis-austerity-strike-university-accreditation.

Herlihy-Mera, Jeffrey. 2017c. "Hemingway's Cuban English." *Chronicle of Higher Education*, July 20, 2017. https://www.chronicle.com/blogs/linguafranca/hemingways-cuban-english.

Herlihy-Mera, Jeffrey. 2017d. "Christopher Columbus's Catalan-Inflected Language." *Chronicle of Higher Education*, October 8, 2017. https://www.chronicle.com/blogs/linguafranca/christopher-columbuss-catalan-inflected-language.

Herlihy-Mera, Jeffrey. 2018a. *After American Studies: Rethinking the Legacies of Transnational Exceptionalism*. New York: Routledge.

Herlihy-Mera, Jeffrey. 2018b. "Puerto Rican in Spain: 2 Grad Students Reflect on Language and Spanish Higher Education." *Chronicle of Higher Education*, July 31, 2018. https://www.chronicle.com/blogs/linguafranca/puerto-rican-in-spain-2-grad-students-reflect-on-language-and-spanish-higher-education.

Herlihy-Mera, Jeffrey. 2019a. "Islamic Spain in American Travel Writing." *Revista de Filología de la Universidad de La Laguna* 38:125–39.

Herlihy-Mera, Jeffrey. 2019b. "Latinx Multilingualism and 'American' Modernism: Concealed Transcultural Depths in William Carlos Williams's English." *Voces del Caribe*, Otoño, 1059–96.

Herlihy-Mera, Jeffrey. 2020. "Post 'American' Hemingway Studies: Multicultural Approaches and Redefinitions of Expatriation." In *The New Hemingway Studies*, edited by Suzanne del Gizzo and Kirk Curnutt, 221–40. Cambridge: Cambridge University Press.

Herlihy-Mera, Jeffrey. 2021. "A New Future for Humanities Funding?" *Inside Higher Ed*, May 14, 2021. https://www.insidehighered.com/views/2021/05/14/grant-makers-should-broaden-support-beyond-elites-opinion.

Herlihy-Mera, Jeffrey, and Vamsi Koneru. 2013. *Paris in American Literatures: On Distance as a Literary Resource*. Lanham, MD: Rowman & Littlefield.

Hernández, Ariana. 2015. "Identidad rasgado y la lengua perdida: The Impact of a Traditional Literary Canon on Latino Perceptions of Identity." Honors College thesis, Texas State University, San Marcos.

Hoey, Michael. 2012. *Lexical Priming: A New Theory of Words and Language*. New York: Routledge.

Holbraad, Martin. 2008. "Proposing the Motion." *Ontology Is Just Another Word for Culture*. Debate. Meeting of the Group for Debates in Anthropological Theory. Manchester, UK: University of Manchester.

House Resolution 789. 116th Congress, Second Session. January 10, 2020.

"How Good Students from Poor Families Get Pushed out of Elite Colleges." 2016. *Think NC First*, January 19, 2016. https://thinkncfirst.hifistaging.com/research/how-good-students-from-poor-families-get-pushed-out-of-elite-colleges.

Hüppaf, Bernd. 2018. "A Witch Hunt or a Quest for Justice: An Insider's Perspective on Disgraced Academic Avital Ronell." *Salon*, September 8, 2018. https://www.salon.com/2018/09/08/a-witch-hunt-or-a-quest-for-justice-an-insiders-perspective-on-disgraced-academic-avital-ronell/.

Ibrahim, D. N. 2013. "Being Bilingual . . . Multilingual Identities." *British Council Blog*, May 13, 2013. https://www.britishcouncil.fr/blog/being-bilingual-multilingual-identities.

Irizarry, Ylce. 2016. *Chicana/o and Latina/o Fiction: The New Memory of Latinidad*. Champaign, IL: University of Illinois Press.

"Ivy League Admissions Are a Sham: Confessions of a Harvard Gatekeeper." 2015. *Gawker*, March 18, 2015. https://www.gawker.com/ivy-league-admissions-are-a-sham-confessions-of-a-harv-1690402410.

Jarrett, Michael. 1996. "Ground Zero Project." *My Writing*. Accessible at http://www2.york.psu.edu/~jmj3/cre_gz.htm.

Jarvis, Scott, and Aneta Pavlenko. 2008. *Crosslinguistic Influence in Language and Cognition*. New York: Routledge.

Jay, Gregory S. 1991. "The End of 'American' Literature: Toward a Multicultural Practice." *College English* 53 (March): 264–81.

Jegić, Denijal. 2019. *Trans/Intifada: The Politics and Poetics of Intersectional Resistance.* Heidelberg: Winter Verlag.

Jordens, Peter. 2016. "Lorgia García-Peña Explains her Approach to *The Borders of Dominicanidad.*" *Repeating Islands*, December 26, 2016. https://repeatingislands.com/2016/12/26/lorgia-garcia-pena-explains-her-approach-to-the-borders-of-dominicanidad/

JTA. 2014. "Muslims Demand Equal Terms for Citizenship in Spain." *Times of Israel*, February 20, 2014. https://www.timesofisrael.com/muslims-demand-equal-terms-for-citizenship-in-spain/.

Kecskes, Ivan. 2014. *Intercultural Pragmatics.* Oxford: Oxford University Press.

Kecskes, Ivan, and Tünde Papp. 2000. *Foreign Language and Mother Tongue.* Hove: Psychology Press.

Keeley, Graham. 2010. "Muslims Arrested for Trying to Pray in Córdoba's Former Great Mosque." *Sunday Times*, April 3, 2010. https://www.thetimes.co.uk/article/muslims-arrested-for-trying-to-pray-in-crdobas-former-great-mosque-3t6mxq278bm.

Kendi, Ibram X. 2019. *How to Be an Antiracist.* New York: Random House.

Kharkhurin, Anatoliy. 2016. "Multi-Competence as a Creative Act: Ramifications of the Multi-Competence Paradigm for Creativity Research and Creativity-Fostering Education." In *The Cambridge Handbook of Linguistic Multi-Competence*, edited by Vivian Cook and Li We, 420–44. Cambridge: Cambridge University Press.

Koneru, Vamsi K. 2007. "Acculturation and Mental Health: Current Findings and Recommendations for Future Research." *Applied and Preventive Psychology* 12(2) (November): 76–96.

Koneru, Vamsi. 2013. "Through Migrant Eyes." National Endowment for the Humanities Lecture. Reading, PA. March 25, 2013.

Kovelman, Ioulia, Stephanie A. Baker, and Laura-Ann Petitto. 2008. "Bilingual and Monolingual Brains Compared: A Functional Magnetic Resonance Imaging Investigation of Syntactic Processing and a Possible 'Neural Signature' of Bilingualism." *Journal of Cognitive Neuroscience* 20(1) (January): 153–69.

Kramsch, Clair, and Lihua Zhang. 2018. *The Multilingual Instructor.* Oxford: Oxford University Press.

Krogstad, Jens Manuel, and Ana González-Barrera. 2015. "A Majority of English-Speaking Hispanics in the U.S. are Bilingual." *Factank: News in the Num-*

bers, March 24, 2015. https://www.pewresearch.org/fact-tank/2015/03/24/a-majority-of-english-speaking-hispanics-in-the-u-s-are-bilingual.

Lamont, Michèle. 2009. *How Professors Think: Inside the Curious World of Academic Judgment*. Cambridge, MA: Harvard University Press.

"Latinx/Hispanic Communities and Mental Health." 2019. *Mental Health America*. https://www.mhanational.org/issues/latinxhispanic-communities-and-mental-health.

Lavinas Picq, Manuela. 2018. "Imagine Otherwise: Manuela Lavinas Picq on Indigenous Futures Interview." *Ideas on Fire*, September 26, 2018. https://ideasonfire.net/72-manuela-lavinas-picq/.

Ledwith, Margaret. 2011. *Community Development: A Critical Approach*. Bristol, UK: Policy Press.

Leeman, Jennifer. 2006. "The Value of Spanish: Shifting Ideologies in United States Language Teaching." *ADFL Bulletin* 38(1–2): 32–39.

Leeman, Jennifer, and Ellen J. Serafini. 2020. "'It's Not Fair': Discourses of Deficit, Equity, and Effort in Mixed Heritage and Second Language Spanish Classes." *Journal of Language, Identity & Education*, July: 1–15.

Lemus, Juan Carlos. 2003. "Escritor Luis E. Rivera." *Prensa Libre*, April 27, 2003, 34.

Lévi-Provençal, Evariste. 2009. *Früher mit d. Zusatz: Revue d'études arabes, Volume 56*. Leiden, Netherlands: Brill.

Lipski, John. 2009. "Which Spanish(es) to Teach?" *ADFL Bulletin* 41(2): 48–59.

"Loi portant reconnaissance de la Nation et contribution nationale en faveur des Français rapatriés." 2005. XIIe législature de la Ve République. Loi n° 2005–158 du 23 February. https://www.senat.fr/application-des-lois/pjl03-356.html.

Loomba, Ania. 2009. "Race and the Possibilities of Comparative Critique." *New Literary History*, Summer: 501–22.

López-Baralt, Luce. 1997. "The Secret Literature of the Last Muslims of Spain." *Islamic Studies* 36(1) (Spring): 21–38.

Lovato, Roberto. 2008. "Juan Crow in Georgia: Immigrant Latinos Live under a Matrix of Oppressive Laws, Customs and Institutions." *Nation*, May 26, 2008. https://www.academia.edu/4243233/Juan_Crow.

Lowney, Chris. 2006. *A Vanished World: Muslims, Christians, and Jews in Medieval Spain*. Oxford: Oxford University Press.

Kaplan, Caren. 1987. "Deterritorializations: The Rewriting of Home and Exile in Western Feminist Discourse." *Cultural Critique* 6 (Spring): 187–98.

Macedo, Donaldo. 2019. *Decolonizing Foreign Language Education: The Misteaching of English and Other Colonial Languages*. New York: Routledge.

Macguire, Eoghan, and Andrew Stewart. 2017. "The Spaniards Rediscovering Their Nation's Long-Lost Islamic Heritage." *CNN*, July 21, 2017, https://www.cnn.com/2017/07/21/middleeast/spain-islam-andalucia-influence/index.html

Macía, Reynaldo. 2014. "Spanish as the Second National Language of the United States: Fact, Future, Fiction, or Hope?" *Review of Research in Education* 38 (March): 33–57.

Mackey, A. 2014. "What Happens in the Brain When You Learn a Language?" *Guardian*, September 4, 2014. https://www.theguardian.com/education/2014/sep/04/what-happens-to-the-brain-language-learning.

Maitreyee, Ramya, and S. P. Goswami. 2009. "Interlingual Homophone Retrieval in Bilinguals." *Journal of Indian Speech and Hearing Association* 23:33–41.

Majid, Anouar. 2009. *We Are All Moors: Ending Centuries of Crusades Against Muslims and Other Minorities*. Minneapolis: University of Minnesota Press.

Maldonado-Torres, Nelson. 2008. *Against War: Views from the Underside of Modernity*. Durham, NC: Duke University Press.

Maldonado-Torres, Nelson. 2016. *Outline of Ten Theses on Coloniality and Decoloniality*. Cape Town: Institute for Creative Arts.

Maldonado-Torres, Nelson. 2017. "On the Coloniality of Human Rights" *Revista Crítica de Ciências Sociais*, December: 117–36.

Marinoff, Lou. 2009. "Inside a Search." *Inside Higher Ed*, August 31, 2009. https://www.insidehighered.com/advice/2009/08/31/inside-search.

Marjanovic-Shanea, Ana, Sohyun Meachamb, Hye Jung Choic, Samanta López, and Eugene Matusov. 2017. "Idea-Dying in Critical Ontological Pedagogical Dialogue." *Learning, Culture and Social Interaction* 20:68–79.

Martínez, Alberto, Jorge Cañizares-Esguerra, Emilio Zamora, Gloria González-López, Francisco González Lima, Martha Menchaca, Fred Valdez Jr., and John Moran González. 2019. "Hispanic Equity Report." Independent Equity Committee at the University of Texas at Austin. October 8, 2019.

Martínez, Rogelio. 2017. *México en la obra de John Steinbeck*. Palibrio.

Mayhew, Jonathan. 2016a. "OK." *Prosedoctor*, June 24. http://prosedoctor.blogspot.com/2016/06/ok.html.

Mayhew, Jonathan. 2016b. "An Experiment." *Prosedoctor*, September 14. http://prosedoctor.blogspot.com/2016/09/an-experiment.html.

Mayhew, Jonathan. 2017. "10 Things about Me." *Prosedoctor*. September 20. http://prosedoctor.blogspot.com/2017/09/10-things-about-me.html.

McKee Irwin, Robert, and Mónica Szurmuk. 2009. "Cultural Studies and the Field of 'Spanish' in the US Academy." *A Contracorriente: Una revista de estudios latinoamericanos* 6(3) (Spring): 36–60.

McNeill, William Hardy. 1986. *Polyethnicity and National Unity in World History.* Toronto: University of Toronto Press.

Mejías-López, Alejandro. 2009. *The Inverted Conquest: The Myth of Modernity and the Transatlantic Onset of Modernism.* Nashville, TN: Vanderbilt University Press.

Melamed, Jodi. 2011. *Represent and Destroy: Rationalizing Violence in the New Racial Capitalism.* Minneapolis: University of Minnesota Press.

Meléndez, Pilar. 2015. "United States Has More Spanish Speakers than Spain Does." *CNN*, July 1, 2015. https://www.cnn.com/2015/07/01/us/spanish-speakers-united-states-spain/index.html.

Meltzer, Françoise, and Jas Elsne, eds. 2011. *Saints: Faith without Borders.* Chicago: University of Chicago Press.

Mendoza, Rubén. 2017. "Perception / Poïesis: Neosophist Pedagogy for a Neoliberal Age of Technoscience Empire." PhD diss., University of California, Riverside.

Menéndez Pidal, Ramón. 1918. "La lengua española." *Hispania* 1:1–14.

Menocal, María Rosa. 2004. "Beginnings." In *The Cambridge History of Spanish Literature*, edited by David Gies, 58–74. Cambridge: Cambridge University Press.

Menocal, María Rosa. 2006. "Visions of Al-Andalus." In *The Literature of Al-Andalus*, edited by María Rosa Menocal, Raymond P. Scheindlin, and Michael Sells, 1–25. Cambridge: Cambridge University Press.

Meraji, Shereen Marisol. 2015. "Why Many Smart, Low-Income Students Don't Apply to Elite Schools." *NPR: All Things Considered*, March 16, 2015. https://www.npr.org/2015/03/16/393339590/why-many-smart-low-income-students-dont-apply-to-elite-schools.

Mignolo, Walter D. 2005. *The Idea of Latin America.* Hoboken, NJ: Wiley-Blackwell.

Mignolo, Walter D. 2007a. "Coloniality and Modernity/Rationality." *Cultural Studies* 21(2–3): 155–67.

Mignolo, Walter D. 2007b. "Delinking: The Rhetoric of Modernity, the Logic of Coloniality and the Grammar of De-Coloniality." *Cultural Studies* 21(2): 449–514.

Mignolo, Walter D. 2013a. "On Pluriversality." *Thoughts on Modernity/Coloniality, Geopolitics of Knowledge, Border Thinking, Pluriversality, and the Decolonial Option.* October 20. http://waltermignolo.com/on-pluriversality/.

Mignolo, Walter D. 2013b. "On Comparison: Who Is Comparing What and Why." In *Comparison Theories, Approaches, Uses*, edited by Rita Felski and Susan Stanford Friedman, 99–119. Redwood City, CA: Stanford University Press.

Mignolo, Walter D. 2018. "Decoloniality and Phenomenology: The Geopolitics of Knowing and Epistemic/Ontological Colonial Differences." *Journal of Speculative Philosophy* 32(3): 360–87.

Mol, Annemarie, and John Law. 2005. "Guest Editorial." *Environment and Planning D: Society and Space* 23:637–42.

Momplet Míguez, Antonio. 2008. "El Islam en el arte del Camino de Santiago." *La corónica: A Journal of Medieval Hispanic Languages, Literatures, and Cultures* 36(2): 125–43.

Monteiro, George. 2000. "Hemingway, Faulkner, and the Nominatives." In *Travelling across Cultures*, edited by Constante Gónzalez Groba, Cristina Blanco Outón, Patricia Fra López, and Susana Jiménez Placer, 95–113. Spanish Association for American Studies. Universidad de Santiago de Compostela.

Moore, John K. 2008. "Juxtaposing James the Greater: Interpreting the Interstices of Santiago as Peregrino and Matamoros." *La corónica: A Journal of Medieval Hispanic Languages, Literatures, and Cultures* 36(2): 313–44.

Moore, John K. 2015. "Two Religions on One Road to Santiago: Polyethnicity and Syncretism on the Camino in Saint Jacques . . . La Mecque." In *The Camino de Santiago in the 21st Century: Interdisciplinary Perspectives and Global Views*, edited by Samuel Sánchez and Annie Hesp, 123–47. New York: Routledge.

Moore, John K. Jr., and Spaccarelli, T. D. 2008. "The Road to Santiago and Pilgrimage." *La corónica: A Journal of Medieval Hispanic Languages, Literatures, and Cultures* 36(2): 5–14.

Morales, Alfredo. 2013. "El autor colombiano Fernando Vallejo: 'España ignora a esa América que colonizó y tiranizó.'" *Tribulaciones de un Sudaka en La Corte de Madrid*, August. https://tribulacionesdeunsudaka.blogspot.com/2013/08/el-autor-colombiano-fernando-vallejo.html.

Morales, Yudes, C. Gómez-Ariza, and M. Bajo. 2015. "Bilingualism Modulates Dual Mechanisms of Cognitive Control: Evidence from ERPs." *Neuropsychologia* 66: 157–69.

Moraña, Mabel. 2006. "Latin American Cultural Studies: When, Where, Why?" In *Debating Hispanic Studies: Reflections on Our Disciplines*, edited by Luis Martín-Estudillo, Francisco Ocampo, and Nicholas Spadaccini, 31–36. Vol. 1 of *Hispanic Issues Online*. Minneapolis: University of Minnesota.

Moraña, Mabel. 2016. "Postscriptum: Decolonial Scenarios and Alternative Thinking: Critical and Theoretical Explorations." In *Decolonial Approaches to Latin American Literatures and Cultures*, edited by Juan Ramos and Tara Daly, 215–25. London: Palgrave.

Murahata, Goro, Yoshiko Murahata, and Vivian Cook. 2016. "Research Questions and Methodology of Multi-Competence." In *The Cambridge Handbook of Linguistic Multi-Competence*, edited by Vivian Cook and Li Wei, 26–49. Cambridge: Cambridge University Press.

Muthyala, John. 2012. *Dwelling in American: Dissent, Empire, and Globalization.* Hanover, NH: Dartmouth College Press.

Newcomb, Robert Patrick. 2018. *Iberianism and Crisis: Spain and Portugal at the Turn of the Twentieth Century.* Toronto: University of Toronto Press.

Novoa, Alfredo, Andre Greene, and Rosa Hwang. 2013. "Mechanisms of Liberation: Towards an Inclusive Pedagogy." *Online Publication of Undergraduate Studies.* New York: New York University Press.

O'Keefe, Sarah. 2012. "The True Cost of Incumbency Bias." *Scriptorium*, July 15, 2012. https://www.scriptorium.com/2012/07/the-true-cost-of-incumbency-bias/.

Orlando, V. 2017. *The Algerian New Novel: The Poetics of a Modern Nation, 1950–1979.* Charlottesville: University of Virginia Press.

Orr, Lisa. 2016. "The Real Reasons Why Low-Income Students Don't Apply to Elite Universities." *Huffington Post*, August 31, 2016. https://www.huffpost.com/entry/the-real-reasons-why-low-income-students-dont-apply_b_57c6c563e4b0b9c5b7360446.

Ortega, Mariana. 2017. "Decolonial Woes and Practices of Un-Knowing." *Journal of Speculative Philosophy* 31(3): 504–16.

Owen, Kendal. 2017. Comment on Herlihy-Mera, Jeffrey. "Hemingway's Cuban English." *Chronicle of Higher Education*, July 21, 2017. https://www.chronicle.com/blogs/linguafranca/hemingways-cuban-english.

Pappas, Christopher. 2015. "Modern & Contemporary American Poetry." *Ida Brandão Space for MOOCs*, October 11, 2015. https://idabrandaomooc.wordpress.com/modern-poetry/.

Paquian, Rubén. 2018. "What's in a Name? Texas SBOE Tentatively Approves 'Ethnic Studies: Mexican American Studies.'" *Texas Observer*, June 13, 2018. https://www.texasobserver.org/whats-in-a-name-texas-sboe-tentatively-approves-ethnic-studies-mexican-american-studies/.

Pardon, Pablo. 2006. "Aznar se pregunta por qué los musulmanes no se disculpan 'por haber ocupado España ocho siglos.'" *El Mundo*, September 22, 2006. https://www.elmundo.es/elmundo/2006/09/22/internacional/1158945858.html.

Patel, Eboo. 2019. "What Do We Really Mean When We Say We Are Hiring for Identity." *Inside Higher Ed*, May 7, 2019. https://www.insidehighered.com/blogs/conversations-diversity/what-do-we-really-mean-when-we-say-we-are-hiring-identity.

Pavlenko, Aneta. 2001. *Negotiation of Identities in Multilingual Contexts*. Bristol: Multilingual Matters.

Pease, Donald E. 2011. "Introduction." In *Reframing the Transnational Turn in American Studies*, edited by Winfried Fluck, Donald E. Pease, and John Carlos Rowe. Hanover, NH: Dartmouth College Press.

Peralta, Eyder. 2011. "Judge Says Mexican-American Studies Program Violates Ariz. Law." *NPR*, December 28, 2011. https://www.npr.org/sections/thetwo-way/2011/12/28/144394127/judge-says-mexican-american-studies-program-violates-ariz-law.

Pérez, Jefferson. 2004. "El país deja atrás el pesimismo y marcha con esperanza." *Hoy*, January 1, 2004, 1ª.

Phillipson, Robert. 1992. *Linguistic Imperialism*. Oxford: Oxford University Press.

Phippen, J. Weston. 2015. "How One Law Banning Ethnic Studies Led to Its Rise." *Atlantic*, July 19, 2015. https://www.theatlantic.com/education/archive/2015/07/how-one-law-banning-ethnic-studies-led-to-rise/398885/.

Planes, Roque. 2013. "Arizona's Law Banning Mexican-American Studies Curriculum Is Constitutional, Judge Rules." *Huffington Post*, March 14, 2013. https://www.huffpost.com/entry/arizona-mexican-american-studies-curriculum-constitutional_n_2851034.

Pollard, Amy. 2008. "The Discussion." *Ontology Is Just Another Word for Culture*. Debate. Meeting of the Group for Debates in Anthropological Theory. Manchester, UK: University of Manchester.

Ponce, Cristian. 2017. "Salinas Teacher Explores John Steinbeck's Mexican Influences in New Book." *Californian*, November 10, 2017. https://www.thecalifornian.com/story/life/2017/11/10/john-steinbeck-mexican-influences-mexico-en-la-obra-de-john-steinbeck/852456001/.

Pons, Marc. 2018. "Nebrija publica la 'Gramática castellana,' para imponerla a bárbaros pueblos." *El Nacional*, August 18, 2018. https://www.elnacional.cat/es/efemerides/marc-pons-nebrija-publica-gramatica-castellana_297210_102.html.

Prádanos, Luis. 2016. "Exploring the Political Ecology of Iberian Studies." *Ethics of Life: Contemporary Iberian Debates Hispanic Issues*, On-Line Debates 7:49–54.

Putz, Orsolya. 2019. *Metaphor and National Identity*. Amsterdam: John Benjamins Publishing Company.

Querejazu, Amaya. 2016. "Encountering the Pluriverse: Looking for Alternatives in Other Worlds." *Revista Brasileira de Política Internacional* 59(2): 1–16.

Quesada-Embid, Mercedes C. 2008. *Dwelling, Walking, Serving: Organic Preservation along the Camino de Santiago*. Ph.D. thesis, Antioch University.

Quijano, Aníbal. 2000. "Coloniality of Power, Eurocentrism, and Latin America." *Nepantla: Views from South* 1(3): 533–80.

Quijano, Aníbal. 2007. "Coloniality and Modernity/Rationality." *Cultural Studies* 21(2–3) (March/May): 168–78.

Quijano, Aníbal. 2014. "Colonialidad del poder, eurocentrismo y América Latina." In *Cuestiones y Horizontes: Antología esencial de la Dependencia Histórico-Estructural a la Colonialidad/Descolonialidad del Poder*, edited by D. Assis Climaco, 777–832. Caba, CLACSO.

Ramos, Juan G., and Tara Daly. 2016. "Introduction." In *Decolonial Approaches to Latin American Literatures and Cultures*, i–xxv. London: Palgrave.

Ramos, María Christina. 2011. "Literary Cartographies of Spain: Mapping Identity in African American Travel Writing." PhD diss., University of Maryland, College Park.

Raulston, Stephen B. 2008. "The Harmony of Staff and Sword: How Medieval Thinkers Saw Santiago Peregrino & Matamoros." *La corónica: A Journal of Medieval Hispanic Languages, Literatures, and Cultures* 36(2): 345–67.

Reis, Richard M. 2000. "The Basics of Cover Letter Writing." *Chronicle of Higher Education*, March 3, 2000. https://www.chronicle.com/article/the-basics-of-cover-letter-writing/.

Renfrow, Peter. 2013. *Geographical Psychology: Exploring the Interaction of Environment and Behavior*. Washington, DC: American Psychological Association.

Resina, Joan Ramon. 2009. "Post-Hispanism, or the Long Goodbye of National Philology." *Transfer. Journal of Contemporary Culture* 4:25–37.

Resina, Joan Ramon. 2013. *Iberian Modalities: A Relational Approach to the Study of Culture in the Iberian Peninsula*. Liverpool, UK: University of Liverpool Press.

Reyes-Barriéntez, Alicia M. 2019. "Lessons from a First-Gen, Working-Class Latinx Student." *Inside Higher Ed*, December 20, 2019. https://www.insidehighered.com/advice/2019/12/20/what-first-generation-working-class-latinx-student-wishes-shed-known-she-went.

Riding, Alan. 1989. "As Spain Heeds Europe's Call, the Americas Fret." *New York Times*, May 10, 1989. https://www.nytimes.com/1989/05/10/world/as-spain-heeds-europe-s-call-the-americas-fret.html.

Righi, Andrea. 2021. *The Other Side of the Digital: The Sacrificial Economy of New Media*. Minneapolis: University of Minnesota Press.

Rivera Cusicanqui, Silvia. 2012. "Ch'ixinakax utxiwa: A Reflection on the Practices and Discourses of Decolonization." *South Atlantic Quarterly* 111(1): 95–109.

Roberson, Jennifer. 2007. "Visions of Al-Andalus in Twentieth-Century Mosque

Architecture." In *Revisiting al-Andalus*, edited by Mariam Rosser-Owen and Glaire Anderson, 247–71. Leiden, Netherlands: Brill.

Roberts, Laurie. 2014. "John Huppenthal: All Spanish Media Should Be Silenced." *Azcentral*, June 24, 2014. https://www.azcentral.com/story/laurie-roberts/2014/06/24/john-huppenthal-anonymous-blog-posts-latino-comments/11312133/.

Rodríguez, Michael. 2021. Interview with the author. July 15.

Rogers, Gayle. 2015. "'Spanish Is a Language Tu': Hemingway's Cubist Spanglish." *Novel: A Forum on Fiction* 48(2): 224–42.

Rolón Collazo, Lissette. 2014. "De la @ a la x." *8ogrados*, April 14, 2014. https://www.8ogrados.net/de-la-a-la-x/.

Rorty, Richard. 1998. *Achieving Our Country*. Cambridge, MA: Harvard University Press.

Ross, Lilian. 1950. "The Moods of Ernest Hemingway: The Writer, Unenthusiastically, Visits New York." *New Yorker*, July 21, 1950. https://www.newyorker.com/magazine/1950/05/13/how-do-you-like-it-now-gentlemen.

Russo Rodríguez, Maureen. 2016. "The Urgency of Teaching Medieval Iberia." *La corónica Commons: Medieval Iberian Languages, Literatures, and Cultures*, November 8, 2016. https://lcc.ku.edu/open-access/the-urgency-of-teaching-medieval-iberia/.

Saffo, Paul. 2007a. "U.S.A. to Disappear in 50 Years." Video lecture. *Uberpulse*, August 29, 2007.

Saffo, Paul. 2007b. "Six Rules for Effective Forecasting" *Harvard Business Review*, July–August, https://hbr.org/2007/07/six-rules-for-effective-forecasting

Said, Edward. 2000. *Reflections on Exile*. Cambridge: Harvard University Press.

Saldívar-Hull, Sonia. 2003. *Exploring Borderlands—American Passages: A Literary Survey*. Films Media Group and WW Norton.

Salloum, Habeeb. 2015. "Arabic Contributions to Spanish Music, Song and Dance." *Arab America*, November 15, 2015. https://www.arabamerica.com/arabic-contributions-spanish-music-song-dance.

Salvatore, Ricardo. 2015. "On Knowledge Asymmetries and Cognitive Maps: Reconsidering Hemispheric American Studies." *MLN* 130, no. 2 (March) (Hispanic issue): 362–89.

Sánchez, Alberto. 1997. *Cervantes: Bulletin of the Cervantes Society of America* 17: 7–24.

Sánchez-González, Lisa. 2001. *Boricua Literature: A Literary History of the Puerto Rican Diaspora*. New York: New York University Press.

Sánchez Prado, Ignacio. 2020. "Academe's Shameful Neglect of Spanish." *Chron-*

icle of Higher Education, March 13, 2020. https://www.chronicle.com/article/academes-shameful-neglect-of-spanish/.

Schwartz, Adam Frederick. 2009. "On Imagination and Erasure: Investigating Undergraduate Spanish Language Education in the U.S. Southwest." PhD diss., University of Arizona, Tucson.

Scott Hanway, Nancy. 2015. "7 Hazards of the Campus Interview." *Chronicle of Higher Education*, January 26, 2015. https://www.chronicle.com/article/7-hazards-of-the-campus-interview/.

Seixo, Maria Alzira. 2016. "A View from Comparative History I, Comparative Literature and Literary History." In *Comparative History of Literatures in the Iberian Peninsula, Volume 2*, edited by César Domínguez, Anxo Abuín González, and Ellen Sapega, 650–53. Amsterdam: John Benjamins Publishing Company.

Shenker, Sarah Dee. 2012. "Towards a World in Which Many Worlds Fit? Zapatista Autonomous Education as an Alternative Means of Development." *International Journal of Educational Development* 32(3) (May): 432–43.

Shott, Michael. 2022. "Merit and Placement in the American Faculty Hierarchy: Cumulative Advantage in Archaeology." *PLoS ONE* 17(1): 2–28.

Shumway, Nicolas. 2005. "Hispanism in an Imperfect Past and an Uncertain Future." In *Ideologies of Hispanism*, edited by Mabel Moraña, 163–90. Nashville, TN: Vanderbilt University Press.

Sleeter, Christine. 2011. *The Academic and Social Value of Ethnic Studies*. Washington, DC: National Education Association.

Soria Mesa, Enrique. 2012. "Los Moriscos que se quedaron: La permanencia de la población de origen islámico en la España Moderna—Reino de Granada, siglos XVII–XVIII." *Vínculos de Historia* 1:205–30.

Stavans, Ilan. 2003. *Spanglish: The Making of a New American Language*. New York: Harper.

Steves, Rick. 2010. "Northern Spain and the Camino de Santiago." *Rick Steves' Europe*. Oregon Public Broadcasting.

Steves, Rick. 2019. "A Medieval Pilgrimage in Modern Times" *Rick Steves' Europe*. https://www.ricksteves.com/watch-read-listen/read/articles/a-medieval-pilgrimage-in-modern-times.

Stewart, Devin. 2006. "The Identity of 'the Muftī of Oran.'" *Al-Qanṭara* 27(2): 265–301.

Suda, Ana. 2019. "Border Patrol Detained Me for Speaking Spanish in Montana. Then My Town Turned Against Me." *ACLU blog*, February 14, 2019. https://www.aclu.org/blog/immigrants-rights/ice-and-border-patrol-abuses/border-patrol-detained-me-speaking-spanish.

Suh, Serk-Bae. 2013. *Treacherous Translation*. Berkeley: University of California Press.

Swartz, E. 1992. "Emancipatory Narratives: Rewriting the Master Script in the School Curriculum." *Journal of Negro Education* 61(3): 341–55.

Sydera. 2011. "I'll Share My Experience with ACLS New Faculty Fellows." *Chronicle of Higher Education*, Disqus forum, "Teaching in the Postdoc Space," April 21, 2011. https://www.chronicle.com/article/teaching-in-the-postdoc-space/.

Sylvester, Bickford. 1996. "The Cuban Context of the Old Man and the Sea." In *The Cambridge Companion to Ernest Hemingway*, edited by Scott Donaldson, 253–68. Cambridge: Cambridge University Press.

Taboada, Hernán. 2004. *La sombra del Islam en la conquista de América*. Mexico City: Universidad Nacional Autónoma de México.

Tasos, Michailidis, and Gina Paschalidou. 2018. "Creative Discourse as a Means of Exploring and Developing Human Creativity." In *Applied Psycholinguistics and Multilingual Cognition in Human Creativity*, edited by Bryan Christiansen and Ekaterina Turkina, 55–82. Hershey, PA: IGI Global.

Thompson, Gregory, and Edwin Lamboy. 2012. *Spanish in Bilingual and Multilingual Settings around the World*. Leiden, Netherlands: Brill.

Tlapoyawa, Kurly. 2018. "Latinx? No Thanx!" *Mexika*, September 28, 2018. https://mexika.org/2017/10/14/chicanx-no-thanx/.

Train, Robert. 2011. "Postcolonial Complexities in Foreign Language Education and the Humanities." In *AAUSC 2010: Critical and Intercultural Theory and Language Pedagogy*, edited by Glenn Levine, Alison Phipps, and Carl Blyth, 141–61. Boston: Cenage.

Trownsell, Tamara, Amaya Querejazu Escobari, Giorgio Shani, Navnita Chadha Behera, Jarrad Reddekop, and Arlene Tickner. 2019. "Recrafting International Relations through Relationality." *E-International Relations*, January 8, 2019. https://www.e-ir.info/2019/01/08/recrafting-international-relations-through-relationality/.

Tyx, Daniel. 2013. "The Year I Didn't." In *The Best American Travel Writing*, edited by Jason Wilson and Elizabeth Gilbert, 60–65. Boston: Houghton Mifflin.

"US Study Abroad: Leading Destination." 2007. *Institute of International Education*. Data available at https://opendoorsdata.org/data/us-study-abroad/leading-destinations/.

Vaid, Jyutsna, and Renata Meuter. 2016. "Not through a Glass Darkly: Refocusing the Psycholinguistic Study of Bilingualism through a 'Bivocal' Lens." In *The*

Cambridge Handbook of Linguistic Multi-Competence, edited by Vivian Cook and Li Wei, 77–96. Cambridge: Cambridge University Press.

Verdecchia, Guillermo. 2013. *Fronteras Americanas: American Borders*. Vancouver: Talonbooks.

Veronelli, Gabrilla. 2016. "A Coalitional Approach to Theorizing Decolonial Communication." *Hypatia* 31(2): 404–20.

Versteegh, Kees. 2001. *The Arabic Language*. New York: Columbia University Press.

Viveiros de Castro, Eduardo. 2003. "And: After-Dinner Speech Given at Anthropology and Science, the 5th Decennial Conference of the Association of Social Anthropologists of the UK and Commonwealth, 2003." Manchester Papers in Social Anthropology 7. Manchester: Department of Social Anthropology, University of Manchester.

Volek, Emil. 2006. "Under the Spell of Magic: US Latin Americanism and Its Others." In *Debating Hispanic Studies: Reflections on Our Disciplines*, edited by Luis Martín Estudillo, Francisco Ocampo, and Nicholas Spadaccini, 37–46. Vol. 2 of *Hispanic Issues Online*. Minneapolis: University of Minnesota.

Wacks, David. 2013. "Cultural Exchange in the Languages and Literatures of Medieval Spain." Lecture. Abu Dhabi Institute, New York University, October 29.

Wacks, David. 2016. "How Christian Was Iberia in the Middle Ages?" *Arcade: Literature, Humanities & the World*, May 9, 2016. https://arcade.stanford.edu/blogs/how-christian-was-iberia-middle-ages.

Wacks, David. 2018. "Sefarad for Hispanists." *David A. Wacks Research and Teaching on Medieval Iberian and Sephardic Culture*, September 3, 2018, https://davidwacks.uoregon.edu/2018/09/03/sefarad/.

Weber, Eugene. 1976. *Peasants into Frenchmen: The Modernization of Rural France, 1870–1914*. Redwood City, CA: Stanford University Press.

Weiss, Jason. 1995. "Héctor Biancotti." *Itineraries of a Hummingbird*. https://www.itinerariesofahummingbird.com/hector-bianciotti1.html.

Weiss, Jason. 1998. "Eduardo Manet." *Itineraries of a Hummingbird*. https://www.itinerariesofahummingbird.com/eduardo-manet.html.

Weiss, Jason. 1999a. "Luisa Futoransky." *Itineraries of a Hummingbird*. https://www.itinerariesofahummingbird.com/luisa-futoransky1.html.

Weiss, Jason. 1999b. "Silvia Baron Supervielle." *Itineraries of a Hummingbird*. https://www.itinerariesofahummingbird.com/silvia-baron-supervielle.html.

Weiss, Jason. 2003. *The Lights of Home: A Century of Latin American Writers in Paris*. New York: Routledge.

Weiss, Jason. 2010. "Edgardo Cozarinsky." *Itineraries of a Hummingbird*. https://www.itinerariesofahummingbird.com/edgardo-cozarinsky1.html.

White, Francisco-Luis. 2018. "The Decolonial Potential of NEITHER." *Tedx Talks*, April 5.

White, Lawrence. 2018. "A Map of Geographical Psychology." *Psychology Today*, July 1, 2018. https://www.psychologytoday.com/us/blog/culture-conscious/201807/map-geographical-psychology?collection=1119326.

Whorf, Benjamin Lee. 1940. "Science and Linguistics." *MIT Technological Review* 42(6) (April): 229–31.

Williams, Jeffrey J. 2016. "American Literature in the World: An Interview with Wai Chee Dimock." *boundary 2* 43(2): 163–78.

Williams, William Carlos. 1925. *In the American Grain*. Cambridge, MA: New Directions.

Wolfson, Nessa, and Joan Manes. 1985. *Language of Inequality*. Berlin: Degruyter.

Wright, W. 2007. *Crisis of the Black Intellectual*. Chicago: Third World.

Wynter, S. 1990. "America as a 'World': A Black Studies Perspective and Cultural Model Framework." Paper submitted to the California State Board of Education, September 9.

Yarger, Lynette, Fay Cobb Payton and Bikalpa Neupane. 2019. "Algorithmic Equity in the Hiring of Underrepresented IT Job Candidates." *Online Information Review* 44(2): 383–95.

Yaycioğlu, Mukadder. 2010. "El uso del aljamía por Cid(e) Hamet(e) Benenegel(i), autor(a) del *Quijote* disfrazado/a de mujer/hombre." *Siglia*, no. 26: 97–113.

Yépez, Heriberto. 2017. *Transnational Battlefield*. Tijuana: Commune Editions.

Young, James Edward. 1993. *The Texture of Memory: Holocaust Memorials and Meaning*. New Haven, CT: Yale University Press.

Young, Robert. 2012. "Postcolonial Remains." *New Literary History* 43(1) (Winter): 19–42.

Zambrana, Rocío. 2021. *Colonial Debts: The Case of Puerto Rico*. Durham, NC: Duke University Press.

Zamora, Javier. 2019. "[Immigration Headline]." *Poetry*, June. https://www.poetryfoundation.org/poetrymagazine/poems/150066/immigration-headline-5ce31b771668c.

Zarnecki, George. 1966. "The Monastic World: The Contribution of the Orders." In *The Flowering of the Middle Ages*, edited by Joan Evans, 35–61. London: Thames and Hudson.

Zeldin, Theodore. 1977. "New Loyalties in Europe." *Listener* 97:663.

Zinn, Howard. 1980. *A People's History of the United States*. New York: Harper & Row.

INDEX

accents: changing, 78, 83, 162; as colonial apparatus, 9, 73, 164; and identity, 106, 161; in Spanish, 4–5, 32, 114, 115, 199
apology, colonial and Eurocentric use of, 45, 152, 154, 171, 173
appointments, scholarly, 16, 20, 32, 34, 40, 50, 91, 193n4; cultural biases in, 85, 87–89, 209n36, 225n20; and educational credentials, 68, 73
American Council of Learned Societies, 95, 179–82, 187–88, 190–91
Americanism, 79, 171, 208n29
Arabic: inflection in Peninsular culture, 126–27, 133, 141–42, 144, 218n16; influence on Castilian Spanish, 140–41; language in Iberia, 129, 131–32, 145–46, 219n23; in Peninsular literature, 133–35
area studies: and influence on "Spain", 122–23, 125, 216n2, 218n14; national and regional, 40, 56, 99 196n11; post-area studies, 49–50; theoretical presumptions, 17, 26, 31, 194n9
awards, scholarly, 55, 149, 180, 188, 225n20

bilingualism, 76, 81, 99–100, 140, 151, 166; in pedagogy, 161, 170

Camino de Santiago, 136, 138, 218n18, 220n35
canon, canonization, 8, 23, 34, 172, Peninsular literary, 41–42, 44, 52, 67, 78, 132, 201n17
Celtic, traditions and culture, 122, 137, 202n27, 220n30, 220n33, 221n40
Christianity: cultural appropriation and occupation of Iberia, 139–40, 143–46, 217n5, 220n29; pre-Christian tradition, 122, 138
citizenship, 21, 78, 144, 149, 152, 166
city-state, epistemes and theoretical frames, 4, 68, 71–73, 173
class, economic, 159, 174, 208, 215n23, 224n8
cognitive imperialism and localism in pedagogy, 23–24, 73, 84–85
competition, as a western paradigm of human relations, 47, 54, 86–87, 92, 180, 189
colonialism, academic, 16, 25, 166, 170; and Eurocentrism, 31, 49, 176
coloniality, 2, 11, 22, 63, 76, 159, 199n1
conquest, 138–39, 143, 171, 176, 218n18, 219n21
Creoles, 33, 220n30, 220n31, 223n3

cross-lingualism, 108, 113–14, 116–17, 150, 156, 215n24, 215n29
critical pedagogy, 53–55, 177
cultural and colonial violence, 81, 130, 138–39, 155, 166, 173
cultural and social appropriation, 139, 143, 155, 220n31, 221n39
cultural engineering, 57, 221n39
cultural neurology, 14, 27, 160–62, 196n12
cultural psychology, 11, 65, 71, 160

decoloniality, 63, 67, 90, 174, 203n2
democratization, 33, 51–52, 67, 188
de-territorialization, 2, 67, 69, 143
digital culture, 3, 173, 177, 205n10
discrimination, 28, 52, 60, 73, 94–95, 128, 173, 175
diversity, 23, 197n18, 203n1, 204n2
doctoral programs and studies, 67–70, 73, 86, 92, 94–95, 174, 200n11

emancipatory programs and praxes, 27, 60, 79, 84, 156,
English-only institutions and best practices, 110–11, 151–56, 162, 167, 174
enrolment, 17, 149, 178
entanglement, conditional nature of, 4, 6, 8, 12, 156, 203
exceptionalist paradigms, exceptionalism, 27, 55, 89, 110, 121, 184, 191

field imaginary, 8, 59, 67, 89
foreignization of Spanish, 8, 23–24, 151, 167, 169, 182, 198n29
Frenchification, 123–24, 217n9
frontier thesis and myths, 175–76

gendered approaches, 3, 54, 100, 102, 117
Geographical Psychology, 61, 62–63
grammar: epistemic, 13–14, 31, 56, 64, 66, 69–70; linguistic 13, 47

heritage languages and cultural frames, 22–23, 44–45, 76
hiring: and course design, 67–68, 85–87; practices and traditions, 2–3, 7, 9, 20, 31, 34; and prestige bias, 89–90, 92, 94

humanistic evaluation, 94–96
humanities grant competitions, 145, 153, 178–81
hybridization, 13–14, 40, 58, 112, 159–60, 193n5, 196n10
hyphenation, 23, 170, 223n5

idea-dying, process and impact, 121–24
imagined communities, 33, 50
incumbency bias, 17–18, 46, 97
institutionalizing, institutionalization, 7, 15, 18, 28, 43, 85
Islamophobia, 142–43, 219n20, 219n24

jamming, cultural, 7, 24–25, 55, 102
Juan Crow laws, 21, 173

Latinx usage in English and Spanish, 116–18
linguistic relativity, 100, 105
linguicide, 172, 174
localization, localizing epistemes, 24, 59, 92, 157, 178, 194n9, 204n2, 206n12

mapping, conceptual, 33, 91, 122, 129, 139, 171, 199n7
martial conscription, 125, 217n9
masterscripts, scripting identity, 105, 170, 211n8
Mellon Foundation, 155, 179, 180, 186, 188
memory-making, 2, 4
Mexican American studies, 24–25, 82
military, military invasions, 130, 133, 139, 173, 202n24, 214n17, 217n9
modernity, colonial, 6, 9, 11, 15, 54, 56–57, 63, 197
monotheism, secular monotheism, 46–47
multi-competence linguistics, 98, 100, 109

naming and interpellation, 24, 211
National Endowment for the Humanities, 94, 180, 184
nationalism, 48, 139, 214
neoliberalism, 54, 96
Nobel Prize, 113–14, 187
nostalgia, 108, 132, 144–45

ontology, 6, 15, 57–58, 60, 63, 90, 93, 121, 166
oppression, 24, 28, 49, 75, 176

periods, 1, 67, 70
pilgrim, pilgrimage, 137–39, 220n35, 221n38
pluriversality, 58, 60–61, 206n13
post-area, 3, 10, 49
post-national, 49, 218n4
prestige system, 88–89, 225n22
pronoun use, 5, 139, 225n21
purity myths, 60, 62, 73, 84, 99, 111, 202n25

racialization, 123, 170
radical epistemes, 1, 4, 21, 63, 84, 86
relational epistemes, 9, 12, 15, 59, 70–71, 206n12

ser and estar, 66, 122, 196n11
settler myths, 82, 132, 143, 221n39
Schengen agreement, 48–50
silence, production and use of, 11, 57, 81, 96, 119, 158
situational analysis, 3, 58, 69, 153, 196n12, 203n2

social engineering, 28, 173
Spain-centric modes, 1, 17, 26, 45, 55, 68, 177–78
Spanish-only initiatives and institutions, 99, 101, 104–5, 111, 119, 151, 162
study away practices and tendencies, 32, 43–44, 46, 58, 68, 121, 225n13
syntax, 5, 109, 111–12, 118, 151, 215n29

temporal, conditional critique, 71, 104
tenure, 3, 73, 85, 96, 172, 186,
topics courses, 36, 40, 85
top-ranked institutions, myths about and fetishization of, 85–86, 95
transatlantic approaches, 50, 69, 119, 171, 192, 200n10, 206n12
translingualism, 99, 104, 151

unknowing, 95–96
unhyphenated-American culture and language, 58, 110, 112–13
US Visa Waiver Program, 48, 50

worlded approaches, 13, 54, 62, 79, 203, 204n2
worldview vis-à-vis world, 61, 63, 75